Coming Together

Coming Together

The Cinematic Elaboration of Gay Male Life, 1945–1979

RYAN POWELL

The University of Chicago Press   Chicago and London

The University of Chicago Press, Chicago 60637
The University of Chicago Press, Ltd., London

For more information, contact the University of Chicago Press, 1427 E. 60th St., Chicago, IL 60637.
Published 2019
Printed in the United States of America

28 27 26 25 24 23 22 21 20 19   1 2 3 4 5

ISBN-13: 978-0-226-63423-4 (cloth)
ISBN-13: 978-0-226-63437-1 (paper)
ISBN-13: 978-0-226-63440-1 (e-book)
DOI: https://doi.org/10.7208/chicago/9780226634401.001.0001

Library of Congress Cataloging-in-Publication Data

Names: Powell, Ryan, author.
Title: Coming together : the cinematic elaboration of gay male life, 1945–1979 / Ryan Powell.
Description: Chicago ; London : The University of Chicago Press, 2019. | Includes bibliographical references and index.
Identifiers: LCCN 2018056058 | ISBN 9780226634234 (cloth : alk. paper) | ISBN 9780226634371 (pbk. : alk. paper) | ISBN 9780226634401 (e-book)
Subjects: LCSH: Homosexuality in motion pictures. | Gays in motion pictures. | Motion pictures—Social aspects.
Classification: LCC PN1995.9.H55 P69 2019 | DDC 791.43/6526642—dc23
LC record available at https://lccn.loc.gov/2018056058

♾ This paper meets the requirements of ANSI/NISO Z39.48–1992 (Permanence of Paper).

For Tim

Contents

Acknowledgments

The research for this project began in the Film Studies Department at King's College London. I'm immensely grateful to Richard Dyer, whose vast knowledge, unique perceptive capacities, and thoughtful guidance helped to shape this work in countless ways. His patience, care, and engagement, especially early on, has helped to sustain and invigorate this work. A great deal of thanks is due to John Howard, who kept me asking hard but necessary questions, and directed me toward strategies of archival practice that have left me with a profound respect for the urgency of recognizing and engaging with disappearing bodies of work.

There are a number of others whose intellectual guidance has marked this work; I am deeply thankful for the many long conversations I have had with Sarah Churchwell. Her intellectual vitality is unparalleled. Thomas Waugh has been extraordinarily generous over many years with both ideas and materials. I admire his unwavering commitment to the politics of eros. Matt Cook's thoughtful reading of my work has impressed upon me the importance of description in recovering a feeling for time and place.

King's College London offered financial support in the form of a travel grant that funded the international research on which this project relied. A travel grant provided by Yale University allowed me to attend a workshop on Postwar Queer Cinema, at which I was able to workshop what was to become an important part of this book. I am especially grateful for valuable feedback and discussion with coparticipants Ron Gregg, Juan Suárez, and Lucas Hilderbrand. This project also benefited greatly from the lively research culture generated by the Queer@King's research group, and I am especially thankful to Robert Mills for inviting me to present my work and receive valuable feedback from the group.

There are numerous institutions, organizations, and individuals without whom this work would not exist. A great deal of the material that forms the historical basis of this work has come from the following archives. Thanks are due to the Hall-Carpenter Archives at the London School of Economics and especially to John Verrill, who assisted with the retrieval and reproduction of copious amounts of archival material; to the Archives and Special Collections at the Thomas J. Dodd Research Center at the University of Connecticut, where the Foster Gunnison Jr. Papers are held, with a particular thanks to Valerie Love for her assistance; to the Leather Archives and Museum in Chicago, with much gratitude to Christina Court and Rick Storer for helping me in sorting through their incredible collection; and to the ONE Archives Los Angeles, with particular gratitude to Michael C. Oliveira; to Joel Fisher of Scarecrow Video in Seattle, who helped me to find films that I had long thought had fallen off the face of the planet; to Bijou Video and Steve Toushin, who generously assisted me with accessing so many of the films explored here; to Pat Rocco, who provided me with copies of his own work and that of other key filmmakers, and with whom I so enjoyed speaking; to Brad Confer at Bloomsbury Books, whose careful preservation of theater ephemera allowed me to engage with these precious artifacts; to the Kinsey Institute, and to Shawn Wilson for getting out all those Beta tapes and actually having a player to play them in; to the British Film Institute, and to Brian Robinson, whom I will never be able to thank enough for introducing me to the extraordinary Peter de Rome; to Joe Gage, whose generosity and time has helped to make the history of this project come alive; to Irwin Swirnoff, curator of "my gaze///yr gaze: a queer film series," for contributing the book's final image; and to Sam Ashby, for so many wonderful and important conversations about film and life.

This book has been completed while I have been working in cinema and media studies at Indiana University, first in the Department of Communication and Culture, then in the Media School. Thanks to Greg Waller who read early drafts and has offered expert advice and mentorship throughout my time at IU; to Stephanie DeBoer, for thoughtful feedback on early parts of this work and for making life in

Bloomington wonderful right from the start; to Scott Herring, whose response during some of the most challenging times in the writing process was invaluable; to Shane Vogel, for expert advice on all aspects of the process; to Joshua Malitsky, for his excellent suggestions during the book-writing process; to Raiford Guins, for being a seemingly endless resource of scholarly knowledge; to Cara Caddoo, for her focused feedback on my work and being an all-around great pal; and to Joan Hawkins, whose intelligence and wit has helped to grow and sustain a vibrant film culture at IU, of which I feel lucky to be a part.

The completion of this research and writing would not have been possible without the impeccable assistance of Landon Palmer, to whom I am extremely grateful for his close eye and sharp mind. Thanks also to Shadia Silliman, who assisted with sorting through the more unwieldy elements of the filmography. I am most grateful for the excellent work of Theresa Wolner, whose sharp mind as an indexer greatly increased the utility of this work.

My editor, Doug Mitchell, has shepherded this project through its journey to publication. His enthusiasm for the material and his wide-ranging and dexterous intellect has made discussing this book with him deeply satisfying. Conversations with him, whether about work, film, or music, always leave me looking forward to our next exchange. Many thanks to Kyle Wagner for attentive and clear guidance in helping me move through the ins and outs of the publication process. I have been lucky to benefit from the impeccable editing expertise of Mark Reschke to whom I am most grateful for treating this work with such care and interest. Many thanks to Tyler McGaughey for his assistance and coordination. A special thank-you to Susan Bielstein, who helped see this work through to completion. An enormous heartfelt thanks to Kevin Quach, whose incredible design talents are responsible for the cover of this book.

I have received perceptive feedback from many peers and colleagues. Thank you to Greg Youmans for helping me to draw out crucial lines of inquiry. Thanks to David Church for bringing his lucid thinking and clever historiographic mind to bear on this work. Thanks to Jenny Gavacs, who was instrumental in helping me to tell this story and saw the larger picture at moments when I couldn't. My deep appreciation goes to Dafna Zur for her unwavering support, perspective, collegiality, and friendship. I am extremely grateful for the level of engagement and creative response offered by the two anonymous readers from whom I received feedback. Their close attention helped to bring the work to life.

This book has been enriched and enlivened by conversations with the following people: Peter Alilunas, Matt Bell, Mark Betz, Matthew Beuckelaere, Pamela Carpio, Nicolaus Chaffin, Lisa Charbonneau, Christine Cornea, Glyn Davis, Corin Depper, Melody Deusner, Stephen Deusner, Aaron Deveson, Caitlin Doyle, Meghan Doyle, Brad Duncan, Elizabeth Ellcessor, Jon Evans, Brittany Friesner, Patrick Gay, Melissa Giannini, William Goodie, Jane Goodman, Elena Gorfinkel, Mary Gray, Paige Gresty, Duncan Harris, Alex Haynes, Jennifer Hodgson, Laura Horak, Nadine Hubbs, Mark Jancovich, Colin R. Johnson, Daniel Kahn, Daniel Kane, Cáel Keegan, Athena Kirk, Barbara Klinger, Michael Lawrence, Shana Lessing, Joseph Lovett, Charles Lum, Emily MacDonald-Korth, Melinda McDowell, Konstantinos Menelaou, Quinn Miller, Andrew Moisey, Josh Morrison, Gary Needham, Diane Negra, Bradford Nordeen, Andy Owens, Michele Pierson, Jim Richards, Scott Richmond, Lisa Robertson, Dena Rothstein, Jeffrey Saletnik, Olivia Schelts (of Scheltzies), Allison Schroeder, Mark Shiel, Marc Siegel, Louise Smith, Phyll Smith, Yvonne Tasker, Nick Trask, Marketa Uhlirova, Anjali Vats, Jon Vickers, Nick Wasserman-Beal, Leilah Weinraub, Sarah Winter, Ellen Wright, and Damon Young.

The support of my family has been crucial to this project and to my life more generally. Through the years, conversation with my brother David Powell has generated much thinking and much laughing; his intellectual curiosity and agile mind are truly inspiring, and his readings of early drafts of this work were invaluable. Thanks to my dad, Richard Powell, for his humor, his problem-solving skills, and his unwavering support (especially in sticking up for me in the face of the homophobic priest at my high school). My brother Richard J. Powell has been a source of great advice, insight, and compassion. It has been a great pleasure to discuss the experience of writing with my cousin Sandra Prysby. Last, but far from least, I can only hope that the inspiring spirit of perseverance that marked the character of my dear aunt, Judith Ann Hartley (1942–2018), who passed away as I was completing this book, has left its impression upon the pages that follow.

There are certain people who have been instrumental in making this book what it is. During the early days of research, I was lucky to meet and spend time with Peter de Rome, whose wit, frankness, and gentle manner I will always remember. You are missed. I am eternally grateful for a certain day when Professor Sheila Lloyd told me to just get on with it at the exact moment I needed to hear it most. To my mother, Gayle Marie Powell (1947–2015), whose beauty of heart and mind changed the lives of all those she came into contact with. Her special combination of realism, goofiness, curiosity, and care has infused my life with warmth and wonder. This book is dedicated to Timothy Alan Bell, whose love, humor, and generous spirit have helped me to keep it together through the ups, downs, and in-betweens of making this book. His mere presence makes everything feel bright and alive.

Introduction

When male-desiring men in the United States began assembling as a sociopolitical entity in the late 1940s and early 1950s, it was prohibited to make, watch, or possess direct cinematic representations of male-male desire. While a small number of homoerotic photography and homosexual rights magazines began to circulate, images of male-male desire were far from direct. Images that placed men *together* within a mise-en-scène that could easily be read as demonstrative of erotic and romantic interaction could land the maker, exhibitor, or owner in prison.

Some men persisted despite the raiding of homes, the arrest of audiences, and the imprisoning of filmmakers. By the early 1960s, scattered independent filmmakers, physique photography studios, and a Los Angeles–based filmmaking collective comprised a constellation of underground film production and reception that engaged participants with censorship-defying images of male-male desire and the social milieus in which they were fostered and protected. While male-desiring men may not yet have "come out" in the post–gay liberation application of the term, they were by no means invisible. Male-desiring men in the postwar years were active participants in the cinematic elaboration of male-male desire.

Coming Together recovers this cinema made by, about, and for male-desiring men, bringing attention to a cinematic corpus that has been overlooked, both critically and historically. Many of the films and film materials considered here have not been seen since the moment of their initial circulation; and some, no longer even in existence, can only be explored through the small traces of writing or promotion that have been left behind. Recovering this material means unearthing images and sounds that carry a multitude of philosophies, political perspectives, social histories, emotional intensities, and sexual and romantic customs and experimentations. Recovering the textures of thought and feeling that make up this cinematic corpus means, above all else, an opportunity to see, think, and feel from a position that may complicate and call into question the widespread dominance of presentist, progressive narratives in our society. Many of the films explored here bring to us a past that is made up of a great deal more than retrograde perspectives—they help to make recognizable a past that may be much closer at hand and less "behind us" than it may seem.

Why have so many of these films fallen out of circulation, failing to reappear despite the recent technological advancements that have helped to re-circulate older media? This is not just a matter of general oversight or neglect. The occlusion of this media serves certain retellings of LGBTQ+ history at the expense of others. Central here is the place of HIV/AIDS and the way it has shaped LGBTQ+ life and experience, and responses to it, over the last nearly forty years.

More specifically, the mapping of tragic HIV/AIDS narratives that place blame on gay sociosexual activities of the 1960s and 1970s has, unfortunately, not been a minor or occasional historical problem, but a powerful structure of feeling that colors how people understand the past and even the ontological status of the artifacts they encounter. For example, the documentary *Gay Sex in the 70s* (Joseph Lovett, 2005) incorporates utopian images of gay sociosexual practice derived from 1970s gay porn as part of a time of dangerous naïveté and innocence not possible following the educating moment of HIV/AIDS. In the film, photographer Tom Bianchi ruminates that "it's the purpose of having been alive at this time [in the 1970s] and having gone through what I've gone through and, you know, part of the purpose is I get to transcend the kind of limitations that we had . . . that I needed to fuck mindlessly or unconsciously . . . to get to a place where I could do it with more sensitivity and more joy." Whole histories of desire are recast and reduced through a retroactive lens of tragedy and risk, foreclosing other ways of seeing. This reconstitution of mid- to late twentieth-century gay sociosexual practice also functions to recast older forms of gay cinema as mired in a sort of pre-HIV Dark Age. For example, Daniel Harris argues that "homosexuals' internalized guilt" accounts for the aesthetics of gay cinema in the years after Stonewall:

Haunting dreamscapes in which darkness served as a psychical analogue of the depravity of gay sex struck a deep chord with a subculture that's always been marginalized as a promiscuous underground, a hellish world of furtive cruisers, condemned to anonymous sex, who flitted in and out of parks and rest rooms in pursuit of unmentionable passion. Over the subsequent two decades, however, the eroticizing of gay oppression lost its control over our sexual fantasies as homosexuals acquired greater confidence about the healthiness of their preferences and thus responded less and less to the dated conventions of the nightmarish tableaux. In fact the entire history of gay self-acceptance since Stonewall can be discerned from the changes that have occurred in the lighting of gay films, from the spectral setting of the 1970s to the brilliant clinical lighting of present days, which take place in spaces free of guilt, of the erotics of sin.[1]

Harris fashions the entirety of not only 1970s gay film but also gay liberation into a pre/post Stonewall narrative about how gay men made a painful trek from darkness to light. In this logic, gay cinema is required to bear the truth of "the closet," with the whole cycle reduced to the single element of lighting. It comes to stand as visual evidence of a mass gay pilgrimage from disease ("taint"), guilt, judgment, and silence ("unmentionable passions") toward a redemptive state of plenitude and individual well-being (confidence, healthiness, self-acceptance). The description equates 1970s cinema with an "erotics of sin" that can be moved past through ostensibly less distorting, more "honest" forms of cinema ("brilliant clinical lighting"). This narrative is far more than a flattening of film history and aesthetics; it reduces the very social, political, and cultural contours of liberation as a lived experience propelled by the repeated interaction and *movement* of people as they took up the project of gay world-making together, often with little certainty of where it would lead.

Similarly, the centrality of "coming out," as both a cultural phenomenon and a narrative trope, has also contributed to the positioning of older forms of LGBTQ+ media as antiquated. Since the 1990s, a steady stream of films have been organized around the drama of LGBTQ+ people coming out to those around them, changing hearts and minds with their courage and making clear to audiences far and wide that they, too, are as human as everyone else. Recent examples span genres as disparate as comedy (*The Broken Hearts Club* [Greg Berlanti, 2000], *4th Man Out* [Andrew Nackman, 2015], *Love, Simon* [Berlanti, 2018]), drama (*The Trip* [Miles Swain, 2002], *Normal* [Jane Anderson, 2003]), and horror (*Pitchfork* [Glenn Douglas Packard, 2017]). Casting coming out as a necessary process of confrontation that LGBTQ+ people must undergo, these films construct this paradigm as *the* means to achieving a meaningful and healthy life.

As with the moralistic reconfiguration of the 1970s through the lens of certain HIV/AIDS narratives, the dominance of coming out as a paradigm has also meant the recontextualization of earlier films in relation to this model, reading closetedness back on to history. Popular film histories such as Steven Paul Davies's *Out at the Movies* position earlier films as footnotes in a progressive history of healthy integration. As Davies puts it in the introduction to his history of gay film, for example:

> From the late 1950s through to the 1970s, gay characters always seemed portrayed as emotional wrecks, many of them suicidal. These images of tormented individuals left a lasting legacy, as they not only told straight people what to think of gay people but also gay people what to think of themselves. . . . Throughout the decades there were always a handful of films that broke new ground—*Victim* (1961), *Making Love* (1982) and *And The Band Played On* (1993), to name just a few. On the whole, films with a homosexual theme were full of anguish.[2]

Limiting the history of postwar LGBTQ+ cinemas to a "handful" of films, Davies dismisses most films as unfortunate causalities of an earlier time, requiring a progressive canon to clear the way and move us into the future. This narrative culminates in what he later refers to as the "break out from the gay, indie-film subculture."[3] Davies's use of "out"—which dovetails the psychosocial meaning of coming out with the commercial sense of successfully moving into mainstream cultural production—marks a similar trajectory to Harris's redemptive arc from darkness to light. Coming out here means gaining access to a larger world that is characteristically straight. What these narratives marginalize is not a small or occasional body of films but well over three hundred widely circulated and seen films in the US alone (or more than three thousand, if mail-order physique films are counted). What is lost when we assume that these films didn't make much of a difference to anyone at the time or that they don't have anything to say to viewers today? The exploration of media forms taken on in *Coming Together* aims to help us think through this pressing question.

The intermedial close analysis undertaken in this book involves examining an eclectic range of archival materials for the recovery of quiescent ideas and practices of which there are few traces today but which are nonetheless worth reawakening. Doing this work involves pursuing certain ways of seeing and recognizing—of coming into contact with—the materials of history. Oscillating between film history and social history, I look at a range of archival materials to consider the role of cinema in social change. This is not a history that can be drawn from any one place or contextualized only through canonical films, particularly given the complex workings of erasure that have long followed LGBTQ+ cultural production. In line with what Tim Dean refers to as "counterarchival practice," the history work undertaken here relies "less [on] a determinate place or archival content than . . . [a] strategic practice or particular style of constituting the archive's legibility."[4] Thus, moving through the individual case studies of films that comprise this book, I bring a multiplicity of archives into a state of discursive play as they prove helpful in clarifying phenomena both large and small, momentary and persistent. As such, this history makes flexible yet careful use of material culled from personal archives of a wide variety (organized and made available by directors, collectors, and noninstitutionally affiliated archivists) as well as commercial repositories (video stores, bookstores, distributors) alongside official university archives and an international constellation of nonprofit LGBTQ+ archives and resource centers.

Approaching Gay Life

The counterarchival approach privileged here invites a reconsideration of gay life that extends beyond a representational discourse that has too often relied on dichotomies of positive/negative and affirmation/degradation and, in the process, often missed how culture may be produced through uncertainty, instability, and ambivalence. It is not only through affirmative paradigms or the transvaluation of negative ones that culture is made. Just as with present-day gay, queer, or trans* positionings, people who understood themselves to be homosexuals or queers (in the negative, postwar usage of the term) worked within as well as against these terms, in the process fostering a world of social, cultural, and political action. During this time, there was no one category or framework of identification employed by the male-desiring men who came together to make and/or watch these films. Homosexual, homophile, gay, queer, camp, and drag all circulated. The use of these terms here forms an important part of this book's historiographic approach, which seeks to stay alert to the way that these terms have been used, revised, and negotiated over time within the everyday lives and cultural productions of male-desiring men. While "gay life" is a major framework explored in this book, it is not a given stable entity but is mediated, performed, anticipated, refused, and embraced in relation to its many layered, divergent, convergent, and overlapping meanings and capacities.

Though gay did not come into usage as a popular designation for a politics of affirmation and coming out until the coalescence of the gay liberation movement of the late 1960s and 1970s—emblemized by concepts such as "gay is good," "gay power," "gay liberation," and "gay consciousness-raising"—this does not mean that the term "gay" only came to have meaning or representational power for male-desiring men from this "inaugurating" moment on. Building on the work of George Chauncey, who has explored how sex and gender discourse has operated for male-desiring men across the early to mid-twentieth century through layered, polyvalent, and divergent social, psychological, and philosophical paradigms, the relational analysis of cinema and social life undertaken in *Coming Together* demonstrates how many of the facets of the term "gay" were operative well before the large-scale consolidation of gay and lesbian leftist politics in the early 1970s.[5]

Gay has meant several things to both male-desiring men and within society as a whole in the context of the twentieth- and twenty-first-century US, and the many meanings it contains and expresses do not cleanly or clearly supersede one another. For instance, in the first half of the twentieth century, gay was commonly used to designate an experience of pleasure or a joyful disposition. Increasingly into the 1940s, it came to be used among male-desiring men as a term of self-naming and designation meant to iterate gay life as a "social category" comprising male-desiring men, many of whom formally identified as "queer" or were younger men who increasingly felt queer was a derogatory term.[6] By the late 1960s and early 1970s, gay was rapidly coming to more exclusively designate sexual orientation (as opposed to either gender transgression, pleasure, or joyfulness) both among gay men and in wider public discourse.[7] Yet, as many cinematic representations of gay men in mid-1970s attest, gay men are often shown as both given to expressions of gaiety and as subjects of a gay male sexual orientation. Likewise, the utility of the word "gay" in signaling group affiliation and sociality among same-sex and gender nonconforming subjects from the 1970s on can also be seen in earlier examples of its usage. This is particularly so in the case of its deployment in designating social spaces or scenes catering to male-desiring men. For example, Chauncey chronicles a 1951 advertising slogan used by New York's Cyrano restaurant declaring "Where the Gay Set Meet for Dinner."[8] More explicitly, a

1966 editorial in the magazine *Pursuit and Symposium* read "We—using, by your leave, a gay editorial 'we' from here on—have grown more blas[é] in the years since our timid out-coming into the 'gay world.'"[9]

Twentieth-century gay life might involve expressions of joy, representations of bachelorhood, participation in camp humor, a sense of shared desire with other men, a sexual orientation, a cultural and/or aesthetic sensibility, a philosophy for living, or a mode of consciousness or certain forms of sociosexual practice, to name just a few possibilities. While there is no question that certain meanings become dominant—with gay becoming a nearly universal signifier for same-sex male sexual orientation by the 1970s—this does not mean that other valences and applications disappear. By staying attentive to the many hues of meaning contained within and conceptualized through the term "gay," this book shows how cinema was used to construct and envision modes and ways of living within the eclectic and multifarious parameters of gay life.

The Coalescence of Gay Male Life on Film

Cinema became a productive site for image making and storytelling by, for, and among male-desiring men between the mid-1940s and late 1970s for a number of reasons. First, there was Hollywood's self-regulation via the production code; in place between 1930 and 1968, it stipulated that no film should contain images of "sex perversion."[10] As explored by Ronald Gregg, the code, strictly enforced from 1933 on, put an end to "the industry's experimentation with homosexuality to solicit fans and establish 'brand' loyalty."[11] This censorship of male-male desire on film helped to define and generate demand for such representations, inviting audiences to *imagine* what a feature-length film dedicated to showing forms of sex and gender dissidence might be, including (1) what might have been excised from any given movie, (2) how movies before this moment might have offered something different, (3) how movies might contain covert and connotative references to and characterizations of male-male desire, and (4) how other cinematic contexts—such as foreign, avant-garde, amateur, and illicit film—might offer a corrective to mainstream film.[12]

Within this climate, the first films to play at screenings put on by male-desiring men in homes, bars, and a handful of willing theaters were rescreenings of precode films and avant-garde films. In the case of the former, for example, the films of Mae West offered both comedic performances ripe for camp reception and (occasional) direct representations of male-desiring men. Multiple avant-garde films, meanwhile, began strongly implying the existence of male-male networks of desire. These films put before audiences those things they understood to be repressed and forbidden. In doing so, they also began to crystallize conventions of representation that male-desiring filmmakers would draw upon and rework over the next thirty years and beyond. Censorship helped to strengthen and create a repository of conventions that inspired, and continues to inspire, gay cultural producers and audiences alike.

Amateur, avant-garde, and illicit films were in a unique position to respond to and make something out of the representational lack imposed by the hardening of censorship. Following World War II, smaller gauge cameras and film stocks were becoming more widely available as the production of lightweight 16 mm cameras designed to be used for documenting and intelligence purposes during the war created a surplus of low-cost cameras. This catalyzed a growing culture of filmmaking by individuals working outside the dominant film industry.[13] Expanding on this territory, by the 1950s companies such as Bell and Howell, the Revere Company, and Bolex were manufacturing cameras and projectors for home use, with increasingly affordable prices—the Revere 50 8 mm camera sold for $49.50 in 1953—making it possible for films to be made virtually anywhere and at any time by the general public.[14] Nearly all of the male-desiring male filmmakers making films between the 1940s and the commercialization of home-video cameras in the late 1970s utilized formats such as 16 mm, 8 mm, and Super 8 mm.

It was not only male-desiring men who lived this set of relations between social life and cultural production. As Patricia White has shown, the popularity of the "woman's picture" of the 1930s, 1940s, and 1950s offered audiences numerous connotative images of female-female desire and gender nonconformism.[15] The importance of this imagery can occasionally be glimpsed in the ways that film iconography shows up within lesbian vernacular culture, as explored, for instance, in Amy Villarejo's account of a Philadelphia lesbian bar named "Hepburn's" after the actress Katharine Hepburn, in particular as an ode to her cross-dressing role in the film *Sylvia Scarlett* (George Cukor, 1935).[16] Likewise, nongender-conforming subjects—including (both overlapping and stratified) positionalities such as trans*, drag, and gay femininity—found common ground through shared interests in and feelings about images of gender nonconformism, however limited in supply.[17]

Through drag and female impersonation at bars and clubs, numerous performers invoked and wove their stage material out of their interest in popular Hollywood iconography that bent toward gender and sexual nonconformism.[18]

At the same time, the privileges guaranteed through the patriarchal, paternalistic, heterocentric, and homosocial organization of US life, especially in the commercial sphere, have bestowed upon normative, masculine-presenting, cisgender men numerous advantages in the realm of cultural production. While female-desiring women may have had popular films with which to identify or find resonance, this did not translate to the creation of a proto-lesbian cinema or social contexts in which cinema exhibition played a programmatic role as the screening of films at bars and cinemas for male-desiring men did. Film would not come to be a programmatic part of the social lives of female-desiring women until the 1970s, when filmmakers such as Barbara Hammer, Jan Oxenberg, and, later, Su Friedrich began screening and discussing their films through an alternative circuit of lesbian events at college campuses, bookstores, bars, and, later in the decade, art museums.[19] In fact, it was not until the gay and lesbian film festivals of the late 1970s and early 1980s that a more organized, industrialized, and accessible "lesbian cinema" would get off the ground.

Similarly, while male-desiring men were beginning to make and screen films aimed at audiences of male-desiring men, trans* people had no site of their own for cinematic production and/or exhibition. While contexts of drag performance and female impersonation did, in some instances, provide a space for trans* performers and audiences to come together, until recently this was largely contained to the level of stage performance in gay male bars and female impersonation shows patronized by largely straight audiences interested in the slumming thrills of a "different" night out. While there were a few films that attempted to capture this culture from an inside or backstage view that focused on the performers, such as *The Queen* (Frank Simon, 1968) and *Outrageous!* (Richard Benner, 1977), these tended to frame the experience of gender nonconformity primarily through a homosocial "gay nightlife" perspective.

The absence of a cinema organized around female-female desire or trans* representation at this time is first and foremost a product of who had access to both the means of production and control over sites of exhibition. By the mid-twentieth century, in mainstream film production, women rarely had the kinds of access available to men via roles such as director, producer, and studio executive. The same is true of the burgeoning hard-core porn sector, which would become, as explored in chapter 2, a highly generative site for the production of male-centered cinema but rarely accommodated women working in the kind of administrative or production positions that would enable them to develop female-centric (or even just non-male-centric) films. Male-desiring men, on the other hand, had a level of access and control in all these areas even if they had to work in underground ways to utilize it. By the 1960s, numerous male-desiring men, with various degrees of support (offered or purloined) from commercial filmmaking industries, were using their access and knowledge to make the films that the mainstream film industry refused to make.

However, this story about the intersection of cinema and gay life is not only one of access. It is just as much about how the deeply homosocialized contexts that made up everyday twentieth-century life in the United States manifested in particular cultures of thinking, feeling, making, and doing. From the beginning of the homosexual rights movement in the US with the first meetings of the Mattachine Group in Los Angeles in the early 1950s to the numerous homophile organizations of the 1960s, many of the most sociopolitically active male-desiring men understood themselves to exist as part of a fraternal brotherhood based on the shared experience of oppression and a belief that their desires for men gave them an important kind of similarity, even intersubjectivity.[20] This model of homosociality and its placement of male-desiring men as bound together within an exclusive framework of camaraderie, sociosexual activity, and, importantly, love (homophile means, after all, love of the same) did not disappear with the emergence of the gay rights movement of the late 1960s and early 1970s. While there were certainly important strands of gay movement politics that sought to dissolve the homosocial divide and build a movement based on the overthrow of what liberationists often referred to as "sex roles," gay life during this period remained overwhelmingly structured around homosocial divides, as evidenced by the commonality of the construction "gay and lesbian."[21]

Representation and Elaboration

Overall, the films explored in this book tend to evoke and participate in a cultural register of "going to the movies" as opposed to looking to disregard or break down the divisions between film and other kinds of visual or aural experience, as with some forms of avant-garde and experimental work. These movies worked within the classic "escape" model that positions cinema as time away from everyday life—time to get into the story of other people's lives via fictional characterizations and scenarios. For male-desiring men of the 1960s and '70s, cinema, even porn, was typically aligned with popular cinematic conventions, both textually and contextually speaking. Like any trip to "the movies," these first screenings of films made explicitly by and for audiences of male-desiring men involved showing up to see *stories* about how people live or might live their lives.

The movies explored in this book—whether products of the postwar homosexual underground, the first gay film programs, feature-length independent films about gay life, or gay hard-core porn features—all share in common a deep investment in the circulation of *fictional* stories about the lives of male-desiring men and their participation in and engagements with proto-gay and gay life and philosophy. Fiction is what drives this body of work, and it overwhelmingly defines the corpus of proto-gay and gay cinema, with fiction films far outnumbering documentaries during this period. These fiction films demonstrate that putting male-male desire on film was not simply a matter of trying to capture an existing social population. It required envisioning the numerous ways male-male desire might be inhabited and practiced. Film became a means for imagining how to forge, sustain, and expand social contexts, even when those contexts might seem impossible to bring to fruition. The filmic elaboration of a multitude of fictional scenarios organized around male-male desire became a way to ask audiences "what if?"

What if cowboys back in the olden days romantically coupled as men? What if the window washer of the skyscraper I live in came through the window and fellated me on my couch? What if there were a place where only gay men go to vacation together and where they dance and fuck all night long on the beach? What if my girlfriend thought I would be hipper if I slept with men? What if movie theaters were full of men who, in addition to watching movies, also make out up in the balcony? What if some Native American men had fewer hang-ups about same-sex desire than white men? What if I could fall in love and wander around the entire city with my lover, feeling completely at ease in the absence of violence or sanction? What if there were a guy who likes the same clothes as me and might also think I'm hot because of it? What if the businessman in this empty subway car with me would enjoy having sex, right here, right now? What if a trucker and farmer could fall in love and live happily ever after? What if my mom called and told me she knows I'm gay and it really is just fine?

The films discussed in this book don't only pose these "what ifs," they develop narratives to answer them. Through these films and the trailers, print advertisements, press kits, posters, reviews, photo series, and novelizations that accompanied them, audiences were invited into a realm that pivoted on the promise of contact, the actualization of desire, and above all else the emotional, psychological, and sexual engagement that comes with getting to see forms of interaction that society at large has worked to regulate and curtail. This is one of the chief reasons why it is so important to explore these films as *both* representational and elaborative. Like nearly all fiction films, these films represent people through processes of characterization. It's unsurprising, then, that the prospects and pitfalls of representing male-desiring men have long stood as a primary focus of interpretations, reviews, and responses. In fact, many of the first analyses of these films, undertaken by activist-reviewers such as John Marvin, Boyd McDonald, and Vito Russo, alongside scholars such as Richard Dyer and Thomas Waugh, focused on questions of representation. How to avoid and challenge stereotypes, where to find politically vital characterizations, and how to create and locate shared cultural experiences and alliances through filmic representations and their reception were fundamental questions driving this first generation of critical film response.

Dyer and Waugh have also informed this project's methodology in a number of specific ways. From his pioneering analysis of stereotypes in *Gays and Film* to his pathbreaking intermedial work on queer cultural production, spanning areas from video porn to film noir to postwar pulp novels, Dyer has developed a rigorous form of close reading that insists on keeping questions of context and text in a state of dynamic play. This books builds on the methodological groundwork laid by Dyer while directing it toward a more historiographic and industrially oriented project. The work of Waugh has been similarly influential in shaping the methodological commitments of this book. In particular, Waugh's detailed research on how legal regulation prohibits, enables, and marks forms of cultural production guides this book's attention to how temporary practices may result in deeply codified and lasting forms of expression. This study also seeks to sustain the scale of analysis Waugh developed in his pioneering work *Hard to Imagine: Gay Male Eroticism in Photography and Film from Their Beginnings to Stonewall*. Inspired by Waugh, I have made every attempt here to sustain a careful and calibrated balance between both long and short views of changing regimes of sexual representation.

This book emphasizes questions of cinematic elaboration. It asks: how do these films *detail* gay life, and how does this process privilege and develop certain ways of thinking and feeling about it? What audiences for these films experienced when they looked up at the screen from the seats of a darkened auditorium or came across a full-page movie advertisement in *The Advocate* was not only the entry of representations of male-male desire into the public sphere but also the converse: an invitation to enter a specific domain where male-male desire might move beyond representational notions of transparency, elaborating thoughts, feelings, and desires.

Cinematic elaboration involves all of the forms, techniques, and processes across the domains of film production, advertisement, distribution/circulation, exhibition, ancillary production (novelizations, soundtracks, etc.), and critical response (reviews, scholarly analysis, etc.). Cinema is not only film itself but is also carried and shaped through each of these domains. At the same time, cinematic form and technique—what is there *on* film to begin with—dictates and directs much of what is privileged in this elaboration, as the participants involved in each of these domains works to make sense of the event of the film for viewers and readers. Many times, contact with an advertisement is where a viewer's experience of story begins, guided by what it foregrounds aesthetically, generically, and philosophically. Even where the movie is showing may work to shape the cinematic elaboration of its diegesis. To bring clarity to this set of relations, this book employs close reading techniques, such as descriptive analysis of how formal film elements work to give shape, meaning, and texture to viewer experience. In line with Eve Kosofsky Sedgwick's model of reparative reading, I use close reading in the hopes of a deeper understanding of "the many ways selves and communities succeed in extracting sustenance from the objects of a culture."[22]

Michael Warner has explored the importance of elaborative processes as a part of what he calls counterpublic formation. For Warner, a society is not made up of one public sphere but rather numerous publics brought into being, at least in part, by the forms through which they are addressed. Publics are constituted through "intertextual frameworks for understanding texts against an organized background of the circulation of other texts, all interwoven not just as citational references but by the incorporation of a self-reflexive circulatory field in the mode of address and consumption."[23] Thus, the textual forms of address—from print and photography to film and television—place strangers in a relational position, prompting them to imagine and grasp themselves as part of a public. Counterpublics are a particular kind of public whose activities are characterized by their marginal status in relation to dominant publics. Delineating this relationship, Warner notes, "dominant publics are by definition those that can take their discourse pragmatics and their lifeworlds for granted, misrecognizing the indefinite scope of their expansive address as universality and normalcy. Counterpublics are spaces of circulation in which it is hoped that the poesis of scene making will be transformative, not replicative merely."[24]

Elaboration is central to the way in which what Warner refers to as "gay or queer" counterpublics are constituted. He writes that "homosexuals can exist in isolation; but gay people and queers exist by virtue of the world they elaborate together."[25] While, as chapter 1 of this books argues, "homosexuality" also provided a context for counterpublic formation during the postwar years, the point is salient. Gay people and queers come to understand themselves as such through the processes of elaboration and mediation they undertake and participate in together, even, if not especially, when they may not be in the same location. For someone flipping through a newspaper or magazine who realizes that an advertisement for a film *elaborates* and excites desires that are resonant and identificatory for them, the very fact of mass address invites them to imagine that they are unlikely to be alone in this. They are coming into contact not just with their own desire, but the possibility of its public circulation. A small advertisement in the corner of an out-of-circulation magazine or a limited flyer made for a party can reveal much about how and why people have come together as gay and the ways they have done so in particular places and times.

Spatiality and Outness

The cinematic elaboration of gay life works through the articulation of the relationship between character and space as a way to situate gay life as a counterpublic formation in a variety of contexts. Elements such as mise-en-scène, framing, film editing, sound recording and editing, musical scoring, scripting, and acting all work as part of this elaborative process, articulating and making legible what it might mean to be gay. These elements construct and, in the process, philosophize about what being out in the world might be for viewers with variable experiences of being out. In a variety of ways, they work to *spatialize* male-male desire as an experience to be found *out there* in the world at large.

Outness is a complex paradigm with an unstable history. It has not always operated through the logic of the closet, whereby the process of disclosure moves a subject from a place of secrecy and lies to one of truth and transparency. Before the 1970s, "coming out" was typically employed as a term to indicate one's participation in subcultures organized around same-sex desire and gender dissidence. The term expressed a spatio-social meaning: meeting up and being part of a social life.

Scholars such as George Chauncey, Richard Dyer, and Samuel R. Delany place the shift toward an "out" that signifies the psychosocial process of "coming out of the closet" as part of the emergence of gay liberation politics in the late 1960s/early 1970s.[26] Delany even laments this shift, arguing that "before one came out *into* the gay community. Now, coming out had become something entirely aimed at straights. . . . Since it had been a case of displacing a term, rather than adding a term, hadn't we perhaps lost something by that displacement?"[27] Where coming out once carried the ontological force of being out with others for the sake of being together, it now meant identifying yourself to others for the purpose of being grasped as an individual with a given sexual orientation.

As a complex form of mediation, cinema rarely, if ever, directly "reflects" historical change, and this is especially true in the case of these paradigmatic shifts in the status of coming out. The cinema explored here evinces sustained and overlapping uses of the concept of outness. Critically, the spatio-social model of coming out does not fall by the wayside but remains a dominant structuring trope, if not *the* dominant structuring trope, working across these films. Whether in homemade fiction films made for fun at gay parties and retreats in the early 1960s or more commercial, higher budget porn features from the late 1970s, gay life becomes discernable through the use of spatialized elaborations. Outness is shown as a social experience shared among male-desiring men.

The films explored in this book feature few representations of heterosexual families or home life and almost no moments of coming out to family, friends, or coworkers. The men who populate these films typically appear within and as part of the world at large or as active participants in a subcultural world too expansive and publicly engaged to be construed as a closet. Instead, male-male desire appears as a rhizome, transpiring across a vast array of locations spanning town/city, region, country, and across domains of the public, semipublic, private, and semiprivate.

This image of what can feel like an unfettered flowering across sites is central to both the cinematic elaboration and the lived experience of male-male desire. That is, as opposed to the figure of containment on which the closet paradigm rests, male-desiring men utilized and moved within and through a multiplicity of locations—visible, semivisible, and hidden—as they actualized their desire in space and time. As explored in chapter 1, from the late 1940s onward, male-desiring men increasingly engaged in assembly and socialization (whether they identified as homosexual, as queer, with some other category, or with none at all). This was not only relegated to closeted environs of basements or "after hours" at the office but also took place across and through a number of known networked domains spanning homes, bars, restaurants, parks, and beaches. Some, such as hotel bars, even overlapped with spaces that catered to the public at large.[28]

Using the means available to cinema, the films explored here elaborate relationships between space and character that work to amplify certain patterns of movement. The composition of space and the orchestration of spatial movement in these films create numerous connections between sites, often as means of rallying participation in gay life. Annette Kuhn argues for a model of the analysis of space in cinema that takes into account the way that different groups of people use spaces differently from one another and gives attention to the way certain films articulate less dominant, or less commonly represented, uses of space. Looking at the ways that space is used by children in the film *Ratcatcher* (Lynne Ramsay, 1999), for instance, she points out that

> [in] many societies there is an active, vibrant, independent childhood culture organized around the exploration of non-home spaces. . . . Children also have their own "path-networks": these are entirely independent of routes used by adults, the main objective not to get from A to B; for the journey is frequently the purpose of the trip.[29]

Male-desiring men have a long history of creating their own geographies, carving out "path-networks" that are not always given much attention. Through trial and error, male-desiring men have learned over time which spaces are safe to meet in, building cultures of knowledge around how to find and use such spaces. While this may be obvious in the use of semipublic spaces, such as parks used for cruising or public toilets used for sex, it is also true of a wider constellation of sites such as bars, restaurants, and beaches that men come to employ for the circulation of gay life, even if only temporarily.

In these films, as in Kuhn's example, "the journey is frequently the purpose." Even in films that are invested in narrative resolution, such as *Pink Narcissus* (James Bidgood, 1971) and *L.A. Tool and Die* (Joe Gage, 1979), the majority of screen time is spent showing male protagonists moving through a kaleidoscopic collection of spaces. Gay life is often elaborated as an expedition that, weaving through a variety of interior and exterior spaces, offers a sense of movement *through* the tributaries and pathways that make gay life possible.

Chapter 1, "Picturing the Underground," begins with an examination of postwar Los Angeles, looking at how male-desiring filmmakers used cinema to "picture" and elaborate a homosexual underground as a vital domain for fostering social, sexual, political, and cultural activity. Through three case studies—Kenneth Anger's avant-garde short film *Fireworks* (1947), the mail-order physique films of Bob Mizer's Athletic Model Guild, and the amateur films of the Gay Girls Riding Club—this chapter asks how each film worked to construct an image of proto-gay and gay life informed by the figure of what I call "outlaw spatiality." I explore how these films draw on and/or cultivate connotative representations of male-male desire as part of a topography of underground space.

By the end of the 1960s, a number of filmmakers were making films that would become part of the first film programs, events, and screenings marketed to a gay audience. Chapter 2, "The Cinematic Authoring of Gay Life," explores how a cycle of films made between the late 1960s and the early 1970s engaged with discourses of authorship as a way of addressing audiences interested in the possibilities of gay life. As a newly deployed paradigm of public address, gay authorship of the gay liberation era began to operate through cinema and the print media connected to it in a more denotative way. Through four cases studies—James Bidgood's *Pink Narcissus* (1971), Steve Arnold's *Luminous Procuress* (1971), and the films of Peter de Rome and Pat Rocco—I trace a textual shift from affective codings of desire to direct and overtly political articulations of gay personhood as the male author/onlooker moves on screen.

At the same time that de Rome and Rocco were creating scores of short films, another crop of filmmakers and producers with ties to the mainstream film industry began to develop the first feature-length dramatic films about gay life, made for distribution to a wider audience. Chapter 3 explores three films—*Song of the Loon* (Andrew Herbert,

1970), *Some of My Best Friends Are . . .* (Mervyn Nelson, 1971), and *A Very Natural Thing* (Christopher Larkin, 1974)—that aspired to larger audiences. These films all constructed representations of male-desiring men as part of a "gay people." Through their foregrounding of gay men as one cluster of social types among others, these films seek to clarify and make drama out of the ways in which gay men as a group may be oppressed by or liberated through the spaces in which they move and the ways in which they do it. This chapter analyzes the emergence of a more psychologically driven, individualist focalization of gay life.

Gay hard-core pornographic feature films were the most prolific area of gay cinema, with over 250 films made for release between the beginning of theatrical hard-core in the early 1970s and its decline in the late 1970s. Chapter 4, "Liberation Porn," explores a dominant thematic that is threaded through 1970s gay hard-core features: the politics and philosophy of the gay liberation movement at a moment when it was extremely unsettled, highly variable, and capable of producing many different ways of thinking and feeling about questions of sex, gender, and world making. This chapter elucidates how gay hard-core modeled numerous versions of gay life. From the avant-garde formal experimentations of *L.A. Plays Itself* (1972) and *American Cream* (Jean-Claude van Itallie credited as Rob Simple, 1972) to the gay utopias of *Boys in the Sand* (Wakefield Poole, 1971) and *L.A. Tool and Die* (Joe Gage, 1979), this chapter shows how gay hard-core films invited viewers to feel, think, and imagine the place of sexual interaction in building practices for gay liberation.

ONE

Picturing the Underground

The Terrain of the Homosexual Underground

In the mid-twentieth-century United States, the figure of the underground was repeatedly deployed to describe two forms of activity in spatialized terms: small organizational meetings held by political dissidents in clandestine spaces and art, music, and film events arranged in out-of-the-way locations such as lofts, old cinemas, apartments, and wilderness settings. The underground operated as both a figure of popular paranoid imagination—a way of imagining invisible groups of others who threatened to destabilize normative civil life from beneath—and as a designation for an actual cultural geographic formation. Underground sites were spaces in which groups came into new constellations of counterpublic formation in private, semiprivate, and appropriated public domains.

A number of key events occurred between the early 1940s and the mid-1960s that changed how Americans perceived their place in wider society. This had particular ramifications for the coalescence of LGBTQ+ social and political life. Primed by the gendered division of labor among soldiers in World War II, many women and men returned from the war after living in sustained conditions of sex segregation. For returning service people, particularly but not only same-sex desiring individuals, this made the prospect of coming back to either begin or resume nuclear family life more challenging.

At the same time, and at least in part as a response to growing sex segregation, a public discourse developed around fears that homosocial contexts might operate as the breeding grounds for dangerous forms of social, political, cultural, and sexual dissidence. During this time, a variety of phenomena fostered the notion of a "homosexual" underclass in the mass media. In a precursor to later paradigms of "outness," official bodies began to register homosexuality as a ubiquitous and often invisible phenomenon that needed to be rendered visible.

The first of these phenomena was the US military's discharge of thousands of personnel believed to be homosexual, officially implemented in 1944 with Regulation 615-360, Section 8. This permitted the government to subject military personnel to psychiatric testing in order to determine if they might be diagnosed as homosexual: a term that at this point was almost exclusively meant to designate a form of psychopathological disease and disorder. With an estimated four to five thousand personnel fired, these discharges had the effect of moving homosexuality into the public eye.[1] It also promoted the notion that homosexuality was something that could be identified through diagnostic psychiatric testing, even if a subject had never participated in same-sex sexual activity. It became conceivable to the public at large that one could unknowingly harbor latent forms of homosexuality that were fully diagnosable to the expert eye.

Another key phenomenon that worked to pedestrianize homosexuality was Alfred Kinsey's 1948 study *Sexual Behavior in the Human Male*, in which the sexologist reported that 37 percent of the male American population had participated in same-sex activity at some point in their lives.[2] As a result of the media attention given to Kinsey's study (as well as the repeated emphasis on what came to be known as the Kinsey Scale, according to which everyone registers somewhere on a continuum between heterosexual and homosexual extremes), it became possible to conceive of any person as having a history of or a continued interest in same-sex sexual activity. While not necessarily constructing homosexuals as an underclass, per se, the treatment of the Kinsey Report as a scandalous revelation presented same-sex desire as something always potentially underneath the facade of everyday American life.

Postwar panic around the specter of homosexuality peaked with the US government's purging of its employees in what has since come to be called the Lavender Scare.[3] Occurring in tandem with Cold War paranoia, prominent government officials came to believe that homosexuals in the US government compromised national security, in that they were susceptible to blackmail and could be forced to spy on behalf of

Communist infiltrators. By the 1960s, this purge reached "well into the thousands."[4]

The combination of these three events encouraged a figuration of homosexuals as existing "underneath" in a variety of ways. Psychologically, homosexuality was a pathologized persona existing just below and working in contrast to an otherwise unsuspecting, presentable self. Socially, it might be gathering just beneath the veneer of governmental institutions from the military to the White House and beyond. Homosexuality, as produced in the postwar discourse of panic and paranoia, was amplified as a spatialized figure that spanned the literal and metaphoric. It threatened to poison normative life from below: invisible but also potentially anywhere and everywhere. While this paranoid figuration resulted in the abuse and persecution of male-desiring men, it also ignited the imagination of people across the US, prompting them to imagine what kinds of activity might be taking place around them. Some men began to move from just imagining to carving out spaces and creating networks of contact. The imagination of social possibility did not end once they began meeting, but became central to facilitating the mobilization of large groups of male-desiring men.

During the postwar years, two nexuses of social organization came into being within and through the figure of underground cultural formation. Each of these nexuses fostered new ways of structuring and experiencing sex and gender, though in somewhat different ways. In the first case, underground social/political groups, such as the Mattachine Society, One Inc., and the Daughters of Bilitis, organized around the interests of same-sex desiring participants. In the second case, the same period saw the emergence and expansion of experimental cinema groups, organized around fostering US avant-garde filmmaking and film events. As Juan Suárez has noted, the underground was an important figure for dissident artistic formations both in Europe and America even before the 1960s, evoking "a certain glamorization of marginality, a desire to thrive outside (or underneath) the mainstream."[5] Spearheaded in Los Angeles in the late 1940s by filmmakers such as Kenneth Anger, Maya Deren, and Curtis Harrington, experimental film culture, like underground gay organizations, quickly came to work as a national (though largely bicoastal) cluster of sites and activities that sponsored non-heterocentric forms of sociosexuality among participants.

These two prominent "undergrounds" are not typically thought about in more than a cursory relationship to one another, and there are many reasons for this. Their goals were different: one sought to advance the freedoms of people at risk of being ostracized and stigmatized as the agents of criminal, pathological homosexuality, while the other sought, first and foremost, to advance challenging new forms and arrangements of filmmaking and film reception. However, if we think of the underground less in terms of culturally located, specific groups and more as a *process* of sociopolitical world-making taken up among a wide range of individuals and groups, then we can see how numerous strands of postwar social activity start to become legible as key contributors to the postwar construction of social life among male-desiring men, both on film and off. In other words, the increasing mobilization of male-desiring men as a recognizable social constituency not only operated through the prerogatives of institutionalization but also developed within a world of overlapping and layered sites of activity, broadly informed by notions of underground dissidence. The same could be said of the avant-garde cinema culture that showed some of the first censorship-challenging images of same-sex desire in the US—one site of overlap in which these undergrounds spoke to and informed each other.

This chapter considers the place of postwar underground cultural production in the United States between the late 1940s and the mid-1960s and asks how the production, circulation, and screening of films worked as a rallying point for the expansion and elaboration of social and political life among male-desiring men. While a number of conceptual frameworks operated as a means for identification and affiliation among male-desiring men during this period—including camp, homophile, queer, homosexual, and gay—in this chapter I explore the increasing popularization of homosexuality as a discourse during the postwar years in fostering new forms of social formation and cinematic experience. While the concept of homosexuality medicalized individuals and groups as pathological and disordered, it also facilitated contacts and connections, enabling social and political organization. People classified as homosexuals not only suffered at the hands of psychiatrists, the law, and phobic citizens, but also came together *as* homosexuals. As Martin Meeker has noted, "before people who erotically and emotionally preferred the same sex could organize to confront and challenge their antagonists, they have had to coalesce around an identity and gather themselves into collectivities, into communities, into specific places, and around certain ideas."[6]

The underground functioned as a figurative trope central to the coalescence of homosexual social organization during the postwar years. Quite different from the metaphor of the closet, which suggests a wholly concealed location that renders certain behaviors and interests invisible to society as a whole, the underground signals a shifting constellation of sites between and through which people move and congregate. Whether bikers like the Satyrs Motorcycle Club barbecuing in a state park, drag queens chatting backstage at Finocchio's in San Francisco, or a group of friends out for a night of cruising at the Windup bar in Hollywood, male-desiring men participated in sophisticated networks of underground sociality. Their energy was directed less toward the possibility of inclusion and acceptance within the world at large and more toward developing sites and networks of sociosexual activity on their own terms.

Cinema and cinema culture offered a fertile ground for the gathering of male-desiring men. Going to, making, and exhibiting movies brought men together in basements, bars, rented movie theaters, apartments, and homes and at special event screenings in art theaters. This chapter explores the place of cinema in the underground world-making activities of male-desiring men during an era when "homosexuality" became a central feature of popular discourse in the United States. At the same time that popular magazines were locating and exploring the features of US homosexual culture, these underground networks themselves were growing, resulting in more complex and enculturated forms of togetherness. The cinemas of the homosexual underground imagined ways of living and being in the world that both echoed the growing collectivizaton of people around models of same-sex desire and imagined mechanisms for inspiring new forms of collectivity, bridging the distance between the imagined and the possible.

Yet, the history I want to recall here does not only describe an emergent group of people coming into visibility through self-representation. It is just as much, if not more, a history of the role of movements, industries, technologies, spaces, and locations in both imagining and bringing into being new social contexts and formations as well as revitalizing and repurposing old ones. In order to elucidate the terrain of the homosexual underground, this chapter considers three areas: avant-garde film shown at art theaters and "private" screenings, mail-order homoerotic physique films viewed in homes and at special events, and amateur/home movies made and screened among groups of friends in homes, apartments, and bars. These films act as documents of participation in cultures of same-sex desire at a time when these cultures, and the films they made, risked bringing participants up against the persecution of the law, family, and the medical/psychiatric establishment. At the same time, they also act as affective repositories that demonstrate how male-desiring men produced, shaped, and participated in particular currents of feeling.

The homosexual underground is a spatially centered cinema; this is a key facet of how these films articulate the complicated relationship between alienation, sexual endeavor, and sociality. Over and over, these movies use the movement within and between certain kinds of space to dramatize how male-desiring men might end up: tragically alone, coupled with another man, or aligned with a group of male-desiring men. They use a variety of spaces—from on-location urban sites to exotic "fantasy" sets—to position male-male desire as a worlded experience. That is, space in the homosexual underground film becomes a means for asserting that male-male desire is capable of claiming a whole domain. Even when characters are shown as isolated and alone, they are rarely figured only in close-up, but rather shown as part of an environment. In the homosexual underground, male-male desire is thus pictured as having the weight and significance that comes with the spatialized constitution of characters placed in the world and thus, at least theoretically, capable of acting upon and changing that world.

This chapter considers the role of space and location in a set of films made in and around Los Angeles and Southern California. It begins by looking at how homosexual discourse fostered certain forms of social and political contact among male-desiring men starting in the mid- to late 1940s and goes on to explore how this in turn fostered certain practices of underground filmmaking and cinema-going culture. It then establishes the relationship that existed between dominant and independent forms of filmmaking, looking at three case studies: the avant-garde trance film *Fireworks* (Kenneth Anger, 1947), the early films of the Athletic Model Guild, and the work of the filmmaking collective the Gay Girls Riding Club. Each of these studies considers how these films undertake negotiations with mainstream film tropes as a means to advance inventive elaborations of underground spatiality.

Across Town: Three Sites in Underground Los Angeles

In December 1945, with his mother's permission, twenty-two-year-old Bob Mizer began taking photographs of muscular men, naked save for posing straps, at their family-owned rooming house under the company name Athletic Model Guild. Located at 1834 West Eleventh Street in the Pico-Union neighborhood of Los Angeles, the 1898 craftsman house offered ample space, inside and out, for Mizer to work with his models, store his equipment, and set up a lab to develop prints. Following the commercial success of his individual photographs with a network of in-the-know customers, as well as his release from six months at the Saugus Prison Farm for sending his photographs through the US mail in 1947, Mizer launched the first issue of his magazine *Physique Photo News* in May 1951 (permanently renamed *Physique Pictorial* in November of that same year).[7] From this point until his death in 1992, Athletic Model Guild operated as a boarding house for models and actors, a screening venue, a distribution hub for AMG's films and magazines, and a photography and movie studio, serving an international audience. Subsequent to his mother's passing in September 1964, Mizer began running the house as a compound that accommodated models.

Between 1945 and the rise in gay visibility in the late 1960s and early 1970s, thousands of men around the globe saw their first overt images of same-sex sexual and romantic desire between men thanks to Mizer. From his corner of Los Angeles, he generated inexpensive, fantastical visions of male-male desire that posited his studio space as a utopian oasis of homoeroticism.

One May afternoon in Los Angeles, 1948, three men met during a lunch break at an industrial office where one of them, Harry Hay, worked as a secretary. Hay, an actor and Communist Party organizer, and Bill Lewis, Hay's coworker, were speaking to their friend Chuck. Chuck, in town for a brief visit, was a secretary in the State Department in Washington DC and was clueing them in to the sudden spate of firings of suspected homosexuals from the State Department. Concerned about this spike in persecution, Hay began planning for more formal meetings to discuss tactics of political and social mobilization. Proposed and provisional names for this group included "Society's Androgynous Minority" and the "International Bachelors' Fraternal Order for Peace and Social Dignity" before the name Mattachine was settled on for the group's first official meeting in November of 1950.[8] The inspiration for the name was the Mattachinos of the Italian Renaissance, masked jesters who were able to use their concealed identities as a means to stage criticism and challenge the dominance of monarchal power.[9]

The Mattachine Society began meeting clandestinely in homes, offices, and apartments throughout the greater Los Angeles area. At these meetings they socialized and strategized for political action. They increasingly merged Communist Party organizational strategies, arranged around small cells, with publicity strategies such as the circulation of magazines and, later, appearances in news and television documentaries. The society created a series of leaflets to warn of homosexual entrapment by police and circulated them across the city at "beaches in Santa Monica . . . bars in Los Angeles, in restrooms cruised by gay men, and at park benches and bus stops in homosexual parts of the city."[10] By the mid- to late 1950s, the Mattachine Society had chapters throughout California, as well as in most major cities across the Midwest and East Coast. Emblematized by the metaphor of masked rebels, from its beginnings the group sought to draw power from its own invisibility, using anonymous meetings at low-key locations as a means to build its membership. This in turn catalyzed the propagation of other homosocial organizations: the breakaway group One, Inc. developed in Los Angeles by Mattachine members and responsible for creating a magazine under that same name, and the women's group the Daughters of Bilitis, started in 1955, which promoted meetings in homes as an alternative to bars, where harassment by police and others was a persistent problem.[11] Between the 1950s and the early 1970s, numerous fraternal groups proliferated across the US, offering social connection and political mobilization for homosexuals based around models of same-sex sociality and desire.

One night in 1947, knowing that his parents were away for the weekend, twenty-year-old University of Southern California student Kenneth Anger gathered together a combination of friends, acquaintances, and (solicited) marine corps members to make a 16 mm movie in his parents' Beverly Hills bungalow. The resulting film, *Fireworks*, meshes dream and reality in telling the story of a young protagonist (played by Anger) who, through the course of the film, sleeps naked, alone and erect (dreaming of himself in the arms of a sailor); cruises the clandestine streets, bars, and public restrooms of a Los Angeles cityscape at night; is brutally beaten by a gang of strapping sailors on a filthy street; is seduced by a single sailor back in his home; and, at the film's end, wakes up naked in bed with a man. While the screening history of the film is somewhat uncertain, reports by both the filmmaker and viewers suggest that it first played at a midnight screening at the Coronet Theatre in 1947.[12] Located in Los Angeles at 366 North La Cienega Boulevard, the Coronet was a hub for experimental and dissident film and theater. It had a significant following of male-desiring men in part due to its willingness to risk legal ramifications for showing explicit images of male-male desire. *Fireworks* made its way to West Hollywood in 1948, where it showed at the home of composer and educator Pauline Schindler alongside another homoerotic trance film, *Fragment of Seeking*, made by Anger's friend and fellow USC student Curtis Harrington. *Fireworks* became arguably the highest profile homoerotic film of the postwar years, playing at numerous arthouse screenings in the US and Europe throughout the 1950s, and becoming the focus of the obscenity trial of the manager of Los Angeles's Coronet Theatre following a 1957 screening (he received a guilty verdict that was then reversed). As a guerrilla film made without permits across the Los Angeles area (including, for example, by the busy roads running through Cahuenga Pass and at a public restroom in Olive Park, where Anger filmed himself nude on the floor in nothing but a sailor's cap), the film—both in its production and exhibition—charts an underground topography of nonnormative desire that positions Los Angeles as a diffuse, though potently charged, sociosexual zone of underground movement and activity.[13]

Taken together, the work of Mizer, the Mattachine Society, and Anger demonstrates an indexically and metaphorically rich emergent topography of underground sites in Los Angeles. These sites and the images produced from them operated as a nexus for the mobilization of direct contact between male-desiring men. They demonstrate an interest not only in facilitating the meeting of people with similar or affiliated senses of desire, but in situating that desire through underground spatiality.

Outlaw Spatiality, Minor Cinema, and the Homosexual Underground

Same-sex desire began to figure in film with increasing regularity from the 1940s onward—often as a form of pathologized homosexual desire—in a combination of crime films, avant-garde films, and physique films. With the Motion Picture Production Code in full effect, which meant a prohibition on direct representations of same-sex desire in Hollywood films, and a patchwork of uneven local obscenity laws across the country, representing same-sex desire carried with it a constant risk of censorship and prosecution.[14] Putting same-sex desire on film could only happen through figuratively undergrounding its representation. That is, to be represented at all, it had to be—like the Mattachine meetings—folded into and submerged within the ordinary workings of everyday life in such a way as to keep it from becoming a focal point.

While nonconformist behavior often resulted in some form of moralizing discouragement at the level of narrative and plot (ostracization, destitution, death), certain genres used location filming and studio back lots to construct a sense of outlaw spatiality: space away from the disciplinary gaze of the legal and medical establishment. This was, in turn, picked up and elaborated on in the first films geared toward addressing male-desiring men as an audience in their own right.

As scholars such as Harry Benshoff, Sean Griffin, and Richard Dyer have explored, homosexuality appeared as part of the iconographic makeup of many key villain characters of the first noir cycle.[15] Criminal undergrounds were often inflected by coded implications of an illicit sexual underground, from the conspiratorial gatherings of the florally scented Joel Cairo (Peter Lorre), teen "gunsel" Wilmer (Elisha Cook Jr.), and aesthete Kasper Gutman (Sidney Greenstreet) in *The Maltese Falcon* (John Huston, 1941), to the inseparable thugs Fante (Lee Van Cleef) and Mingo (Earl Holliman) in *The Big Combo* (Joseph Lewis, 1955). These popular thrillers widely circulated recurring motifs of homosexuals as a threatening criminal underground, unseen but active from the beach to the bookstore, the casino to the boxing arena. Distinct from the pansies of 1930s comedies, these homosexuals were defined less by gender dissidence and personal eccentricity and more by the social networks and positions they inhabited and animated. They were dangerous in part because they were connected.

Meanwhile, in film series like *Tarzan*, story collections such as *Teenage Stories of Action* by Frank Owen (New York: Grosset & Dunlap, 1948), comic books like *Batman* (featuring Robin the Boy Wonder), movie serials such as *Terry and the Pirates* (James W. Horne, 1940) and *Jungle Queen* (Lewis D. Collins, Ray Taylor, 1945), and hugely popular features such as *The Thief of Bagdad* (Michael Powell et al., 1940) and *Arabian Nights* (John Rawlins, 1942), teenage males were frequently figured within a paradigm that Jeffrey P. Dennis has called "the homoromantic." Locales such as magical islands full of alcoves and hideaways, byzantine cityscapes, deep lagoons, and underground cave networks marked a romantic, Arcadian (often Technicolor) mise-en-scène in which male bonds flourish away from the dominant social order without, as Dennis puts it, "being hidden, denied, or drowned out by the roar of heteronormative expectations."[16] Within these fantastical Arcadian spaces, heterosexuality takes a break, and outlaw activity finds a home.[17]

A similarly homoromantic Arcadian space is also on display in the cycle of teen rebel films of the early to mid-1950s, addressing the youth audiences who were quickly becoming the primary audience for film. Films such as *The Wild One* (László Benedek, 1953), *Rebel without a Cause* (Nicholas Ray, 1955), *East of Eden* (Elia Kazan, 1955), and *Blackboard Jungle* (Richard Brooks, 1955) all focused on disaffected, almost exclusively white teenagers who, like youth audiences themselves, developed complex social contexts away from the nuclear family, aided in some cases by the growing accessibility of scooters, motorcycles, and automobiles. The teen rebel cycle elaborates an outlaw topography of romanticized spaces separate from the dour everyday world of adult heterosexist convention that works to accommodate and foster new forms of bonding where feelings of sameness, at times rooted in notions of biological sex, might be accorded a great deal of social, sexual, and psychological power.

Michael De Angelis has explored the sense of equivalency that marks the relationship between James Dean's Jim Stark and Natalie Wood's Judy in *Rebel without a Cause*. Unlike other male-female movie couplings, the two invest in a kind of buddy relationship wherein they seem more invested in their shared sense of alienation than in the kind of opposites-attract model of desire through which heterosexual relations are dominantly figured. Even more, as a threesome they share physical closeness and affection with their friend Plato (Sal Mineo). As De Angelis notes with regards to an evening the three of the spend hanging out in an abandoned house and sarcastically enacting a role-play of the traditional American family:

> What is valued within this reconfigured family is not the demonstration and enforcement of parental authority, but a spirit of equivalence—a sameness of oneself and to others, and a spirit of mutual understanding, that becomes possible whether one elects to enact the role of parent, child or both.[18]

This sense of sameness—of what De Angelis refers to as a "utopic state of equivalence"[19]—constructs new arrangements of sex and gender relations. Established conventions, set loose into an arrangement of play, foster affective relations whereby the three become closer through their shared demotion and dismissal of the heteropatriarchal culture in which they have been raised. In short, they find themselves bonded together through their shared sense of the absurdity and grotesque limitation imposed by conventional roles.

This overlap of outlaw sexuality and outlaw spatiality running through dominant cultural production offered opportunities for independent and/or avant-garde cinemas to use and rethink popular imagery. Building on Deleuze and Guattari's writing on minor literature, David E. James has noted how subaltern groups have utilized independent cinema as a means for minor cultural production. Minor film and minor cinema culture, for James, repurpose the tropes and conventions of dominant commercial cinema as a means of reading or speaking back to it in such a way that fosters certain forms of group consciousness among viewers. Through this process, a group of people come to "counter their representation in the commercial cinema: and filmmaking and film viewing become rituals by which the group invents and understands itself, communicates with others, extends its influence, and makes new recruits . . . minor *films* are created—even as they create—avant-garde or minor cinemas."[20] James has explored the specific place of Los Angeles in the proliferation of minor filmmaking in avant-garde, amateur, and other forms of independent production and exhibition during the postwar years. He notes:

> The role of spatiality [in minor avant-garde cinema] is double, involving the representation of spatiality and also the role played by spatiality in their production . . . the link between the two geographies are integral, and often avant-garde films manifest or inscribe the relationship between the environment in which they are produced and that which they represent.[21]

The inscription of this relationship, between the actual environment of Los Angeles and its representation on film, was a key aspect of putting male-male desire on screen and, even more so, a key facet in the articulation of postwar attachments and associations with popular models of the homosexual by nonnormative subjects (including those who will not come to identify as gay: trans*, queer, men who have sex with men). Through the avant-garde shorts, homoerotic mail-order films, and amateur/home movies made and shown during this period, a cinema began to crystallize around figurative inscriptions of spatial relations. Across the work of Kenneth Anger, Curtis Harrington, Bob Mizer, Richard Fontaine, and Bruce of Los Angeles, environment operates as a metonym for the experience of being homosexual in postwar Los Angeles, a figure through which to articulate, flesh out, play with, and work through that experience.

Though these minor categories—avant-garde, mail-order, amateur—tend to be treated as distinct cinematic arenas in terms of industry, aesthetics, and audiences, they share a great deal in common in terms of how they undertake inventive depictions of male-male desire through recourse to and appropriation of the popular postwar trope of outlaw spatiality. Collectively, these eclectic film types form homosexual underground cinema and, while coming at male-male desire from somewhat different perspectives (and having different uses), all showcase how outlaw space could be taken up by male-desiring men.

However, unlike the major movies they drew on, these films also worked to develop outlaw space in real life by bringing audiences together as part of a public constituency meeting in the spaces of the homosexual underground. Anger's *Fireworks* brought male-desiring men together through screenings starting, purportedly, in 1947 at the Coronet Theatre in West Hollywood, a theater known for being, as Whitney Strub has noted, a "gay male social hub."[22] Even the mail-order homoerotic physique film—typically thought of as only for discrete, individual home viewing—was recommended for collective and semipublic screening. The April 1961 issue of magazine/mail-order catalog *Physique Pictorial* invites its readers to offer feedback: "if you have our films or see them at your gym or other places where physical culturists congregate . . . let us know what we can do . . . to make them more effective."[23] This circulation of physique films contributed to the early consolidation of the homosexual underground.

These film screenings, like the material presented in them, undertook outlaw uses of space, risking and sometimes suffering the consequences of censorship. At the same time, censorship and condemnation meant publicity. For example, the *Fireworks* obscenity trial in Los Angles worked—like a pin stuck into a map—to mark and perversely promote an underground cinema addressing the interests of male-desiring men.

Fireworks and the Glorification of Homosexuality

Contact between sexual outlaws in underground space finds cinematic elaboration in films made by male-desiring men with a small of cycle of avant-garde films produced and screened from the late 1940s through to the 1960s. Work by Anger, Harrington, Gregory Markopoulos, and Willard Maas all featured lone protagonists (often played by the filmmakers themselves) moving through black-and-white, often shadowy, urban landscapes, presenting male-male desire within a circuitry of recessed, tucked-away spaces. Films such as *Fireworks*, *Fragment of Seeking*, *Christmas U.S.A.* (Markopoulos, 1949), and *Narcissus* (Maas, 1956) situate their filmmaker-protagonists within labyrinthine pathways that lead to dramatic, externalized confrontations with internal desires, dreams, and curiosities. In *Fireworks* and *Fragment of Seeking*, Anger and Harrington each traverse mazelike pathways to compartmentalized spaces (in *Fireworks* a bar, a bathroom, side streets, and an apartment; in *Fragment* a series of rooms, gardens, hallways, and courtyards) in which they confront their desire for men and other forms of nonnormative being and expression (Anger's erotically charged sadomasochistic contact with sailors, for example, or Harrington's encounter with a female doppelganger.)

P. Adams Sitney has explored the trope of the wandering filmmaker-protagonist in these films as part of a postwar avant-garde tradition he calls the "trance film." Describing the relationship between mise-en-scène, subjectivity, and confrontation in these films, Sitney writes:

> The trance film as it emerged in America has fairly strict boundaries. It deals with visionary experience. . . . The protagonist moves through a potent environment towards a climactic scene of self-realization. The landscapes both natural and architectural . . . often intensify the texture of the film to the point of emphasizing a specific line of symbolism. It is part of the nature of the trance that the protagonist remains isolated from what he confronts; no interaction of characters is possible in these films. . . . [These films are characterized by] the protagonist who passes invisibly among people; the dramatic landscapes; the climactic confrontation with one's self and one's past.[24]

Sitney observes how mise-en-scène and the protagonist's traversal of space highlight a narrative of self-confrontation. It is interesting to note the way he oddly overlooks the action that defines so many of these films, in which protagonists are repeatedly shown coming into *interaction* with others through shared experiences of nonnormative sociosexual contact (in fact, the final scene of *Fireworks* shows Anger lying in bed naked with another man, his arms affectionately stretched out over the man's torso). As such, attention to the function of outlaw space in the exchange of male-male desire might productively modify our use of Sitney's formulation of the trance film.

The way these films dramatize both isolation and contact in relation to a homosexual discourse that posits male-desiring men, and young homosexual men in particular, as psychologically unwell is a fundamental aspect of how they came to speak to an audience of male-desiring men (and still do). Drawing on the kind of outlaw spatiality seen in teen rebel and noir films, these trance films reconfigure the official discourse of homosexuals-as-sick in socializing terms; if these men are sick, then they are far from sick and alone. What the protagonists of many of these films can't seem to escape is not so much themselves, but the fact that there are others who share or at least exist in relation to their feelings and desires; not that they are bound to an endless, alienated subjectivity but that they are constantly on the brink of experiencing intersubjectivity with others.

This does not mean that these films move toward a purely affirmative stance on male-male desire or attempt to extricate it from the pathologizing discourse of homosexuality. Instead, they refashion the negative discourse of homosexuality, recasting it by adding to it an increased texture of social possibility. Take, for example, a passage from Robert H. V. Ollendorf's popular psychological study *The Juvenile Homosexual Experience and Its Effect on Adult Sexuality,* based on research conducted as far back as the 1920s. Ollendorf explains that "[homosexual neurotics] are forced to adopt a style of life which carries the character of a secret society and, as in all such groups, naturally a great amount of special neuroticisms are developed spontaneously. Emotional histrionics, the formation of pseudofemininity, and an incessant real anxiety over discovery of blackmail inevitably play an essential role."[25] The author also stresses that the neurotic is "inducted" into such a society, emphasizing through italics that *"the noninduced nonconditioned person will not become a homosexual under any circumstances."*[26]

Fireworks offers a virtual compendium of such images of juvenile homosexual neurosis. The story poetically elaborates a single day or so in the life of the protagonist, starting with a medium long shot of the teenage Anger being held in a sailor's arms (which will later reappear as an image in a stack of burning photographs). This is followed by Anger waking up alone in bed with an erection (comically revealed to be a wooden statue). From there he gets dressed, exits through a door marked "GENTS," and traverses a shadowy night city of highways, overlooks, bars, side streets, and public bathrooms. Following an attack at the hands of a sailor he desires, he is shown coming back to his apartment where the sailor lights his cigarette with a burning "faggot" (an archaic word for a bundle of sticks). Cutting to an exterior scene, we see Anger chased on the street by a gang of sailors who beat him to the ground. This is followed by a dreamlike succession of erotic, violent close-ups of milk (a hyperbolic stand-in for ejaculate) spilling down over his lips and neck, and hands ripping open his chest, after which we see him back in his apartment again, this time with the top of a shimmering Christmas tree attached to his upper body, lit candle atop. A subsequent blurred medium shot shows him naked in bed with another man by his side.

As mentioned by Sitney, the trance film "intensif[ies] the texture of the film to the point of emphasizing a specific line of symbolism." In this case, this intensification works to highlight notions of homosexual neurosis. The burning of the images of the protagonist in the sailor's arms suggest incriminating evidence for exposure or blackmail. The burning sticks and shimmering tree render the protagonist in the derogatory terms of "pseudo-effeminacy," a "flaming faggot" decked out "like a Christmas tree." Throughout, numerous elements paint the protagonist as a neurotic overflowing with "special neuroticism developed spontaneously," from his desire to frantically give the cigarettes to other men he finds attractive to a quick shot of him submissively sprawled out naked on a bathroom floor.

What makes this more than merely a portrait of homosexual unwellness is the way cinematographic texture is used to glorify these instances as pleasure filled, beautiful, even revelatory. Much of this effect is achieved through the way outlaw space is presented as ecstatic. The film builds on the kind of images of recessed outlaw space familiar from noir crime films and the rebel cycle, yet it also lifts those spaces out of their role as milieus for character interaction. In *Fireworks*, outlaw space itself becomes energetically arranged and organized through quick cuts, forming a series of lively interconnected sites. The apartment, the bar, the public bathroom, and the street are all braided together, shifting and unfolding into one another choreographically.

If homosexuals "induct" others into male-male desire within the terms of the secret society that they "adopt," then the cinematographic texturing of *Fireworks* takes this clandestine society and intensifies it, creating a terrible world knitted together from outlaw spaces, the entering of which results, paradoxically, in the reward of ecstatic and erotic male-male coupling. This makes the film somewhat unique in the corpus of early postwar trance films. As Juan A. Suárez observes, "by positing some sort of continuity between the communal and the individual aspects of homosexuality, *Fireworks* departed from the films [of Markopoulos, Maas, and Harrington], . . . which tended to focus almost exclusively on its subjective side."[27]

Violence and turmoil here may be the stuff of dreams or a confrontation with reality, but ultimately the vision of this trance protagonist appears to bring him to a space of waking within the glory of his actualized male-male desire, a fact emphasized by the shimmering halo painted on the film negative that graces his lover's head.

Suárez places this reinscription of dominant culture as a tendency running through underground avant-garde cinema more broadly. He notes that "the underground's celebration of a decentered subjectivity based on role-playing and artifice can be read as a maneuver of occultation, governed by the desire to escape the fixity medical and popular journalistic accounts were trying to enforce."[28] Within *Fireworks*, the signs that mark homosexual unwellness are refracted through a rendering of subjectivity that disarms them through their very glorification. Figured as crude manifestations of artifice and perhaps even fetish, homosexuality here is also an avenue for movement toward the actualization of one's desires.

Responsive to a paranoid medical discourse of homosexuality that posits the "secret society" as the locus for the induction and expansion of male-male desire, the mediation of space and location is central to the film's figuration of decentered subjectivity. Focalized as the wandering protagonist's vision, decentered subjectivity also carries with it, in line with the trance film's emphasis on mise-en-scène and formal texture, the articulation of a decentered spatiality that results in a revaluation of peripheral and recessed locales, in a sense recentering them as dramatic focal points in and of themselves. Reconstituted as part of a drama of male-male eros and ecstatic contact, space, in this context—moved toward the hegemonically decentering center of homosexual reverie—comes to deny a heterocentric perspective, picturing in its place a world of underground movement that takes perversity as a cue for coming together.

Outlaw Space and the World of the Athletic Model Guild

Filmed in actual, out-of-the-way spaces such as backyards, wilderness areas, and secluded beaches, and often incorporating stagy scenery and props to construct jungle, desert, and wilderness environments, the homoerotic physique film worked to turn audiences on through fantasy while alerting them to the real possibilities of actualized male-male desire promulgated through a topography of underground space—a sort of psychogeographic map, fusing the imaginary and the actual. The short (typically five to fifteen minute) mail-order films that Bob Mizer produced and sold through his Athletic Model Guild (starting in 1957 and continuing, intermittently, until the early 1990s)[29] drew on the homoromantic imagery found in popular teen rebel and adventure boy films and novels, bringing it together with the more avowedly homoerotic aesthetics of physique photography that Mizer had been producing and distributing since the mid-1940s. From the 1950s through the early 1970s, hundreds of AMG films and their promotional materials facilitated the assembly of male-desiring men. These men engaged with Mizer and each other through letters and phone calls, with many men meeting at his home for making, watching, and buying photographs and films, as well as gathering in parks and other locations for AMG sponsored events. By the late 1960s, screenings of AMG films were part of the first aboveground proto-gay cinema programs to take place at Los Angeles's Park Theatre and received a prominent place in promotional materials.

AMG was not focused on speaking for or about sexual orientation in a straightforward manner. This does not mean, however, that its handling of male-male desire is entirely covert. AMG's output sought to engage its customers by presenting an emphatically hyperbolic and mystified world that blurred the lines between heterosexual and homosexual life. Ranging from the "realist" iconography of military camps, jails, and gyms to the more fantastical adventure boy milieus of the frontier, the Roman slave market, and the harem, AMG engaged viewers in picturing a rich terrain of male-male desire spread out across sites that alternately register as banal and fantastic. This was an outcast, outlaw vision of life that treated male-male desire as, simultaneously, utopian fantasy projection and wholly doable social inclusion. As Thomas Waugh put it in his observation about the 1957 AMG film *Boys in Prison*, "this is not . . . the 'coming out' formula of post-Stonewall fiction, but a utopian fantasy of an outcast's conversion of a whole social environment."[30]

Central to this process of converting the world to an outcast homoerotic perspective was the way in which AMG created a sense of outlaw spatiality through the setup of Mizer's house and its surrounding property. This operated as a compound for AMG incorporating a boarding house, studio spaces, and an outdoor swimming pool. Filled with props and set dressing produced on site by Mizer and his small staff, AMG's production work incorporated the whole of the property, utilizing the backyard, rooftop, parlor room, and swimming pool as sets for the Guild's films.

This use of the Mizer property had the interesting effect of adding an additional layer of self-consciousness to AMG's films. Whereas many of his photographs of posing, showering, and wrestling men were rendered within a modernist studio aesthetic that made use of high-contrast lighting and the sleek lines of minimalist architectural features (geometric sculptures, monochrome backgrounds, and angular shadows were common), Mizer's films had a clumsier, piecemeal aesthetic: quickly fashioned props were made from wood, cardboard, and other cheap, easy-to-obtain materials. The studio kept costs low through its reuse of props so that a backyard rock garden, for instance, could be refashioned to stand in for a number of locales from desert to jungle. The conversion of Mizer's home itself becomes fundamental to the expressive outlaw spatiality of these films. As the quasi-visible spaces of the backyard and the rooftop, for example, become discernable sites for the erotic showcasing of young men, the viewer is invited to imagine real American homes repurposed as living fantasy-scapes of endlessly renewable homoerotic pleasure.

This reimagining of the American home acts as a powerful counterimage to the popular idealization of the home as the locus of the middle-class nuclear family; the Mizer property blurs the boundaries between home and work, labor and leisure, while existing as a space for the social engagement of multiple publics, enabling the growth and expansion of group affiliation and assembly. As Stephen Vider reminds us in his study of postwar gay domesticity, "the home should be viewed not as a sealed private space but as a portal to the public where social connections and political consciousness may be fostered."[31] Mizer's "portal to the public" became the subject of anxiety and interrogation in two court cases: the September 1954 case *People of California vs. Robert Mizer* and the December 1955 case *Donald Thirkill vs. Physique Pictorial* (held before the Superior Court of the State of California, Los Angeles).

In the former, Herbert Selwyn, the defense lawyer, solicited a detailed description of Mizer's home from a vice officer who sought to entrap Mizer by visiting his residence to purchase nude photos. The officer, Phillip J. Barnes, describes being led through the front hall to a porch area; there, he was shown photographs of naked men with their genitalia scratched out or painted over. Barnes reports that he was given time to look at the images and told to ring a bell located on a table when he was ready to make his purchase. Unable to obtain the completely nude photographs required to arrest Mizer, the officer solicited information on where he could attain such items and was given the address of another salesman, Lyle Frisbee, whom he would subsequently visit.[32]

In *Thirkill vs. Physique Pictorial*, plaintiff Donald Thirkill accused Mizer of publishing photographs of him without permission. Mizer's home was again positioned as a portal to underground connections, but an underground defined throughout Thirkill's case not by cloisteredness but permeability. In his testimony, Thirkill outlines an expansive, open world of activity and contact fostered by those who make, sell, and consume homoerotic physique material—an extensive network of male-desiring men across Los Angeles and the world. Thirkill alleged that that the photograph of him in *Physique Pictorial* prompted unwanted contact from numerous male-desiring men from as far away as Australia, writing him letters and phoning him at Babe's, the gym listed as part of his profile in the magazine. As he describes his movement through the world of AMG, Thirkill offers a virtual map of locales through which male-male desire operates, including Mizer's home of Venice Beach, where he met Mizer; Van Ness Park, where Mizer purportedly hosted a Mr. America–style contest between physique models called "Mr. Van Ness Park"; and an apartment near the University of Southern California campus, where a man who contacted Thirkill after seeing him in the magazine expressed interest in spending time with him.[33]

This account of Mizer's home as a network hub resonates with *Physique Pictorial*'s own organization of its material. Alongside AMG's output, the publication promoted work from studios such as Spartan (Los Angeles), Kovert (Los Angeles), Tomorrow's Man (Chicago), and Weaver Studios (Oakland). Post office boxes and, in some cases, the actual addresses of their studios were included. When pooled together, photographs and contact information suggested a panorama of sites across the United States, inviting readers to imagine a world of homoerotic activity. This geographic sprawl was further underscored by the way that the names of studio heads and/or photographers were often tied to locations: Bruce of Los Angeles and Douglas of Detroit were linked to specific cities (and in Al Urban's case, with the figure of the city in general). The pseudo-anonymity of names worked less to protect producers—many of them were openly publishing their home addresses—than to suggest production houses cultivating whole regions. They are the stewards of a culture of homoerotic activity that one can make contact with, whether by mail, phone, or in person.

Mizer's term "guild" suggests a sense of collective, fraternal participation, marking an output as coming from an active community rather than stemming from the labors of one individual. Unlike the subjective cinema of avant-garde filmmakers like Anger, Harrington, and Markopoulos, these films were not constructed to appear as the vision of a single authorial perspective. Films and photographs were not typically sold as being "by Bob Mizer." Directors were frequently uncredited. The images were AMG images.

This places Mizer's work within a tradition of homoerotic image-making stretching back to the invention of photography in the Victorian era. As Thomas Waugh has observed, early homoerotic photography and film kept the presence of the maker decidedly outside of the frame of the image while simultaneously marking the image as part of a dynamic of male-male onlooking. Waugh argues that these images, and in particular the work of Wilhelm von Gloeden, resulted in the signification of a "third body." This is a term Waugh employs to designate "the invisible desiring body of the producer-spectator behind the camera, in front of the photograph, but rarely visualized within the frame," adding that "the third body, the looking, representing subject, stood in for the authorial self as well as for the assumed gay spectator."[34] Unlike the clearly authored work of von Gloeden, however, the often uncredited films and photography of AMG move further into a fantastical blurring between producer and spectator, promoting the sense that anyone—model, maker, consumer, collector, audience member—might be part of this group project of homoerotic picturing.

This sense of collective-yet-anonymous authorship fostered a spirit of participation. Following the guild's addition of film reels for rental and purchase, *Physique Pictorial* began soliciting stories for scripts from customers, promising a free copy of the final product to anyone whose material helped to shape a particular production.[35] *Physique Pictorial* also invoked an editorial "we" in dialogue with its audience: "In this magazine, we try to present a balanced selection of model types, art expression. While we shall never ignore the requests of minorities, we feel our bulk of material should represent what the majority of our readers find desirable."[36]

The spirit of participation cultivated by the guild's many projects is most fully elaborated in their films. After starting with titles such as *Cowboy and the Sailor* and *Pharaoh's New Slave* (both 1958), by 1959 the guild was advertising a mailing list of over a dozen films. This output both works in accord with the third-body paradigm while also stretching and troubling its signifying capacities. Fraying boundaries between the illicit and the permissible, AMG films began placing scenes of wrestling and roughhousing within outlaw and homoromantic settings, echoing teen rebel and adventure boy material through their use of locations and sets centered on a rotating iconography of beaches, county jails, slave markets, and harems. Exciting the imagination of viewers by reconfiguring major movie settings for their unabashedly low-budget and minor erotic skits, the guild made a certain sort of comedic sport out of pushing the limits of third-body representation. That is, the repeated trope of wrestling in a romanticized mise-en-scène of outlawism and/or exoticism played with the notion that popular films were indeed *already* bursting with homoeroticism. The studio underlined this inherent homoeroticism by stripping the plot down to jokey pretexts for action and emphasizing the sensual nature of bodily contact with settings that used popular iconography in a celebratory, decorative manner. In diorama-like constructions, the AMG model appeared like a character from *Tarzan* or *Rebel without a Cause*, but staged and decorated by a mise-en-scène that amplified the pleasure of both production and spectatorship.

AMG's *Booking a Hood* (1957) is a textbook case of the studio's approach. The film comically repurposes the rebel image of Dean and Brando by replacing their usual brooding affects with antics. *Booking a Hood* opens with a Dean-style rebel (Rick Spencer) being booked into jail by two cops: one in full uniform (Brad Allen), the other (Darrell Summers) in nothing more than cap and posing strap. This "interior" is shot in Mizer's backyard and consists of a brick wall, an unattached and incomplete set of bars, handwritten cardboard signs that read "city jail" and "shower," and various props (including a fingerprint station and a camera). The nearly naked cop enters the frame wet, just out of the shower. The second cop enters with the rebel, and the two cops wrestle the playfully (laughing and smiling) resistant youth into handcuffs. The ensuing struggle leads to all three men taking positions that emulate acts of oral sex and anal sex. A close-up of a cop preparing to put his finger in the anus of the rebel as part of a cavity search is followed by a close-up of the rebel's legs and feet as he reacts to this penetration. Right at the end of the cut from the first shot to the second, the cop turns to the camera, breaks character, and laughs, revealing to the filmmakers and the audience the fun he is having with this highly performative moment of transgression. In this moment, it is as if we see the actor reveling in breaking the third-body paradigm that secures the invisibility of the producer/spectator, acknowledging fully the ruse, those involved in it, and his pleasure in dispelling it through overzealous participation.

The scene dissolves into a wrestling match with all three men wearing nothing but posing straps; the rebel wins out, cuffing the cops to the cell door that, comically, appears to be upheld only by the men attached to it. Capping the film is a cut to all three models shown together, playfully smiling while holding up a sign that features their names. In light of the constant threat law enforcement presented to Mizer at this moment, the film reads as a mischievous gesture toward a system that has persistently attempted to deny him, his employees, and his patrons pleasure in homoerotic expression. AMG lampoons that system as the ideal context for the elaboration and enactment of that desire. The film seems to say that there is nothing, no space or situation—even the most official—that is exempt from the circulation of male-male desire.

In a similar spirit, AMG's many mock adventure boy films spectacularized young men facing adversity in quickly assembled sets of other places and times such as Ancient Rome, the jungle, and the "Far East." Films such as *Aladdin* (1956), *The Jewel Thief* (1956), and *Slave Market* (1958) repurposed the orientalizing Hollywood aesthetics that characterize much adventure boy fare, with sword-and-sandal dramas built around plots that would occasion images of young men being captured, enslaved, and punished by other men. *Slave Market* is an excellent example of how the adventure boy formula was extended to elaborate a playful sense of outlaw spatiality in domestic terms. Shot against the brick wall that lined the perimeter of Mizer's backyard, the film constructs an in-film spectacle of men of various ages gathered for the display of other men for their pleasure. Potential buyers are shown grouped together below a stage, across which "slaves" are paraded in various states of undress. However, the shoddiness of the set—with rugs placed over the stage and creased, billowing bed sheets hung behind—evokes the feeling of backyard make-believe. Likewise, the flexing, posing, and grimacing of the "slaves" are so exaggerated that a tone of skit-like antics permeates the scene. The spatial-spectatorial relations analogize the producer-spectator within the frame; a group of men sitting before the stage watch with unshakeable attention.[37]

As the auction ensues, an older man and a younger blond man fight to obtain a teen rebel–styled slave. While the older man wins the auction, the slave and the younger man make a plan for the slave to feign that he is "defective" so that he will be returned. The slave fakes a seizure and is then returned to the auction where the blond man is able to purchase him. The film ends with the two younger men walking off together arm in arm. In *Slave Market*, the outlaw use of domestic space that is Mizer's backyard and the fictional Arcadian space of boys' adventure begins to take on a camp veneer, the overt artificiality playfully highlighting the spectatorial pleasures of homoerotic viewing.

This fantasy space clearly exceeds the pretense of the adventure boys formula: the "buyer's" nearly translucent, tight-fitting lavender toga is cut at mini-skirt length, and the slave's brown scrap of fabric serves to highlight his largely exposed backside.[38] The viewer is invited to take pleasure in the silliness with which this appropriation of popular film imagery allows one to dwell on the nude male body thanks to ad hoc costuming.

In *Boys in Prison*—shot in a mock prison dormitory—a new arrival (Don Klein) with a leather jacket and a Dean-style pompadour is bullied by group of men wearing nothing but white briefs when he puts a male pinup above his bunk; the others all have pinups of women. Having clearly disturbed the status quo, a tall blond "bully" (Keith Rodgers) rips the male pinup off the wall, crumples it up, and throws it to the ground before he begins pushing the new guy around. In the group shower scene that follows, the two men wrestle each other to the ground while a horde of men cheer them on from the sidelines. Having won the fight, the new guy gains the admiration of his prison mates, and the final scene shows all the men including the bully settled into bed, in their underwear, slowly thumbing through an issue of *Physique Pictorial*.

Within this dually marked space that registers as both the world of prison as well as the world of the AMG studio and its models, dominant heteromasculinist discourse is reversed and converted. Viewers are left with a space where male-desiring outcasts become leaders of the pack, inciting them to dissolve the boundary between the homosocial and the homosexual. Within this space, aggression around the pleasure in looking at men is converted into an equalizing affection, suggesting a world were rebel actions have the power to simply flip men away from heterocentrism and homophobia. Like the abandoned house sequence in *Rebel without a Cause*, the refusal of social norms here results in a spirit of equivalence in which, having moved against the status quo together, a new sense of harmony and accord is achieved.

With the 1959 film *The Sailor and the B-Girl*, AMG made an important shift, incorporating two actual all-male bars into the mise-en-scène. The film credits these locations—the Satellite and Explorer—by name in the title sequence, providing viewers with information that invites participation in the homosexual underground. Here AMG's mail-order network worked to actively grow this underground, circulating details about accessing wider male-male networks (however geographically specific) through the (mostly) domestic spaces of its subscribers.

Following an establishing shot of a muscular sailor approaching the doorway of the Satellite, we see him enter into an interior protected from public view by an absence of windows and a small alcove entranceway, where another man looks him over upon entry, as if to make sure he is suitable. Enclosed though it may be, there is evidence of wider and clearly legible social networks: posters for movie events and walls strewn with male pinups show that this is a space marked by activities explicitly aimed at male-desiring men in general, as opposed to a closeted, clandestine space that would require decoding to be read as a place for male-desiring men. The people that make up the bar seem similarly uninterested in pretending this is like any other bar: a tattooed man with a tightly fitted polo shirt leans on a cigarette machine, looking directly into the sailor's eyes as he enters the bar; a muscular drag queen in a billowy dress with ruffles and a fake pearl necklace sits drinking a beer on top of a raised counter. When a fight ensues after the queen tries to steal the sailor's wallet out of his back pocket, her dress gets ripped, revealing a young man with an almost identically muscular physique to the sailor. This becomes all the more evident as the two men tear at each other's clothes until they are wrestling on the floor in only posing straps.

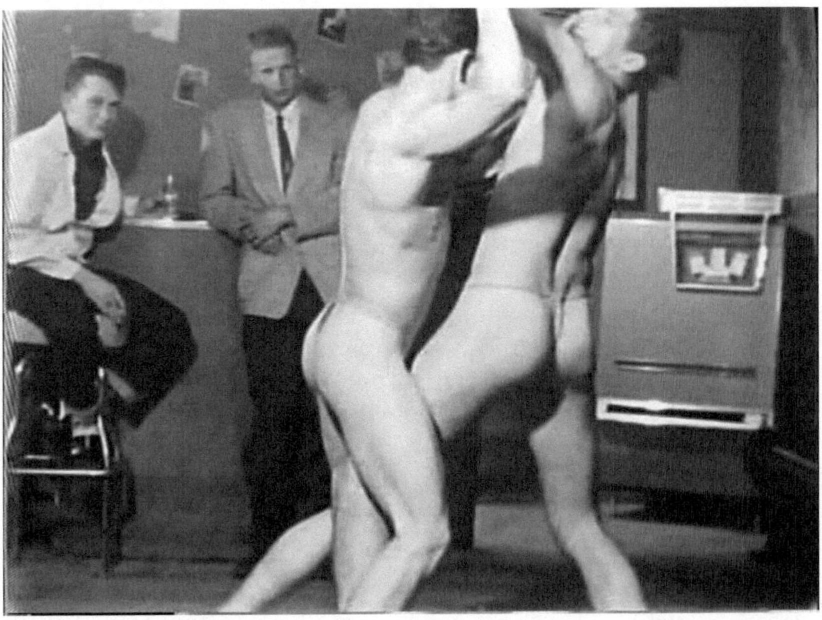

FIGURE 1 The erotics of male-male spectatorship as featured in the 1959 AMG film *Sailor and the B-Girl*. This interior shot was taken on location at a Los Angeles gay bar called the Explorer.

This film indexes a key historical moment by highlighting images of male-male couples and individual men depicted as smiling, excited spectators of male-male erotic performance in a space designated for these activities (fig. 1). The audience breaks the bounds of third-body invisibility, making visible a collective presence of male-male desire without the fantasy alibi of *Slave Market*. Conferring with one another, bringing each other drinks, and behaving with the occasional awkwardness (looking at the camera, etc.) of the nonprofessional, these patrons elaborate the bar as a space for sociosexual connection among men. *Sailor and the B-Girl* illustrates for viewers how spaces such as the bar could be used for communing through the shared act of homoerotic spectatorship. This matches the social ethos expressed in *Physique Pictorial*'s advertisement for a handheld movie viewer: "for those who like to have novelties around to entertain their guests—this is definitely a conversation piece."[39]

While the world of the AMG film does not simply reflect reality, it can, however, respond to or bear upon it. Calibrated to sexually excite viewers, these films also stand as examples of an independent cinema accommodating and working through the lived realities of male-desiring men. As Laura Kipnis notes:

> Pornography is both a legitimate form of culture and a fictional, fantastical, even allegorical realm; it neither reflects the world nor is it some hypnotizing call to action. The world of pornography is mythological and hyperbolic, peopled by characters. It does not and never will exist, but it does—this is part of its politics—insist on a sanctioned space for fantasy.[40]

The AMG films of the 1950s and 1960s constitute a precursor to a whole domain of cultural production and commercial development for and by male-desiring men in which sanctioned spaces for fantasy played a central role. Fantasies of inclusion, unfettered movement across space, and the discovery of sites for group sociosexual activity would all go on to play a major role in how these men collectively actualized their desires.

Cinema and Counterpublic Formation

The relationship between home moviemaking, location, spatiality, and nonnormative performance of sex and gender branches out in the beginning of the early 1960s. Cinema during this time became one of the central techniques of world-making among male-desiring men. Running counter to the overdetermined narrative of a pre-Stonewall/post-Stonewall historical split that asserts the former as a period of isolation and invisibility and the latter as *the* moment of emergence and coming together, homosexual underground cinema from the early 1960s to the late 1960s troubles reductive notions of invisibility and visibility and points toward a culture more invested in making itself visible *to itself* than in constructing an image for a wider audience. These were films for microcultural enjoyment and affiliation as opposed to mass consumption. They were about making new worlds, as opposed to remaking *the* world.

Between the early and mid-1960s, a new cycle of films made by male-desiring men began to appear that were very different from the mail-order physique films and avant-garde films of the 1940s and 1950s. Whereas these earlier films were all short film reels that featured small casts of men who may or may not have been male-desiring men (most of AMG's actors are believed to have identified as heterosexual), a new cluster of slightly longer films began to appear that, by the early 1960s, foregrounded the collective participation of groups of people who were unabashedly connected to scenes in which expressions of nonnormativity in terms of gender presentation and sexual interest, and male-male interest in particular, were central aspects of collective social experience.

Underground films and those conventionally classified within categories of avant-garde and/or art (whether meant to designate a social scene and/or a type of film) provided a primary source for screenings that brought male-desiring men into contact with one another and played a central role in constituting audiences within social and political networks organized around a shared oppositional relationship to dominant bourgeois norms of gender and sexuality. Screenings of work by filmmakers such as Kenneth Anger, Jose Rodriguez-Soltero (*Jerovi*, 1965), Jack Smith (*Flaming Creatures*, 1963), and Andy Warhol (*My Hustler*, 1965) provided a social network that, by the mid-1960s, increasingly acted as a site for the kinds of socialization and politicization that would come to inform the gay liberation movement at the end of the decade. For example, Suárez has detailed how the contentious reception of *Flaming Creatures* worked to bring audiences together around its censorship. While it was initially shown at home screenings, when Jonas Mekas elected to include it in an independent cinema program at New York's Bowery Theatre in March 1964, the film was seized by the district attorney's office and several patrons were arrested.[41] Further busts on the film at movie theaters and on college campuses across the United States helped to elevate the film's countercultural status: as Suárez puts it, "from this moment on, repression and scandal became trademarks of Jack Smith's celebrity . . . and the keys to his important influence on New York's alternative and avant-garde sub-cultures."[42]

Janet Staiger notes that around this time underground film in general came to mark "the emergence of tacit, if not aggressive, gay liberation activities . . . [associated with a] critique of traditional gendered, heterosexual, same race/ethnicity sexual norms," adding that "going to these films after midnight was a declaration of where one stood in these debates . . . the midnight cinema was—like the St. Marks Bathhouse—an expression of community and a site for building a community, which would eventually have its culmination, at least for the mainstream press and for gay men, in the Stonewall events of 1969."[43]

Noting the concomitant relationship between the ideological makeup of the audience for underground film and the textual features of the films themselves, Staiger explains that a staple trope of these films involved "ironic appropriations of popular culture . . . [as] . . . stylistic tactics directed against bourgeois culture but also assertive rhetorical strategies for creating . . . sub-cultural community connections."[44] In *Flaming Creatures*, for instance, a host of performers are used to reference a number of well-known female actors in such a way that distinctly moves beyond any simple adoration-through-impersonation through an emphasis on drag and gender performance that works toward self-consciously grotesque ends: a Marilyn Monroe impersonator is shown engaging in vampirism; performer Mario Montez (whose very name plays on Maria Montez, a Hollywood B-movie actor who was a popular camp icon within postwar queer subcultures) is costumed with allusions to Marlene Dietrich. Similarly interested in the intersection of star persona and camp reflexivity, Kenneth Anger's *Scorpio Rising* (1963) situates a teenage biker as a cult product of his own making, devotedly studying teen magazines in his bed beneath a wall adorned with Marlon Brando and James Dean pinups.

Unlike physique films and homemade/amateur films, the underground was more clearly associated with viewing as a public, social event. This phenomenon, however, was not solely based around the pleasure of gathering to watch images that countered and/or positioned Hollywood iconography in a reverse discourse, but was also part and parcel of a larger, more complex relationship that existed between networks of male-male desire and Hollywood film during the postwar years. That is, while filmmakers like Anger, Smith, and Warhol were undoubtedly working Hollywood imagery into their own dialectics of camp and eroticism, this phenomenon is not particular to this set of filmmakers but is informed by the subcultural viewing practices of postwar networks of male-desiring men, and in such a way that it is key to the development of this group as a public.

The emergence of these collectively driven filmmaking projects was inextricable from the growing coalescence of groups of male-desiring men who were for the first time coming together to watch movies in public. In bars and private clubs, the programming of specific Hollywood films based upon their potential for camp reception among groups of male-desiring men operated as a social activity that fostered a sense of camaraderie and group consciousness through shared practices of viewing and reception. Screenings of Hollywood films such as *Jezebel* (William Wyler, 1938), *The Great Lie* (Edmund Goulding, 1941), and *Some Like It Hot* (Billy Wilder, 1959), situated as camp, played a key role in the development of male-desiring men as a discernable social group as well as in the increasing legibility and visibility of this group within the media at large. This is starkly evident in the 1964 *Life* magazine piece "Homosexuality in America," which deploys a large two-page photograph of a mass of men gathered together for a late-night screening at San Francisco's Jumpin' Frog Bar, the photograph positioned just under a large caption that reads "Rejected by the 'Straight' World, Homosexuals Build a Society of Their Own" (fig. 2).[45]

Contributing to the formation of a counterpublic, these events allowed audiences of male-desiring men to "elaborate a world together" that was "defined by its tension with the larger public."[46] This coalescing counterpublic—defined, at least in part, by participation in specialized movie nights, midnight screenings, and/or underground programs—often assumed a proto-gay liberation rhetoric organized around the prospect of social and political empowerment through the act of assembling to view particular combinations of films with others (fig. 3). In other words, before male-desiring men could become engaged in a political program that stressed the visibility of gay men in public life, they needed to first become visible to each other as a group. Even a cursory look at promotion for these events demonstrates how a variety of film types—from physique and porn loops to classical Hollywood—were brought together and framed in such way as to invite the formation of a publicly constituted group that is interested in a variety of forms of visibility both on and off the screen.

One of the earliest of these programs, the "Camp-Out," was held in 1967 at the Apollo Arts Theatre in Los Angeles (fig. 4). In combining

Mae West's *I'm No Angel* (1933) with a smattering of physique-film titles like *The Hot Harem* and *The Vice and the Badge,* the program combined camp and erotica in a way that would soon come to be characterized as "gay interest." The vernacular of the advertisement indexes the programmers' attempt to appeal to a proto-gay audience through making multiple links between three components that would become staples of a publicly recognizable and industrialized gay cinema: a direct address to an exclusively male audience (in a playful camp tone that signals a sense of group-ness and familiarity between the men addressed with the proclamation "GET READY BOYS"), the move from censorship to visibility (the "original un-TV-cut 1935 [*sic*] version" of *I'm No Angel*) and a conflation of male-male sexuality and cinematic spectacle ("a program of gay, colorful films" "in full living color," "in gayest color"). Other key elements work toward similar ends: the "Out" in "Camp-Out" suggests coming out, "Camp" suggests gathering and camaraderie, with the mass element emphasized through the description of "2 Giant midnite shows"; the invitation to "Camp-Out Again!" adds a sense of the event as ritual.

This camp collectivity was, at the same time, not specific to the context of film reception and moviegoing. As chronicled by Fabio Cleto, camp and drag performance has played a central role in the coalescence of sex and gender dissident social formations dating back to the late nineteenth century, if not earlier, and can be seen as a primary social adhesive across a variety of instances, from the cabaret shows of the Weimar Republic in prewar Germany to the Harlem drag balls

FIGURE 2 "Homosexual" patrons gather at San Francisco's Jumpin' Frog Bar, where meeting up for screenings of Hollywood movies helped them to "build a society of their own." From the *Life* cover story "Homosexuality in America" (June 26, 1964). Photograph by Bill Eppridge/© Estate of Bill Eppridge.

FIGURE 3 New York City's Corduroy Club gets people together in December 1967 for a month-long series of Hollywood movies incorporating "dancing and refreshments." Flyer, "Gala Film Festival" (1967). Image courtesy of Thomas J. Dodd Research Center at the University of Connecticut, Storrs.

of the early twentieth century.[47] However, by the late 1950s and early 1960s, new cultures of camp and drag were beginning to develop that were increasingly informed by and refracted through popular cinematic material.

There are multiple reasons for this: however, one of the most important is the way in which three phenomena worked together to lay the ground for new viewerships: changes in US censorship practice;

FIGURE 4 Addressing a viewership of "BOYS" for a "wild weekend" of camp and erotica. Flyer, "Camp-Out" (1967). Used with permission from the personal archives of Thomas Waugh.

the recirculation and rerelease of older Hollywood films in repertory theaters, in alternative nontheatrical spaces, and on television; and the development and expansion of theatrical production troupes in the US military that fostered and encouraged the camp labors of sex and gender dissident soldiers and that were patronized by audiences of thousands both at home and abroad during and just following World War II.[48]

Whether through valences of laughter, through the recognition of a shared sensibility in the cadence of and ideas proffered in reviews of films and/or plays, or through the sideways and backward glances that made many a theater, lobby, and auditorium an active field of occularity for male-desiring men in the 1940s, '50s, and '60s, male-desiring men were coming to recognize one another in and through the experience of new alternative forms of theatrical consumption and patronage. By the 1960s, mail-order amateur porn and homoerotic avant-garde film began to look like an underground tributary that was bubbling up in alternative spaces: the bar, the rented function room, the independent movie house. Event programming for screenings, with theater programs, posters, and reviews, kept these films in a discourse of the underground by emphasizing them as hard to see and framing this as creating socially powerful, exciting "event" conditions.

Pulling from official culture and dragging it into an underground terrain, gay social life was produced through a camp humor that reconstituted the world "above" on its own terms, "mak[ing] fun out of" it, to borrow Richard Dyer's phrase.[49] Subjects who simply didn't fit in established a particular shared relationship to the world "out there" or, perhaps more accurately, "above." Film played a very particular role here: the underground continued to have an interesting salience different from other cultural corners, largely because the production code itself had driven cinema underground. The beloved camp films of Mae West, for example, were driven out of theaters and only screened in censored form from the mid-1930s through the early 1960s. As a cycle of films that foreground the erotic and often explicitly nonnormative sexual pleasure of West's protagonists, films such as *She Done Him Wrong* (Lowell Sherman, 1933), *I'm No Angel* (Wesley Ruggles, 1933), and *Belle of the Nineties* (Leo McCarey, 1934) had a large following among male-desiring men during the early 1930s, providing these viewers the opportunity to identify with a protagonist who desires men, and gets the men she desires, usually in a way that unabashedly refuses normative gender and sexual roles (often reversing or inverting them for fun and spectacle).

One of the new strands of popular discourse that camp production was engaged with centered on representations of homosexuality itself: in particular, the homosexual exposé. These new postwar models of homosexuality circulating in dominant discourse were informed by an interesting mix of the kind of popular pseudosociology common to homosexual exposés such as the 1964 *Life* cover story or television documentaries and talk shows, like *Confidential File*'s "Homosexuals and the Problems They Present" (KTTV, 1954), *The Rejected* (KQED, 1961), and *The Homosexuals* (CBS, 1967). Through these media, homosexuality was increasingly marked by ever-simpler psychologistic models and reductive bastardizations of Freudian theory. Increasingly, pulp novels, many of which were written by male-desiring men and female-desiring women under pseudonyms, were beginning to demonstrate a salacious and ambivalent tone in relation the image of the sick homosexual. Both in the press and in the pulps, homosexuality was coming to be packaged as though sickness and pleasure might exist in a mutually beneficial relationship: that the "sicker" the desire, the *more* desire there is, and the more desire there is, the greater the potential for pleasure.

Thus, the negative characteristics held together under the concept of "the homosexual" were increasingly repurposed in proto-gay and gay forms of cultural production that resituated homosexual deviancy within a camp dialectic, where alternative constructions of deviant homosexuality began to "speak back" in a growing multiplicity of ways to the dominant medical discourse of deviancy. In many ways, the exposés, with their particular mix of pop psychology, armchair anthropology, and pseudosociology, opened up the door to this.

The Guerilla Films of the Gay Girls Riding Club

In the early 1960s, a small group of Los Angeles area men began meeting as a social group when Hollywood cinematographer Ray Harrison and a few of his friends began reaching out to other men at bars and beaches frequented by male-desiring men. By the early 1960s, the group was meeting regularly on Sundays under the name the Gay Girls Riding Club. Between the 1960s and the 1970s, the club became a mainstay of gay social life and cultural production in greater Los Angeles, sponsoring and hosting parties, drag balls, bar crawls, group vacations, and regular get-togethers (Curtis Harrington was a frequent attendee).[50] Under the guidance of several of its members who, like Harrison, worked in the film industry, they began making films together on 16 mm. By the mid-1960s, the Girls had made a series of four camp reinterpretations of popular films that were shown and reshown many times over at parties in homes, at bars, and at special social events across the Los Angeles area (though often centered around Santa Monica). These parodies include one of *What Ever Happened to Baby Jane?* (Robert Aldrich, 1962) titled *What Really Happened to Baby Jane?* (Connie B. DeMille, 1963), one of *The Roman Spring of Mrs. Stone* (José Quintero, 1961) titled *Roman Springs on Mrs. Jones* (Connie B. DeMille, 1963), one of *Never on Sunday* (Jules Dassin, 1960) titled *Always on a Sunday* (Connie B. DeMille, date unknown), and one based on the James Bond series titled *Spy on the Fly* (Ray Harrison, 1966).

Using real locations, many of them highly public, the Gay Girls Riding Club created films that explicitly placed gay male sociality—including both same-sex coupling and dissident gender performance—as part of both actual city space and within the terms of popular imagery of Hollywood movies. Their films were illegal on multiple fronts, with great risks taken in their production. This was guerilla filmmaking that, shot on the streets, highways, and beaches and in bars and businesses across Southern California, routinely risked being shut down. However, this risk carried with it an even greater one in that they moved about city streets both dragged up and as an array of types: sailors, trade, and go-go dancers as well as feminine gay roles such as the camp and the swish—all of which risked inciting arrest.

Most of the Girls' early 1960s films were made within a year of the films that they spoof, and it is this quickness, in part, that defines how the films work as products of camp labor. The way the Girls worked to revalue popular film material varied depending on the production. In the case of *What Really Happened to Baby Jane?* they offer a close camp reading of the film that retains a notable fidelity to the original. By recreating certain sequences and particular shots almost to a tee, the film worked as camp commentary that sought to bring out and highlight the camp value of the original, pushing it just a little bit further over the edge. It is precisely this doubling up on the camp value of the original text that situates the production within a discourse of gay visibility.

What Ever Happened to Baby Jane? tells the story of two sisters, one an aging former child star named Baby Jane (Bette Davis) and the other a former movie star, Blanche (Joan Crawford), who is now paraplegic and confined to living in the upper level of a home where she is "looked after" by her jealous, controlling sister. Jane's increasingly delusional behavior produces some of the most cited moments in gay camp film reception.[51] Highlights include Jane withholding one of her sister's meals with the infantilizing comment "but you didn't eat your din-din!"; serving her a rat under a cloche; attempting a revival of the childhood stage act that once brought her fame; leaving Blanche tied up in restraints in her bed for extended periods; killing the maid with a hammer; and, in the film's final scene, abandoning her dehydrated and dying sister on the beach while she dances, surrounded by a crowd of onlooking teenagers.

The restaging of these moments of dramatic excess in *What Really Happened to Baby Jane?* uses humor to self-reflexively situate each of them within camp vernacular terms that work as forms of gay performance and address, to be enjoyed by both the makers and the viewers of the film (in the case of the GGRC, often one and the same). For instance, instead of serving a rat, Jane brings Blanche a plate of fire, creating a visual-linguistic pun that positions Blanche as a "flaming queen." In the living room revival sequence, both Jane and her piano player punctuate movement after movement with limp wrists to the point where the very repetition of the movement becomes humorous. For the scene in which Jane kills the maid, the iron hammer of the original has been replaced with a comically oversized cardboard hammer covered in aluminum foil, again suggesting both the physical weakness of the drag version of Jane while also highlighting through exaggeration the fact that all objects in Hollywood productions are, at the end of the day, just props, rendering the naturalizing mise-en-scène of popular film ridiculous. This denaturalizing effect is taken a step further with the blonde Marilyn-esque wig worn by the African American maid, through which the film creates a purposefully failed version of the black maid trope common to Hollywood movies of the period. Here, with the black maid glamorized in terms of ideal whiteness, the film draws attention to the construction of a type whose very purpose is to function (in life and on film) as a background element in relation to white characters.

The conclusion of the GGRC version of *Baby Jane* strays from the original by ending on an optimistic and celebratory note. There are no teenagers here despondently circling around the hysterical Jane, but instead the entire cast has been reprised and dances together, after which Blanche rises up, no longer paraplegic, and hands Jane an Oscar (perhaps a healing gesture referencing a famous bone of contention between Davis and Crawford: when Davis lost the award for her nominated performance in *Baby Jane,* Crawford collected on behalf of winner Anne Bancroft). While different from the kind of affirmative imagery that ends Anger's *Fireworks,* the finale of the GGRC film nonetheless gives viewers a jubilant scene of homosocial gay drag bonding in public (fig. 5). This notion of publicity is further emphasized by the Oscar itself, offering a camp transposition whereby one of the most highly visible moments of prestige in popular culture—the reception of an Academy Award—is given over to a gay man in drag. Here *What Ever Happened to Baby Jane?*'s climactic drama, depicting a sickness that leaves all characters alienated and alone (save for the band of mocking teenagers), is replaced with an affectionate celebration of those that society has deemed hysterical and unwell, a paradoxically affirmative

FIGURE 5 Gay hysteria as group camaraderie.

image in which the performance of a ludicrous notion of sickness—homosexual sickness—is presented as a moment of both individual dramatic achievement and group camaraderie.

While all the GGRC films are centered on gay drag performance, the films *Always on a Sunday* and *Spy on the Fly* document how acts of gender dissidence and same-sex sexuality existed in an interesting relation to one another in the emergent realm of gay cinematic representation. In some instances these elements were presented as part of one and the same cultural experience, while in others same-sex desire and nonnormative gender presentation appear to exist alongside or even at odds with one another. In this way, these films offer an indispensable view into the ways in which relations between sex and gender were changing in the postwar period and, in particular, show how imbricated experiences of gender dissidence and male-male desire worked as elements of world-making in the 1960s.

Never on Sunday, which was a Greek-US coproduction nominated for five Academy Awards, winning one (Best Song) in 1961, tells the story of young carefree prostitute named Ilya (Melina Mercouri) who lives in a Grecian port town and meets a male tourist from Connecticut,

Homer (Jules Dassin), who is obsessed with classical Greek culture. Homer feels Ilya represents the increasing devaluation of a once great culture, while Ilya seeks to help Homer become less of an uptight traditionalist. In *Always on a Sunday,* the Girls primarily repurpose the milieu rather than the plot of the story to create a skit-like film set in a Greek bar peopled with a panoply of sailors, drag queens, and numerous young, handsome male-male couples and single men. Like all GGRC films, this bar is shown to be part of the topography of Los Angeles, as the film's opening credits, shown over an image of waves crashing on the beach, tell us the movie has been filmed in "Hollywood, U.S.A." We see a group of the Girls, costumed as prostitutes, enter the bar and respond with excitement at the discovery that it is packed with young men. Soon after their entrance, another of the Girls, playing Ilya, enters the bar, killing any chance for competition and homing in on the heartthrob of the bar, whom she seduces into a wild dance, stripping his shirt off and prompting the whole bar to take to the dance floor. The short film resolves through two final twists that ensue when a couple of fresh-faced sailors enter the bar. First, the sailors immediately garner the affections of Ilya's catch, with an intertitle that highlights their advantage over the women in the bar with the words "Those Greeks Are All Alike." Following this, the sailor and the man leave the bar, but Ilya does not despair, instead joining the entire bar in a frenzy of dancing and (like the end of *Baby Jane*) group handholding and spinning. The film cuts to the exterior of the bar, where we see the shirtless man arm in arm with the sailors on either side of him, before the shot pans down to reveal that both sailors are wearing high heels (fig. 6).

The film focalizes erotic desire through *both* masculinized and feminized versions of male-desiring men. The film first establishes a world in which if men are going to have access to young, virile, masculine men, then they must do so by presenting and behaving as masculine men themselves or as women. In this configuration, it is heterosexuality itself that is the precondition for getting the guy (though it is, of course, all part of the fun of camp here that we know we are in the realm of masquerade). At the same time, the film demonstrates the historical transition underway in the postwar years, as some male-desiring men moved toward an understanding of their desire for men as more exclusively part of a model of sameness (as opposed to one figured through notions of gender transgression or identification with the "opposite sex").[52] As the sailor gets the guy, it seems this model of sameness wins out. The phrase "Those Greeks Are All Alike," a pun

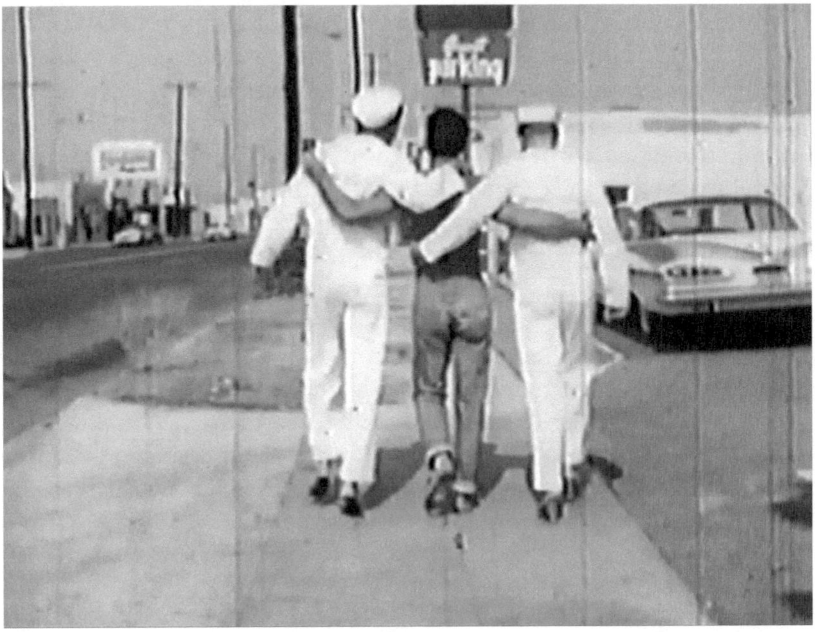

FIGURE 6 Sailors in heels, brothers in arms.

on the stereotype of Greece as a sort of ancestral homeland for love between men, equally suggests male-male desire as an experience of "likeness." The matching sailors and the similarity in build and appearance (toned physiques, short hair, clean shaven) between the three men reinforce the point. Here "Greek" becomes shorthand for a kind of masculine likeness in which homosociality and homosexuality appear wholly compatible.

The departure of the sailors and the young man results not in a sense of failure among the prostitute queens, but instead in an enthusiastic moment of disregard for life lived in the service of normative masculinity as they unite in the center of the bar and begin dancing. With their attention focused only on one another, bar patrons dancing around them, the film moves from idealizing same-sex desire to embracing its absence, creating an atmosphere in which people can truly let loose. It seems that the film establishes a firm polarization between same-sex desiring men and gay performances of femininity: drawing a line between two distinct cultures, we see the drag celebration inside and the three butch men walking arm in arm away from the bar. But with the revelation of the sailor in heels, the Girls leave their distinctive camp mark on the film's resolution. In one way, this is a standard camp transvaluation of gender norms suggesting that all gender presentation can be reduced to the level of play. However, the undercutting of gender norms here takes on another layer of resonance when considered within the bounds of an emergent gay discourse of visibility. That is, the film models a spectrum of different relations between gender and sex, some working together and some against one another, but all of them equally aestheticized as forms of dress-up and display meant to inspire a feeling of wonder and excitement in the audience. The idea here is not "what if sailors really were women?" but rather "what if the difference between a sailor's boots and a prostitute's heels were really not much at all?" This takes on a further valence in camp vernacular terms when considering that many sailors did in fact have sex with, and in some instances were, male-desiring men. Here the sailors' donning of similar shoes to the prostitute queens in the bar works to mark economies of male-male desire that, within the terms of dominant discourse, were rendered so completely invisible as to seem impossible.

Dragging Down Bond

In 1966, the Girls made a radical break with their film *Spy on the Fly*, an ambitious camp send-up of the popular early to mid-1960s James Bond cycle. Whereas the club's previous films had all been credited using camp pseudonyms, this film brazenly opens with a credit sequence putting on screen what appear to be the real names of most of the actors and director as well as a listing of actual locations used, layered on top of aerial images of downtown Los Angeles (though it is also worth noting that sixteen of the forty-four actors' names consist of two male first names [e.g., Rod Arthur, Saul Bernard, Richard Blake, Roger Cody, Jim Daniels, Peter Douglas, etc.], suggesting that if participants are using pseudonyms, they have abandoned women's names and are doubling down on male coding). Regardless, this film is a landmark in the history of gay visibility in that its director, the GGRC organizer Ray Harrison, leaves behind his pseudonym Connie B. DeMille and fully claims producing and directorial credit for the film.

However, the club's expanded use of named actors and public locations in *Spy* does not mean that the group pursued a form of visibility that should be equated with going "aboveground" or going public. This film continued to play within the delimited nontheatrical space of house parties, balls, and bars. Mapping networks of gay social activity through the figure of underground spatiality continued to be *the* dominant pattern underlying the construction of plot and narrative in their work.

Before looking at how *Spy on the Fly* uses the spy-thriller genre as means of showing and spectacularizing California itself as an expansive terrain of underground gay social life, it is necessary to consider, briefly, the place of the Bond films in US popular culture at the moment of the film's making. Between 1962 and 1965, the first four Bond films were released (all of which were adaptations of extremely popular recent paperback novels by Ian Fleming). *Dr. No* (Terence Young, 1962), *From Russia with Love* (Terence Young, 1963), *Goldfinger* (Guy Hamilton, 1964), and *Thunderball* (Terence Young, 1966) were all box-office hits and rocketed Sean Connery to fame as the handsome, infallible, lady-killing spy, winning out in film after film against dangerous international crime syndicates (often a threat to UK and US national security). As agent 007, Connery's brand of masculinity communicated an air of confidence and indestructibility. On one level this was expressed through the plots of these films, where the secret agent is able to outsmart and outfight scores upon scores of other men as well as the numerous machines they deploy in an attempt to destroy him. More generally, though, Connery's physical performance, his gait and gestures, show unshakable certainty and a highly controlled demeanor capable of successfully seducing any woman he wants at any moment. Bond represented a new, modern vision of masculine taste and discernment that was expressed through a calm, controlled body that is always self-satisfied and never reveals any kind of need or desire that cannot amply and immediately be met. Connery's Bond was, above all else, an idealization of masculinity-as-stability.

Spy on the Fly replaces Connery with agent 0069 (Warren Freming). The plot revolves around an assignment 0069 is given by headquarters to meet up with a woman named Fonda Peters at a downtown beauty parlor, with whom he must travel to San Francisco in order to help her deliver top secret plans for an atomic bomb. His plan is foiled when, in a sequence that works as a loose send-up of the opening health spa scene in *Thunderball*, Fonda Peters is electrocuted by a hair dryer. Thus, 0069, with the assistance of a beauty technician named Madame Tussaud, is forced to drag himself up as Peters so he can deliver the note himself. On the way from Los Angeles to San Francisco, he makes a number of quick detours to evade two detectives who are chasing him. In the film's conclusion, 0069 ends up in an opium den in San Francisco where he is nearly raped by a group of orientalized patrons and, throwing a grenade in self-defense, accidentally destroys the all-important note. Luckily, Madame Tussaud shows up just in time (dressed as a drag queen biker), shoots up the den, and reassures 0069, who is feeling like a failure, that the note has also been copied in microfilm hidden on the inside of her press-on nails. Tired of all the trouble caused by life as a special agent, in the final shot of the film 0069 enters the famous female impersonation club Finocchio's, where he intends to seek new employment.

Spy's reinscription of the Bond films in gay camp terms drags down and makes fun out of Connery's 007 through a direct inversion of the role's gendering. Instead of a smooth, contained masculinity (Bond is nearly always in a fitted suit, with short, combed-back hair rendered motionless by a hardening gel), we are given a feminine man, dressed as a woman, whose gestures are frantic and hysterical, who nervously moves through the plot making one mistake after another, who manages to garner no sexual attention along the way. Speaking back to its host films, *Spy* ridicules the absurdity of Bond's stable masculinity by replacing it with an image of failed gender performance that nonetheless serves as a motor to push the generic plot through its set pieces. If the agent need not be a model of stable masculinity for the genre to float, need stable masculinity exist at all?

It would be a mistake to understand the film as only related to the Bond cycle through parody. In fact, the way the narrative operates through a collection of exoticized locations and spaces is, in cultural geographic terms, little different from the Bond films. In fact, *Spy* might be described as pop-camp, in that it contains all the pop-pleasure "nowness" of the Bond films' focus on modern, up-to-date lifestyle consumption (0069 lives in a thoroughly modern apartment building, drives a shiny new black sedan, and is regularly brought in to contact with the spaces of hip youth culture) while at the same time recalibrating the cultural economy of this lifestyle in gay terms.

This recalibration is most pronounced in the film's foregrounding of space. As with the list of dozens of participants involved in its making, *Spy on the Fly* is a historically important production for the way in which it shows an array of gay spaces, charting topographic vectors of movement between and among them. The film's two gay bar sequences, filmed on location in actual bars, are of particular importance in this regard. In the first, 0069 is stuck in Santa Barbara while his overheated car gets repaired. Beginning with an exterior shot, 0069 wanders around outside and eventually stumbles across the gay bar the

Fly, suggesting that gay bars are ubiquitous and accessible spaces. With a cut to the inside of the bar, the film gives multiple horizontal panning shots from behind the bar, showing a range of types associated with queer, homosexual, and gay iconographies: a feminine man ogles a young marine; two similar-looking preppie men exchange phone numbers; two distinguished looking proto-cloneish men with matching haircuts and sweaters unbuttoned at the top sit together talking closely and seriously (fig. 7). Echoing the policing and raiding of bars frequented by drag queens, trans* people, and other gender nonconformists, the detectives come busting in to the bar and lunge at 0069, removing him from the bar and throwing him in the back of their car.

In the film's second bar sequence, 0069, now escaped from his kidnappers and back en route to San Francisco, makes another stop in Carmel at the Club Foot Discotheque. Inside, the club is filled with GGRC members who are dressed as young hip types and are dancing in pairs, performing drag versions of heterosexual coupling. To the sound of rockabilly music, the dancers hop, jump, and gyrate across the dance floor, emulating a youth set taken by the latest dance moves. A go-go boy, dressed in a spandex leotard, pulls 0069 onto the dance floor and

FIGURE 7 A panoramic view of life at the gay bar.

then up onto a stage where he proceeds to strip down, turning his leotard into little more than a cover for his genitals. Medium shots frame each of them dancing separately, and then they are brought together in a two shot. Side by side, these two figures are extremely apt representatives of gay life in 1966: the drag queen who represents a tradition of gender dissidence increasingly informed by masterful mocking of pop-consumer aesthetics and the young, white go-go boy who takes to the platform as an idealized form of same-sex desire.

The film's conclusion follows 0069, still dressed in drag, as he heads through the streets of San Francisco toward his next assignment. Arriving at the club Finocchio's, he swings around the pole that holds up the entranceway awning, catapulting himself into the bar. Holding on the exterior shot of the entrance, the film credits signal the close of the film with the words "The Beginning" sprawled across the screen. Finocchio's was famous for its female impersonators and drag performers as well as for attracting slummers interested in a one-off evening of "something different." Situating this real location as a new beginning works to conclude the film on an expansionist note. Over the course of the film, the viewers have taken in an aggregation of underground locales that cater to male-desiring men, leaving this final move through Finocchio's doorway to promise participation in a more iconic and public site of gay social life.

The early films of the Gay Girls Riding Club document a moment in the years between the coalescence of a homosexual underground in the late 1940s and the emergence of gay liberation politics in mid- to late 1960s. Their very name marks a moment in which the word "gay" was coming to be used to signify a sense of shared social experience. At a time when Hollywood allowed no recourse for male-desiring men to make movies about their own lives, the GGRC constituted a guerilla-style minor cinema out of the film equipment and experience their work in the industry gave them access to. As their films incorporated a larger and more diverse set of locations across California—especially outdoor, pedestrian-oriented locations—the GGRC showcased an engagement with public space that would become central to the gay cinema explored in the following chapter. These are films that begin to people the world with male-desiring men, hinting at possibilities beyond underground networks and toward paradigms of the public and the mass-oriented.

The production contexts, films, and film screenings explored throughout this chapter trace the coalescence of a cinema that, by the 1970s, would be patronized and discussed as "gay cinema." Yet the case studies explored here demonstrate how, as early as the 1940s, filmmakers were using film as a means to elaborate and extend greater possibilities for social and political formation among male-desiring men in the US. While gay liberation discourse and notions such as "gay power" and "gay is good" would soon come to characterize an increasingly popular and populist paradigm of gay life, these earlier films offered an occasion for male-desiring men to gather in the acts of making and viewing cinema, encouraging them to inventively move through and within the spaces around them as part of the process of coming into contact with others. These films took inspiration in not only putting male-male desires on screen, but in elaborating an intricate and interwoven set of worlds for the further generation and enjoyment of these desires.

TWO

The Cinematic Authoring of Gay Life

> We must begin to recognize that we do have a gay media, and we must develop it and break away from their narrow conception of what media is. This will go hand in hand with developing our gay consciousness. We must recognize that we do not simply wa[nt] to be gay people operating their media. We want to expand and extend our gay media with "gay soul" and "gay pride," to include our sense of camp, our flair for a masquerade. This will be revolutionary, th[is] will be our power. JIM CLIFFORD, 1970[1]

By the mid-1960s, groups of sexual and gender dissidents were beginning to assume a new role in relation to dominant social discourse in the US through a succession of moments of civil disobedience. Many such moments were spurred on by intensified policing in major cities across the country. Key examples include May 1959 at New York's Cooper Do-nuts, when male-desiring men, trans* people, female-desiring women, and drag queens threw coffee cups and donuts after being harassed by the police;[2] August 1966 at San Francisco's Compton's Cafeteria, when male-desiring men, trans* people, and drag queens rioted in the streets in response to police harassment;[3] and March 1968, when hundreds of people, called together by local drag queens the Princess and the Duchess, gathered in Los Angeles's Griffith Park for a protest against the entrapment and harassment of male-desiring men and trans* people by the LAPD.[4] In these and dozens more events prior to and following the Stonewall riots, people we now often refer to as LGBTQ+ began to push back and make confrontational demands for their right to assemble and socialize without harassment—to exist as a social body—in public space.

During this time a "gay movement" of mass proportions began to gain traction, with consciousness-raising and media production groups organizing marches, protests, and social and political events of a dizzying variety. Disco parties, biker runs, "gay-ins" at public parks, all-female and all-male nature retreats, movie nights, sex parties, concerts at bathhouses (including those starring Bette Midler), gay beauty competitions, and gay rodeos all began springing up across the US between the late 1960s and the mid-1970s. US cities went from having a relatively small number of sites for male-desiring men to meet and organize to having widely recognizable business districts with gay bars, restaurants, bathhouses, discos, clothing stores, bookstores, lesbian and gay community centers, and sex shops. While areas such as Greenwich Village, New York—the site of the Stonewall Riots—and the Castro District of San Francisco tend to hold a privileged place in historical retellings of this period, it is easy to forget neighborhoods and streets were becoming energetic centers of gay life across the US—for example, Highland Park in Detroit, Halsted Street in Chicago, Live Oak Area (now known as Bryan Place) in Dallas, Miami Beach, and the Capitol Hill area of Seattle. Resort spaces also grew and proliferated. While Fire Island, New York, and Key West, Florida—places with a deep history of patronage by male-desiring men—became more commercially branded for gay travel (working in accord with the development of gay travel agencies), new locations such as the Marlin Beach Hotel in Fort Lauderdale, Florida, the Island House Resort in Key West, and the Bunkhouse in Breckinridge, Colorado, entertained hundreds of male-desiring men in resort complexes that included motel rooms, cabins, campgrounds, discos, cabarets, pools, beaches, and nature trails (often operating as sites for sociosexual encounter). By the mid-1970s, the US was heavily peppered with a world of gay activity geared toward the assembly of larger groups, even crowds of men.

Concepts of media and mediation had a critical place in this moment of political and cultural work. People began to think of themselves affirmatively as *gay people* and to use media forms as a way to elaborate and impress upon each other their sense of gay experience. The potential of media to express or impede gay life was explored through events with names such as "Multi-Gay Liberation Media" and "Gay Activists Alliance Mediazap Dance," public lectures and slideshows by media critics such as Vito Russo, and organizations such as the Gay Media Task Force.[5]

As outlined by a November 1970 list titled "Marathon Suggestions for Our Relationship to The Media" produced by members of New York City Gay Liberation Front, gay liberationists called for a radical rethinking of not only what their relationship to "the media" should be, but what the very concept of media is and how it might best be employed among gay people. Under a subheading titled "Our Media," the document outlines the following:

> (a) Media is a fancy word for communication.
> (b) Re-definition of media to include alternative to the attitude that media is *print*, i.e. dances, demonstrations, coffee houses, leaflets, cruising. . . .
> (c) Our media should recognize honestly all aspects of what it is to be gay, including our "bad" aspects, e.g. trucks, cruising, sexual objectification, etc.
> (d) Portray the gay life style and culture[6]

The document closes with the line "QUESTION: Do you suppose the gay bar is gay media?" Gay activity of all sorts is presented here as cultural mediation. Liberationists and those inspired by them often construed media as extending far beyond popular conceptions, such as television, newspapers, and magazines. Just as film may work through elements such as lighting or set design and figure movement to produce certain understandings, a gay bar (or a demonstration, or a dance, or a coffee house) may be purposely organized to modulate and elaborate certain ways of patterning and seeing gay life. Just as the "gay bar" is a place, it is also an arena of mediated engagement, a cultural location not unlike a film, play, or stage performance wherein what one sees, hears, and feels in and around oneself can become an opportunity for self-reflection and group affiliation—in short, what liberationists referred to as "consciousness-raising."

These media forms were marked by an emergent discourse that sought to challenge medicalizing and criminalizing paradigms of homosexuality through the creation of counterimages that shifted emphasis toward experiences of affirmation, collectivity, and direct, unhindered expressions of same-sex romantic and sexual interaction spanning the individual, couple, and group. At the same time, interests in and uses of media in the gay liberation years should not be understood as only extending outward from a fixed sense of gay self, community, and/or politics. Image constructions and performances by LGBTQ+ people during this time intersected with aesthetic, social, and political practices developed in areas including glam-rock, the hippie movement, the expansion of porn cinema, and that important yet elusive category, the sexual revolution, to name but a few key areas of influence.

Cultural practitioners and participants of a wide variety became makers and mediators—authors—of gay life. Amplifying a range of models for and expression of gay experience, male-desiring men put gay life into action through writing, singing, acting, filming, talking, dancing, clothes making, cruising, site-making, traveling, and demonstrating. Filmmaking and filmgoing brought many of these elements into play, constituting a vital means for the elaboration of gay life. The drag queens seen in the documentary *The Queen* (Frank Simon, 1968) found an audience at some of the first gay film festivals. Likewise, in work such as Peter de Rome's *The Fire Island Story* (1965) and *Encounter* (1971), couples and groups of male-desiring men assembled not only as participants in short erotic dramas taking place in and around beaches, resorts, towns, and unmarked urban spaces, but also as audiences for the films, watched later among friends (fig. 8). At many of the first gay movement events, such as the Gay Activist Alliance held in an old New York firehouse, "film nights" were a central part of gay gathering,

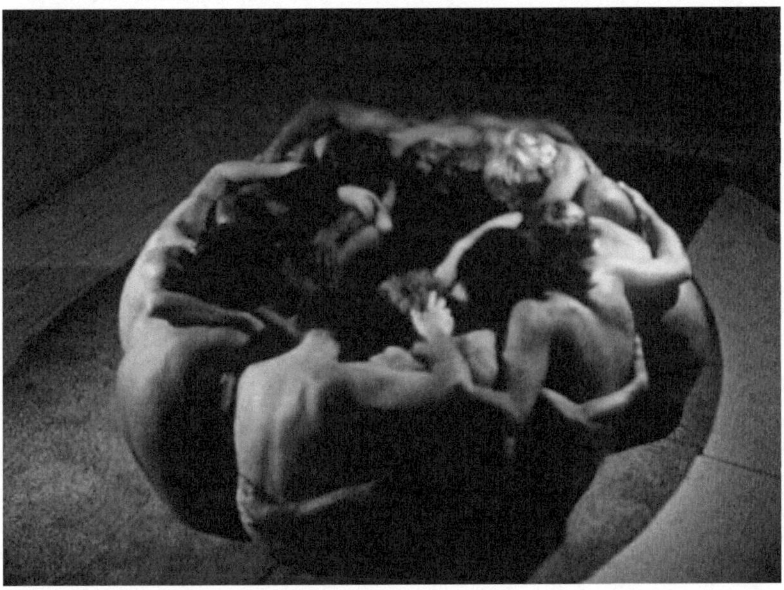

FIGURE 8 The explicit assembly of male-desiring men.

exhibiting French imports such as *This Special Friendship* (*Les amitiés particulières*; Jean Delannoy, 1964) alongside time-tested films of camp reception such as Mae West's *I'm No Angel* (Wesley Ruggles, 1933) and *Three Faces of Eve* (Nunnally Johnson, 1957) (fig. 9). Categories such as "new gay pix," the "great gay movie boom," and "Lavender Cinema" began to bring a variety of films into view as gay cinema (fig. 10).[7]

Filmmaking activities were attuned to the workings of the kind of performative paradigm Janet Staiger has referred to as "rebellious or re-

GAY ACTIVISTS ALLIANCE 5-71

JIM OWLES • PRESIDENT
P.O. BOX 2 VILLAGE STATION
NEW YORK, N.Y. • 10014

FILM SCHEDULE

All Movies On Friday Nights at 8:00 PM AT THE GAA Firehouse, 99 Wooster Street

May 28th - Marilyn Monroe in "Bus Stop" and Ginger Rogers doing the Black Bottom in "Roxie Hart" with Iris Adrian as Two Gun Gertie

June 4 -"This Special Friendship" about two boys in love and Marlene Dietrich in "Dishonored"

June 11 - "The Bride Of Frankenstein" and Bette Davis in"The Anniversary"

June 18 - Special showing after the Gay Pride Dance - "Gypsy" at 3:30 AM Breakfast follows.

July 2 - "Wait Until Dark" and "The Littlest Show" with Margaret Rutherford

July 9th - "The Queen" - a documentary about transvestites and "The Women" with Rosaland Russell, Joan Crawford, Paulette Goddard, Norma Shearer, Joan Fontaine, Marjorie Main and Mary Boland & Hedda Hopper as herself.

July 16 - "Three Faces Of Eve" and "Born Yesterday" plus a very rare short showing the woman that Three Faces of Eve really happened to in an interview, displaying all three personalities.

July 23rd - Mae West in "I'm No Angel" and "Animal Farm"

FIGURE 9 Viewers gathered at the Gay Activists Alliance Firehouse in New York City for regular "movie night" screenings that included a combination of Hollywood movies and independent films. Flyer, GAA "Film Schedule" (1971). Image courtesy of Thomas J. Dodd Research Center at the University of Connecticut, Storrs.

FIGURE 10 "New Gay Pix" for "America's homophile community." Cover, *The Advocate* (July 8–21, 1970). Image courtesy of the Hall-Carpenter Archives at the London School of Economics. Used with permission.

sistant authorship."[8] Gay films gained a special power and intensity that pivoted on "asserting agency against the normative."[9] Whereas earlier films often cautiously subverted what was considered acceptable, many liberation-inspired filmmakers used film to insist on bold, unregulated images of male-male desire, even if only within home movie and amateur film contexts. Film was used not just to put gay people on screen, but elaborated gay feelings, articulated gay philosophies, and modeled gay eroticism and sexual activity. Makers and viewers alike participated in the imagining *and* the social activation of gay life, contemplating a variety of models for living that they brought into the "practice of everyday life," to employ Michel de Certeau's formulation.[10] As people authored their own lives anew as gay lives, filmmakers authored with and alongside them. As people experimented with how to live lives out of accord with the larger heterosexual world, film became a way of modeling and making statements about these experiments. As Staiger puts it, "what an author *is*, is the repetition of statements."[11] In the authoring of gay life, film became a repository for a collection of tropes, references, and conventions that worked as part of a public context for making statements—sometimes vague and abstract, sometimes lucid and direct—about what it means to *live gay*.

As such, putting gay life on film was seldom understood as being solely a matter of personal expression. Directors of liberation-era gay cinema were not simply *auteurs*. This is not to say that they were not marked as directors (or writers, editors, etc.), but rather that these positions were often discursively framed in promotional materials, film credits, reviews, and interviews as emerging out of their role as an active participant in the elaboration of gay life. In tracing the relationship between these authors and the constructions of gay life fostered by their films, it is important to consider how gay authorship was itself deployed contextually: primarily, through the development of the first gay film screenings and film programs around heavily promoted and branded author figures. It is also important to consider how the changing strategies of independent film production and exhibition, working alongside new concerns around film censorship, set the stage for gay cinema.

How was authorship utilized as a means of making gay films legible as such? What did it mean for specific filmmakers, and the distributors and promoters they worked with, to claim—or, in some instances, disavow—a gay film or film program as their own creation? How did the listing of names such as Andy Warhol, Kenneth Anger, Steven Arnold, or Fred Halsted work to position films not just as the products of individual male creators, but as some of the first gay cultural products explicitly marked as gay? A turn to the context that enabled gay cinema will illuminate how gay authorship was mobilized at this particular historical juncture.

A National Market Comes into View

As an industry in its own right, the mass theatrical distribution and screening of overt images of male-male desire began to take shape within the overlapping contexts of art house and adult cinema. Whereas audiences had previously gathered for one-off film events and programs, by early 1968 these programs began to be extended over whole weekends, and by midway through that same year ran as ongoing film seasons. There are three major factors that, between the late 1960s and early 1970s, helped to facilitate the coalescence of gay cinema as it moved from the localized phenomenon of film programs and events in a handful of major cities to a national market working within and through a complex variety of distribution and exhibition contexts specific to this moment: (1) Changes in censorship, obscenity law, and practices of film classification contributed to the expansion of a cinematic marketplace for "adult" and "mature" audiences that, in turn, provided a new context for the expansion of proto-gay/gay films; (2) an increasingly discernable mass audience for gay film worked in tandem with larger factors—such as a film industry recession and shifts in the cultural geography of major US cities—to contribute to the national expansion of proto-gay/gay cinema; (3) shifts in the marketplace for mainstream film worked, in combination with the above, to contribute to the development of gay cinema produced, promoted, distributed, and exhibited with a mass, national audience in mind. Each of these factors played a significant role in enabling gay cinema to move from one-off film programs to a complex web of industrial networks.

The most critical event in the overhaul of censorship practices was the complete abandonment of the production code in 1967. The code had been used to prohibit overt representations of sexual desire in Hollywood film since its instigation in 1930, but since it was not law but merely a set of self-imposed industry regulations, numerous producers, directors, and exhibitors had sought to test the viability of working outside the Hollywood distribution system. One of the most important of these tests came when MGM, the distributor for the film *Blow-Up* (Michelangelo Antonioni, 1966), having been denied certification for full-frontal female nudity, decided to release the film through an independent distribution company anyway.[12] With the film recouping seven times its production cost and receiving two Academy Award nominations, other distributors followed suit, leading to the abandonment of the code by 1967 and the introduction of a classification system created by the newly instituted Motion Picture Association of America (MPAA) in 1968. A system that emphasized classification replaced one that emphasized censorship.

Two further events occurred in 1968 that would pave the way for gay cinema: first, the Supreme Court case *Ginsberg vs. New York*, which was resolved on April 22, 1968; and second, the impact that the outcome of this case had on film classification. The court case emphasized the concept of "variable obscenity" as a means of classifying film. Asserting the idea that what should be deemed obscene is dependent on the intended audience of the work in question, the ruling stressed the notion of age appropriateness, bringing demographic thinking into obscenity law. Central to this case was the prosecution of Sam Ginsberg, after he sold two magazines with nude women in them to sixteen-year-old informants at his Long Island stationary store. Ginsberg argued that the state of New York was stripping those under eighteen of their liberty, but the state ultimately ruled against him.[13] The case was central in informing the code system under development at the time by MPAA director Jack Valenti. On October 18, 1968, when a new regulatory system was established under the name Classification and Rating Administration (CARA), the categories "suggested for mature audiences" (M) and "persons under 16 not admitted" (X) were established.[14]

The concept of the "mature audience" was pivotal in enabling the more sustained development of gay film programming. It provided a legitimizing rhetoric that could be employed to both defend and promote a cinema predicated upon images of interest to male-desiring men as matter of American rights. Accordingly, when the Park Theatre ran its adult-male film program in the summer of 1968, promotional brochures were created in advance to situate the program within a patriotic, rights-based discourse. Asserting the legitimacy of both the films and their audience, the cover of the brochure used austere aesthetics (elegant typeface, photograph of a classical male nude) along with several passages that read like a legal defense, citing the constitutional rights of freedom of speech and freedom to assemble as the very impetus for creating the program. Echoing the "we" of the US Constitution, the final passage asserts:

> We the management of the Park Cinema, announce the very first assemblage of films of interest to the adult homosexual. . . . Freedom to think, to speak, to write and to film—and for the other person to listen and to see—is essential to us as individuals and to the safety of our democratic society. Only in this way can a society

grow from ignorance and irrationality to knowledge and reason, the firmest pillars of public morality.[15]

Within the logic of the advertisement, adult homosexuals are a sector of the American population who (1) are highly literate (think, speak, write, and make and see film, etc.), (2) protect individualism and therefore democracy, and (3) are perhaps even the potential harbingers of a strengthened sense of "public morality." Ultimately, however, the program is positioned as an opportunity to mature—to grow up—by asserting its value as a device to stimulate growth "from ignorance and irrationality to knowledge and reason."

By the autumn of 1968, the weekend festival programming of gay films at the Park Theatre gave way to longer programs lasting several weeks followed by a switch to nonstop seasonal programming by the year's end. These longer programs pivoted on the success of a dependable audience eager to participate in gay cinema. Gay cinema was increasingly garnering a public face as a complex institution in its own right, with a distinct sense of assuredness coming to mark the promotional strategies undertaken by the Park (fig. 11).

Where just months earlier, promotion for the theater was organized around a defensive, legalistic rhetoric vying for the right to exhibit overt images of male-male desire, by the introduction of the film season "Autumn at the Park," the promotion had come to assume an air of confident self-assertion. The cover page was graced with an illustration by Los Angeles artist Harry Bush of a confident-looking muscleboy in a zebra print Speedo placed alongside a series of film stills featuring drag queens standing triumphantly on stage as they accept awards at a drag ball, as well as various actors looking strikingly and even joyfully assertive; two boys stand shirtless together, one just behind the other in the traditional blocking of a couple's portrait, both men with wide, friendly smiles evoking the exuberant quality of a high school yearbook spread or a social club newsletter. Likewise, the names of several production companies now appear as a primary focal point; bold, elegant calligraphy advertises veteran physique filmmaker Richard Fontaine's Zenith Productions and Pat Rocco's Bizarre Productions, one caption celebrating the continuity between tried-and-trusted physique companies and this new public cinema with the announcement of "a 'merger' of two great Physique Studios . . . who combine to offer a truly outstanding program." Another section of the brochure shows the relationship developing between filmmaking and

FIGURE 11 The bold and exuberant announcement of a "continuing program" of gay cinema. Brochure, Park Theatre (Autumn 1968). From the personal collection of the author.

film screening as a gay practice with "L.A.'s first annual male filmmakers competition."

A few forerunners called attention to the possibilities of a lucrative market for gay cinema beyond one-off film programs and events. Beginning in 1967, Mike Getz formed a network of seventeen theaters across the United States for weekend midnight screenings of experimental short films by filmmakers such as Andy Warhol and Jonas Mekas.[16] By 1968, with the inclusion of several features by Warhol—*Bike Boy* (1967), *Nude Restaurant* (1967), and *Lonesome Cowboys* (1968), among others—it became evident that the series was drawing in a large audience of gay male viewers. Thomas Waugh notes:

> An audience of gay men was clearly the decisive factor in Warhol's commercial success. The late sixties saw gay audiences beginning to be publicly constituted in theatrical venues for the first time (not necessarily in 42nd street ambiences either) and expressing community through then-experimental exhibition ideas like midnight showings, and even gay cinemas.[17]

A crucial role Warhol's films played in the public constitution of gay cinema was that large numbers of people were beginning to see them, read about them, and talk about them simultaneously in various parts of the country. Not only was gay film beginning to happen, but also a host of curious entrepreneurs were starting to institutionalize a cinematic apparatus for gay film on a national scale. By 1969, gay cinema was becoming formalized as a cinema in its own right: *Lonesome Cowboys* simultaneously played in an extended release format in two theaters, Manhattan's 55th Street Playhouse and Los Angeles's Cinema Theatre, which were, as noted by Waugh, rapidly "on their way to becoming gay male houses."[18] Signaling, at least on an industry level, a national awareness of an audience of gay male viewers, it wasn't long before theater owners and distributors across the US started to explore the possibilities of instituting a network of cinemas to build on this audience.

Between 1969 and 1971, a number of factors came into play that accelerated a boom in gay cinema. Within this period, several theater owners across the United States invested in gay cinema as a product, developing interstate networks of distribution and exhibition. While this is, to a certain extent, attributable to the success that pioneering film programs experienced on local levels, there are some critical ways in which this expansion was informed by broader national issues of socioeconomic change. There are three primary factors at play here: the severe recession suffered by the American film industry between 1969 and 1971 and the way in which this opened up a space for new kinds of film product on a mass scale; widespread urban decentralization in major cities across the US and its impact on theater ownership, distribution policy, and film exhibition practices; and, lastly, the rise of new kinds of film—such as the counterculture film, hard-core porn, and blaxploitation—that, in shooting for both mass-market appeal and popularity among specific audience demographics, came to shift conceptions of what mainstream film could be.

While Hollywood and its complex networks of production, distribution, and exhibition had been in decline for some time, in 1969 the system took a nearly fatal blow. The outcome of a radical overinvestment in several mid-decade productions that flopped culminated in a recession so severe that between 1969 and 1971 the majors suffered $600 million in losses, leaving, by 1970, 40 percent of Hollywood filmmakers jobless.[19] During this same period, major cities across the United States were suffering from a steep acceleration in suburbanization, intensified by the mass exodus of the white middle classes (also known as white flight) from several cities. With the concurrent development of the suburban multiplex, scores of urban movie theaters—from first-run movie palaces to neighborhood art theaters—moved from the hands of major national chains into those of newly formed, often localized companies and independent business owners.[20] With this shift, hundreds of urban theaters went from exhibiting product that was in some way or another dictated by the major Hollywood studios to more complex, independently oriented kinds of programming.[21] The combination of the decline in available Hollywood product and the increasing availability of urban theaters set the stage for new kinds of cinema culture to take up residency.

Much of the gap left by the recession and suburbanization led to an increase in lower budget films that could be produced quickly and inexpensively, targeted toward specific audience demographics through genres such as blaxploitation, pornography, and horror films.[22] This shift did not go without response from Hollywood. Writing in 1969, the chairman of American International Pictures (AIP), Samuel Z. Arkoff, announced in the *Journal of the Producers Guild of America* that "today the audience is fragmented . . . one must take aim at a special group to be successful."[23] Adult films proved to be one of the largest areas of growth within this context. According to producer David Friedman, the number of theaters showing exclusively adult fare nationwide went from around twenty in 1960 to a total of 750 by 1970.[24] As Jon Lewis notes:

> X-rated exploitation films were at the time making a lot of money—on a screen-by-screen basis, more money than some very big studio releases. . . . The message was clear: even the biggest and best theatres were willing to book hard and soft-

> core titles so long as they made money. While the MPAA refused to acknowledge X-rated films, the nation's exhibitors were anxious to view all films as somehow the same. A good picture was one that made them money.[25]

In fact, many theaters switched their programming altogether in an effort to develop a "parallel marketplace" that was not dependent on the approval of the MPAA.[26] While this boom was well on its way by 1968, expansion in this area picked up substantial speed in 1969 with the outcome of the Supreme Court obscenity trial *Grove Press v. Maryland Board of Censors* regarding the Swedish film *I Am Curious (Yellow)* (Vilgot Sjöman, 1967), which, after having been seized by customs earlier that year for containing uncensored images of male and female genitals and penetrative sex, was now legally protected, stimulating what Eddie Muller and Daniel Farris have referred to as "a tidal wave of sex films."[27]

With a growing sense of confidence that the days of censorship were now behind them, exhibitors and distributors were now ready to institute a national network of gay cinema. Seeking to expand on the success of the film program at the Park in Los Angeles, owner Shan Sayles purchased New York's 1,700-seat movie palace the Henry Miller Theatre, renaming it the Park-Miller.[28] In a full-page "grand-opening" advertisement for the September 1969 issue of *The Advocate*, blocks of text that announce "Look out New York" and "L.A.'s Famous Festival Goes Coast to Coast" are shown raining down like confetti over an image of New York City as if having been thrown clear from one coast to the other.[29] Later that same year, Sayles continued to branch out in a similar fashion with the opening of the Mini-Park in Houston, Texas.

Working within the more time-tested bounds of the sexploitation market, Lou Sher, owner of the Art Guild Cinemas, having experienced success with gay audiences as a result of his distribution of *Lonesome Cowboys*, began to use his nationwide chain of (at least) twenty-five neighborhood art cinemas as reliable sites for the regular exhibition of gay cinema.[30] With theaters in cities and towns across the US such as Cleveland, Champaign, Tucson, and Los Angeles, Sher adopted a similar programming model as the Park, re-releasing recent hits from the underground midnight movie circuit and one-off events into more traditional "first-run" style booking schedules.[31] This resulted in the wider availability of gay-themed underground films from directors like Andy Warhol and Kenneth Anger as well as cult gay sexploitation favorites such as *The Meatrack* (Richard Stockton, 1970) and *Sticks and Stones* (Stan Lopresto, 1970). Sher found these films to be such a successful addition to his programming of horror, heterosexual sexploitation, and experimental film that in the late 1960s and early 1970s, he began investing in the production of gay cinema. The exhibitor gave underground filmmaker James Bidgood funding to complete his film *Pink Narcissus* (1971), a work the director had been painstakingly producing out of his own pocket and filming in his tiny New York apartment over the previous six years. At this point, the production, promotion, and distribution of gay movies was becoming more closely coordinated and thought out, with entrepreneurs like Sher beginning to think more about questions of audience demographic and national circulation.

The Changing Frame

Film promotion was the most ubiquitous means used to mark films as gay and was important not only for framing films for cinema patrons, but also for giving them life outside of the cinema. Readers of newspapers such as the Los Angeles–based papers *The Advocate* and the *L.A. Free Press* or the Houston-based *Nuntius* were invited to envision what a gay film would look like, an important activity for the many readers who had never seen one and perhaps did not have easy access to the cities in which they were beginning to play. Likewise, flyers, posters, and lobby cards, often viewed or picked up on the street or in bookstores, invited the same kind of imaginative speculation.

Such promotion played a key role in more securely establishing the Park Theatre in Los Angeles as an identifiable site for gay cinema, than the scattered one-off film events at the Coronet Theatre or in the disparate bars scattered across Los Angeles that are explored in chapter 1. Starting with the program "A Most Unusual Film Festival," which ran from June 26 to July 2, 1968, theater owner Shan Sayles not only commissioned extensive programs of "all-male" films, but also undertook highly visible promotional campaigns incorporating elegant brochures, newspaper advertisements, and marquee signs.

How did the Park prepare filmgoers to see films as gay? Promotion for the theater's first gay programs worked in the tradition of much homoerotic art, the most salient characteristic of which is the third-body paradigm described by Waugh: a poser/sitter/model who is presented as an object to be transformed into artistic content under the careful gaze of an onlooking male maker. The brochure for the first program positioned this new cinematic experience by foregrounding author-text relations in a way that signaled them as evidence of same-sex desire.

Titles include "Andy Warhol's 'My Hustler'" (1965), "Jack Smith's Notorious Flaming Creatures" (1963), "Warhol's 'B-J'" (1963), "Mike Kuchar's 'The Secret of Wendell Sampson'" (1966), and even Jonas and Adolfas Mekas's "The Brig" (1964), a film not overtly concerned with male-male desire that has been repurposed within a homoerotic frame through an image of a nude actor (fig. 12).

The marking of authorship did more than place these films within a discourse of auteurism. By putting male authors' names to film titles that connote or denote eroticized male characters, the brochure signaled a set of relations whereby the act of one male viewing another is modeled for the viewer: where the figure of director-actor relations is established for the mobilization of one male taking pleasure in the erotics of viewing another. This evidences a modified deployment of the third body. As images of male-male desire became more explicitly contextualized in the 1960s as gay (as opposed to simply homoerotic), a more self-conscious presentation of the third body began to come into view. The desiring male onlooker/producer, once behind the scenes, was increasingly figured as a central part of the story. The program's centerpiece advertisement directly amplifies this through the still taken from *My Hustler*: the image mirrors artist/sitter relations in the way the "john" (Ed Hood) sits close to and looks at the seminaked muscular body of "the hustler" (Paul America) stretched out across the fore-

FIGURE 12 Foregrounding the third-body paradigm. Brochure, Park Theatre (Autumn 1968). From the personal collection of the author.

ground. Together, Hood and America figuratively extend a layered set of significations that not only work to activate a discourse of male-male desire, but also evokes an array of relations within which the viewers can align their own participation: author-text, director-character, hustler-john, and so on. While these films in and of themselves may or may not have been invested in explicit stories about male-male desire at the diegetic level, between the mid-1960s and the early 1970s a number of films began to appear that were more directly devoted to incorporating male-male desire at the level of filmic diegesis.

While the earlier corpus of postwar homosexual underground cinema tended to mute the direct representation of male-male desire, a new cluster of films in the late 1960s modified underground tropes to showcase explicit male-male coupling and group interaction. A landmark example of this shift is Andy Milligan's 1965 short film *Vapors*, which used the real locations of New York's St. Mark's Baths to tell a story centered on experiences of male-male contact within such a space. Here, desire is enacted through direct romantic contact between men and a frank, solemn discussion about one's experience of being a male-desiring man. At the level of dialogue, for instance, the protagonist, alone in a bathhouse cubby with another man, nervously asks, "may I touch your face . . . I just want to put my hand on your skin," prompting the other man to raise his hand and bring the man's hand to his face. *Vapors* pressed beyond the connotation of much earlier filmmaking with a more direct address to male-desiring men who were contemplating or pursuing sociosexual contact with other men. The film played briefly on the art house circuit in 1965, followed by a longer run at New York's Cameo Theatre in 1967, this time promoted by a poster that amplified the film's liberatory nature, featuring a shirtless image of the film's leading men and a tagline reading, "Bold . . . Sensitive . . . Imaginative." Moving beyond the home screenings and special events of the avant-garde circuit, *Vapors* broke ground in the viability of theatrical runs for gay films.

Vapors marks a transitional moment. The late 1960s and early 1970s saw hundreds of films produced and screened that elaborated experiences of male-male social, sexual, and romantic contact alongside performances of radical gender dissidence through celebratory—sometimes dreamy and abstract, sometimes lucid and direct—poetic registers. Like the "visionary cinema"—to use a paradigm employed by P. Adams Sitney—of filmmakers like Maya Deren, Kenneth Anger, Jack Smith, and Stan Brakhage, those making gay cinema at this time were able to use alternative, non-Hollywood sources of funding to carve out an oppositional cinema for the elaboration of new, poetic ways of thinking, seeing, feeling, and desiring. In this sense, they were truly "visionary." Sitney's use of the term is drawn from Harold Bloom's *The Visionary Company* wherein Bloom characterizes the Romanticism that underpins the "visionary" qualities of this tradition by drawing on Wallace Stevens:

> "To live in the world but outside the existing conceptions of it," Stevens writes, and also: "In the presence of extraordinary actuality, consciousness takes the place of imagination." The world of actuality faced first by Blake, Coleridge and Wordsworth . . . afforded no existing conceptions fully acceptable to the imagination, and presented a provocation for a heightening of consciousness so intense that a true awareness of reality inevitably sought for itself the identifying sanction of imagination.[32]

These were films that sought to live outside the existing conceptions of the world, to forge new conceptions that would be acceptable to the imagination. However, gay visionary films must be understood as a kind of gay authorship in which individual poetic sensibility is embedded in concerns about group consciousness. In some cases, these films drew on gay liberation ideas that emphasized the importance of self and group affirmation through actualization of one's nonnormative desires as well as rhetorical frameworks and actions such as gay pride, gay power, and coming out. At the same time, gay visionary cinema rarely, if ever, neatly reflected these formulations. In fact, individual films tend to call the stability of these paradigms into question and point to different ways of understanding and enacting them.

For example, the spatial paradigm of "outness," arguably the most persistent trope of gay visionary cinema, does not designate one consistent spatial idea. How might exploring this moment in cinema help us to understand the many different meanings and uses that outness can have? While little of the material explored in this chapter was made to be received as documentary cinema (*Mondo Rocco*'s [1970] weaving of actual gay social and political events notwithstanding), Greg Youmans's observations about how outness functions in gay documentary of the period is instructive here. Through a comparison of *Word Is Out* (Nancy Adair et al., 1977) and *Gay U.S.A.* (Arthur Bressan Jr., 1978), Youmans elucidates two different approaches to picturing "out gay life."[33] *Word Is Out*'s focus on head shots in bright, sunny, often outdoor locations functions to "articulat[e] a vision of gay and lesbian experience that is no longer riven by conflicts of surface and depth, public and private, light and shadow" in which "coming out is the coming into self-honesty, into political legitimacy and into unremarkable documentary realism."[34] *Gay U.S.A.* puts into formal play a combination of "aerial shots," "street-level photography," and camera movements that "weave in and out of the crowd," giving viewers "a sense of the disruptive potential of gay life."[35] Legitimacy, publicity, exteriority, disruption—outness can be many things and articulated to a variety of differing ends.

In the fiction work of gay visionary cinema, the valences of outness work less to frame ways of understanding actual and particular lives and events than as occasions for exploring different ways of *seeing gay*. In the case studies explored here, figurative employments of gay authorship work to suggest the experience of outness as something that can, and perhaps should, be modulated and shaped, extending ways of imagining and assembling an image of gay life. In the first case study, *Pink Narcissus*, I explore how ideas of anonymous authorship across levels of promotion, narration, and mise-en-scène work to reposition the third body as a spectacularized trope. In the second case study, *Luminous Procuress*, I explore how the film emerged from contexts of collaborative authorship. Combining radical drag with formal film experimentation, the film manifests a poetic quest narrative in which third-body spectatorship is rendered at the level of its diegesis as we see the protagonists move from a place of erotic spectatorship to one of participation in sex and gender dissidence. In these worlds, the postwar sense of coming out as coming into a gay social scene is maintained as the protagonists' journeys unfold through spectacularly explicit scenes of gay sex and transgressive gender performance.

In the subsequent case studies, *The Erotic Films of Peter de Rome* (1973) and *Mondo Rocco*, the figure of the author is used to weave together the notion of coming into a gay scene with the kind of "unremarkable documentary realism" that marks much gay documentary of the period. Rendering the "unremarkable" remarkable, these films merge elements such as on-location filming in everyday environments and nonprofessional actors with dreamlike erotic scenarios that emphasize the actualization of desire between men through a variety of sex acts. In considering how all four cases use the figure of authorship as a means to situate films within a discourse of gay life, the following analyses demonstrate how those involved in the inventive work of gay cinema elaborated entwined visions of group and self to encourage a sense of the ever-expanding parameters of gay life.

Pink Narcissus as Anonymous Homosexual Production

Gay visionary cinema went beyond suggesting the possibility of contact between male-desiring men to (a) indicating the social existence of such activities at discernable sites (as opposed to the often more vaguely figurative, fantastical, or mythical sites of homosexual underground cinema) and/or (b) pushing connotation to its limits, such that it spills over, paradoxically, into a denotation in which homoeroticism is so overcoded that it is recast as a feature of gay poesis. An example of the latter is the "Blue Velvet" sequence of Kenneth Anger's *Scorpio Rising* (1963), in which the camera's gaze, repeatedly panning up and down a nearly naked biker as he changes into his gear, is reciprocated with direct eye contact. The Bobby Vinton rendition of "Blue Velvet," highlighting the sensuality of clothing, positions him as the object of desire. Unlike Anger's earlier *Fireworks*, this sequence does not move quickly through glancing instances of possibility, but rather holds and sustains the act of homoerotic looking, amplifying this act with the camp gender transposition of the song. While the film is still homoerotically coded, here coding comes to take on an overtly desirous perspective that engages and celebrates male-male looking.

Gay visionary cinema, however, did not necessarily even require homoeroticism to undertake such an operation. In two avant-garde films that might be described as proto-gay, Jack Smith's *Normal Love* (1963) and Ron Rice's *Chumlum* (1964), the devotion to an orientalist Hollywood B-movie aesthetic so thoroughly and painstakingly structures these films as to foreground what Ronald Gregg has called their "ever-present sense of joyful absurdity." Gregg explains:

> Becoming ostentatiously and luxuriously dressed harem girls, magicians, slaves, sheiks and other such archetypes, they lingered in their imagined idyllic pleasures, the eroticism (at times transformed into something distinctly unerotic), in the narcissism, violence, polygamy and same-sex intimacy. They teased out these non-narrative moments of play and excess to create an imaginary location for their experiments in subjectivity.[36]

Much of the imagery detailed here by Gregg, appears, by the late 1960s and early 1970s, as part of gay visionary forms of film and photography that position their filmmaker-protagonist (and often other members of their social circle or scene) as members of magical orientalist tableaux in which gender and sex norms are ecstatically, playfully disregarded and/or reconstituted. For instance, in Steven Arnold's *The Liberation of Mannique Mechanique* (1967), scores of models draped and bejeweled in scarves, headdresses, necklaces, and painted with white face-paint and shimmering cosmetic designs are shown lounging decadently in a world of sashed drapery and embroidery. With costumes that render gender indistinct but provide copious views of unclothed body parts, the mise-en-scène reads as a futurist harem where the desire for "experiments in subjectivity" organizes the film's formal composition.

In Charles Henri Ford's *Johnny Minotaur* (1971), the American filmmaker utilized the Greek island of Crete to recreate the archetypical story of the Minotaur in gay poetic terms. The film reformats the island as an exotic mythical paradise, where same-sex desire is rendered as abundant and unrestrained by norms of age, nationality, or location. While loosely following the Minotaur myth (featuring a Minotaur fashioned out of an abundance of fabric), the film features numerous outdoor nude scenes of sexual contact on beaches and rooftops. Though less distinctly "Eastern"-themed than Smith's, Rice's, and some of Arnold's imagery, the film similarly constructs the island as a paradisiacal, phantasmagoric inversion of life in the US, free from the regulation of male-male sexual expression.

By the early 1970s, a cycle of gay visionary films began bringing together the homoeroticism that structured the narrative design of many postwar trance films with the more psychedelic aesthetics of such orientalist fantasias. Informed by the emergence and expansion of hippie culture in the mid- to late 1960s—with all of its confrontational rejection of dominant US conventions of social organization (the nuclear family), self-presentation (traditionally gendered dress), and sexual behavior (restraint and privacy)—the work of directors and performers such as James Bidgood, Steven Arnold, Sebastian, and The Cockettes promulgated radical and poetic images of male-male desire, gender dissidence, and anticonformist sexual behavior. In particular, in Bidgood's anonymously released *Pink Narcissus* (1971) and Arnold's *Luminous Procuress* (1971), the wandering protagonist of the postwar trance film journeys not through hard-edged, black-and-white urban landscapes, but through brightly colored, fantastical studio sets that combine the futurist aesthetics of science fiction, orientalist drag recalling B-movie costuming of the 1940s and '50s (and boys' adventure movies in particular), and an emphasis on nudity characteristic of the rapidly expanding porn industry.

At the time of *Pink Narcissus*'s release in the spring of 1971, several epitextual elements worked to give the film's renegotiation of the Narcissus myth specific resonance for male-desiring male viewers. First and foremost was the widely publicized withdrawal of the director's name from the project and the particular way in which this was incorporated into the advertising campaign. While the film has since been claimed by James Bidgood, a New York–based physique photographer, costume designer, and window display artist, at the time of the film's release the credits for the director, as well as the producer, the writer, and the photographer, were listed as "ANONYMOUS." This credit was emphasized across both film and promotion, inciting curiosity about the film. The question of who made the film became a site for speculation that continued throughout the early 1970s. Engaging in a game of detection and guesswork, Parker Tyler declared, "*Where* it was created, or by *Whom*, remains a secret: it was conceived, written, directed and produced by Anonymous . . . who may be, according to rumor, a VIP."[37] In *Interview* magazine, critic Labrunie Ducasse pondered the motives for this authorial masking, noting that "perhaps it is to conceal a name, perhaps it is to eventually make one . . . but whoever made *Pink Narcissus*, and it doesn't really matter, he is the spiritual grandson of some queer old surrealist couple and he wants to share the credit with all of us . . . for we have all made it."[38]

The emphasis on the veiled and undisclosed author as a trope of homosexual authorship works paradoxically to make legible the film's thematic content as part of a rhetoric of gay visibility. This is most evident in the way magazine advertisements (fig. 13) linked secrecy with explicit homoerotic content, combining stills from the film with the following disclaimer:

> Because of the intense personal nature of PINK NARCISSUS, the filmmaker has chosen to remain anonymous. Despite continuous speculation in the film-world, the distributor respects the director's desire for privacy and will not provide any credit listing.[39]

The promotion for *Pink Narcissus* makes a grand display of what it chooses to leave out, sexualizing that anonymity. This is achieved by playing off the undisclosed against suggestions of maximum visibility inherent in the pornographic syntax of the image. The image of "Bobby"—displayed for the viewer stretched out on the edge of his rococo bed, decked out in white fur and throwing his best come-and-get-it gaze at the camera—is resonant with the erotic register of striptease, provoking the viewers' anticipation with the suggestion

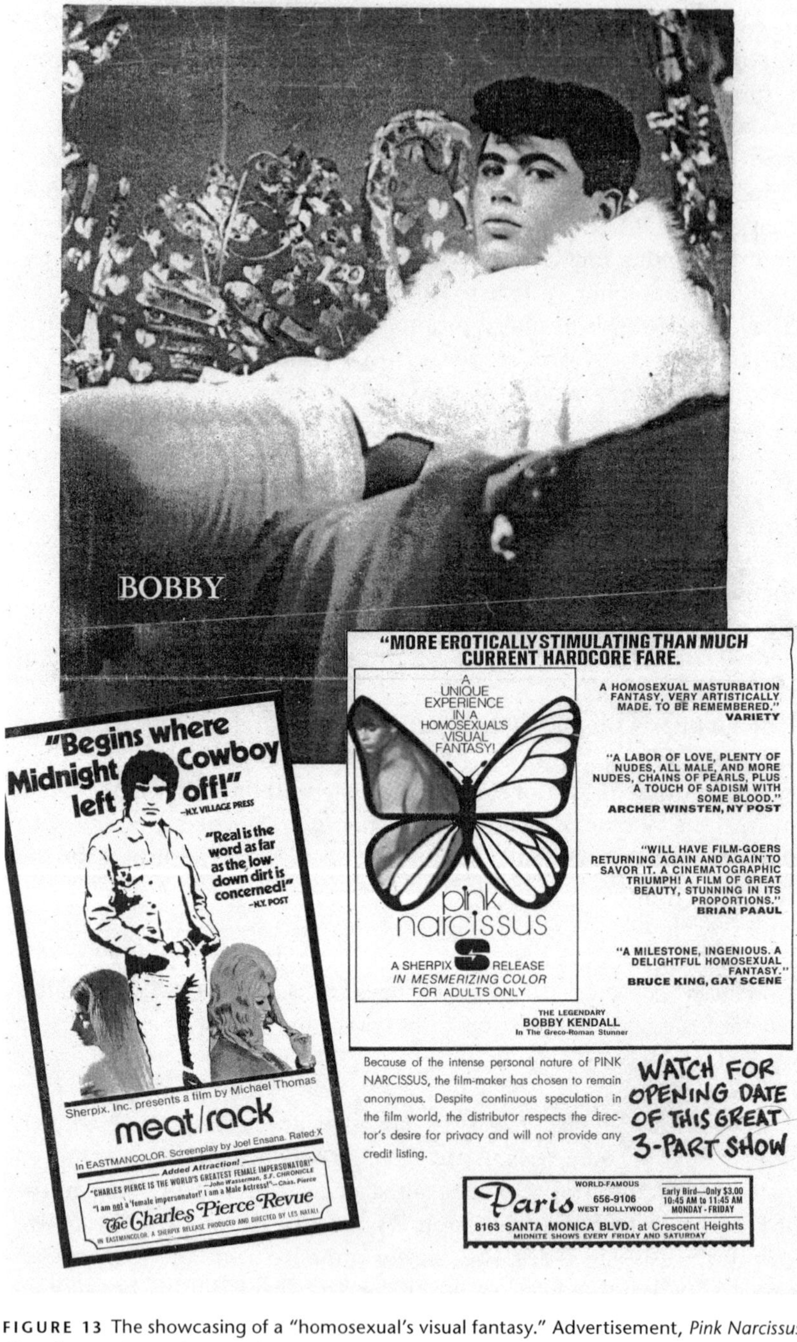

FIGURE 13 The showcasing of a "homosexual's visual fantasy." Advertisement, *Pink Narcissus*, *The Advocate* (December 1971). Image courtesy of the Hall-Carpenter Archive, London School of Economics.

that more flesh is likely to be made visible through admission to the performance.

The incorporation of themes of secrecy into the advertisement also engages a striptease formula by eroticizing the hidden with phrasing like "intense personal nature" and "desire for privacy." Both the withholding of the director's name and the seductive play of the photograph invite the viewer's speculation, not only about the identity of the filmmaker but also the potential relationship between the film's maker, or makers, and the pictured lead actor. Such connections are reinforced by the absence of any typical crediting of actors, replaced with the rather homemade-looking label "BOBBY," evoking the personal, intimate feel of a private scrapbook.

While these playful elements establish a scandalous tone, the branding of the film as "A Homosexual's Visual Fantasy" complicates this. Since the film was primarily advertised (repeatedly, over many years) within the gay publication *The Advocate*, some consideration needs to be made of the kinds of resonance this "homosexual's visual fantasy" might have in the context of the progressive gay discourses privileged by the magazine (at least in its early years) and, by extension, advertisers who took up space within it. The advertisement for *Pink Narcissus* appears in distinct contrast to the other film advertisements. Films like Wakefield Poole's feature-length hard-core film *Boys in the Sand* (1971) were promoted in ways that attempted to amplify their status as exciting and fresh vehicles for positive gay visibility, whether the films themselves were truly invested in positive representations or not. The advert for *Boys in the Sand*, for instance, quotes *Variety* claiming that "there are no more closets."[40]

Conversely, promotion for *Pink Narcissus* often appeared in combination with advertisements for a much smaller group of films that were marketed as "homosexual classics," a category that served to recast the figure of the homosexual as both antiquated and novel, as well as a marker of tried and tested eroticism; this material was often linked with a narrative of the film being brought out from the underground and/or making an aboveground debut. An advertisement for *Seven in a Barn* (1971), for instance, declared "from the underground . . . the famous homosexual story classic."[41] Similarly, an advertisement for *Song of the Loon* promised the opportunity to witness "the famous homosexual classic" on screen.[42] Other advertisements strove to evoke a similar sense of changing mores by citing films commonly read as rich in homosexual innuendo, and then promising a more explicit rendering. For example, the advertisement for the film *The Meatrack* (1970), featured within the *Pink Narcissus* advertisement above, contains the quote "begins where *Midnight Cowboy* left off," suggesting that the homoerotic buddy couple relations of the film's leading males might here be rendered explicit. *Pink Narcissus* offered an example of eroticized homosexual anonymity in an era beginning to think in terms of outness.

This positioning of homosexual authorship and production is extended in the film through specific points of view and ways of seeing, established via framing, editing, and mise-en-scène. These elements are utilized to establish the figure of a homosexual narrator as the dominant visual perspective of the film. While there are multiple perspectives signaled within, all events, actions and, critically, spectacle in the film are oriented around a narrator system that plays on the trope of the homosexual aesthete, evoking a host of figures that associate practices of looking with artistic creation: the painter/drawer, the photographer, the director, the producer, the set designer, and so on. Alongside the title's invocation of pink, these devices are central to how the story's structure is organized in relation to the figure of "homosexual vision."

In the film's opening sequence, the figure of the narrator is established through a self-reflexive emphasis on various kinds of framing and through the repeated use of decorative frames positioned in relation to the overall framing of the shot. Frames for pictures, mirrors, and doors act as compositional devices as well as elements of Bobby's world. *Pink Narcissus* draws attention to the act of framing itself. Through a series of cross-fades, the film transitions from the shot of the frame to a shot of Bobby-as-satyr and then to a shot of Bobby unzipping his coat, maintaining the oval border of the initial frame; increasingly darkened around the edges, the image begins to evoke the spatial dynamics of a peep-show booth or disguised peephole wall portrait, emphasizing the act of peeping from one (darkened) space into another (lit) space (figs. 14–15).

This is the first of many points in the film in which picture frames, studio backdrops, and mirrors are used to conflate practices of voyeurism and artistic production. First, the shot of the empty hanging frame suggests the practices of viewing and curation, as in viewing an object of art or a photograph. However, the zoom in toward the center of the image, and then the match-cut superimposition of the frame-prop image of Bobby-as-satyr, works to promote a sense of the portrait as something willed into being, brought to life by the desiring imagination of an onlooker. The zoom amplifies a sense of third-body spectatorship, bringing homoerotic activity into the frame.

FIGURES 14 and 15 Homoeroticism framed through artifice.

This should alert us to *Pink Narcissus*'s representation of the homoerotically engaged third body during a transitional moment, drawing on both avowedly gay-authored filmmaking that situates it as an explicit narrative component and earlier, more coded forms in which it operates through an implied "producer-spectator." *Pink Narcissus* turns on representing both homosexual anonymity and homosexual artistry as inextricable elements within a dynamic of male-male desire; this works as a means to represent the forms this desire takes, ambivalently, as it comes into being at the intersection of past and present—homosexual and gay—models of sociality and sexual interaction.

Numerous shots combine framing, lighting, and theatrical blocking (of characters and props) in order to establish a sense of parallel viewing distances between Bobby and his mirrors (fig. 16), the camera and Bobby, and the viewer and the mise-en-scène. The film echoes these visual parameters in other situations as a means of implying viewers other than Bobby occupying similar positions. Through these positions, the producer-spectator—"behind the camera, in front of the photograph, but rarely visualized within the frame"—is characterized in both the narrational perspective as well as through Bobby's narcissistic

FIGURE 16 Checking out Bobby checking out himself.

processes of looking. Here, any viewer is invited to become a gay viewer as they watch Bobby within and through the same architecture of desire he visualizes his own desire through, multiplying the point of view in a hall-of-mirrors fashion. This keeps the film within a sustained register of prohibited desire. By continually emphasizing processes of anonymous onlooking, the film trades on the conflation of the unseen viewer and the homosexual artist to establish a figurative economy that exists at a tenuous boundary between anonymity and ubiquity.

Transforming Frames: Participation, Collectivity, and *Luminous Procuress*

In contrast to *Pink Narcissus's* New York production, in which collectivity was fostered fleetingly in apartments and lofts, on the other side of the country more sustained, less cloistered forms of collective world-making were taking off. In restaurants and bars such as San Francisco's Compton's Cafeteria and the Black Cat, and housing collectives and communes such as Haight-Ashbury's Kaliflower house, male-desiring men, drag queens, and trans* people were beginning to assemble in more publicly oriented ways. This was in large part due to the vaster and more loosely organized discourse of underground sexual culture emergent in the mid- to late 1960s, which was increasingly invested in public engagement. Not unlike the earliest California-born homosexual and homophile rights organizations, new organizations looked to non-normative sexual practice as a generative force for public assembly. Organizations such as Berkeley's Psychedelic Church of Venus and publications such as the *Sexual Review Quarterly* were contesting societal norms by encouraging new forms of erotic interaction that countered reproductive heterosexuality.

Although advertising for many theater and film productions undertaken by gay-identifying people in the Bay Area in the late 1960s mimicked mainstream promotional material by crediting directors, producers, and actors, these productions were often produced and received as collaborations. While many of them were not exclusively labeled as gay, much of this work came together through small but subculturally influential gay social networks that were actively involved with San Francisco hippie culture. Unlike the more populist straight-oriented hippie culture that would come to dominate mainstream media representations, gay hippie culture cleaved more closely to surrealist practices that took aesthetic manipulation and negotiation as the starting point for a performance-based approach to everyday life. As with James Bidgood's prop- and costume-filled apartment in New York, gender dissident and same-sex desiring artists such as Hibiscus, Steven Arnold, and Sebastian blurred the lines between street, home, and theater. The lofts, apartments, and communal houses these artists lived in acted as a constellation of sites for alternative forms of artistic practice and sociality, filled with aesthetic-performative devices and materials: orientalist garb, 1950s B-movie makeup, mannequins, sculptures, beads, jewels, and medallions filled the rooms and decorated the bodies of these artists as they moved through San Francisco, recontextualizing interior and exterior space alike into an interconnected series of endlessly unfolding platforms for performance-driven self-presentation and social interaction.

These interconnected spaces enabled a wide spectrum of collaborations across art forms. Filmmakers such as George Kuchar, Mike Kuchar, James Broughton, Steven Arnold, Curt McDowell, and Sebastian undertook a variety of filmmaking projects that brought an ethos of what might be called performative life-crafting to the big screen. In turn, theatrical events promoted the same kind of life-crafting within the spaces of the (typically rented) urban movie theater and home screening. These filmmakers participated in the authoring of particular models of gay life to be taken up by audiences. Through this process, new instances of participation were invited, positioning audience members as coauthors in the making of gay life.

One of the most high-profile collective projects to arise out of this milieu was the proto-glam drag troupe the Cockettes. Formed by Hibiscus, a founding member of the Kaliflower commune, in fall 1969, the Cockettes emerged out of the Bay Area hippie drag of the late 1960s. They were a paradigm shift in gay drag, loosening it from its ties to female impersonation in clubs like San Francisco's Finocchio's and recalibrating it as something more philosophically performative that sought to dissolve lines between audience and performer, bystander and participant, through visually overwhelming styles of dress and gesture. Their drag, coupling science-fiction and futurist aesthetics with diverse dress from earlier eras, radically juxtaposed both male and female and past and future. Lacey burlesque showgirl dresses were combined with metallic face paints applied in angular or geometric patterns and nineteenth-century lumberjack grooming, accentuated with purple or gold pigmentation and glistening gold and silver glitter. The artful decoration of the body with dazzling light-reflecting materials and never-before-seen combinations and applications of color dyes rendered moot signifiers of biological sex. Through this clashing, dialectical use of dress and decoration, the Cockettes placed binaries of both past/future and male/female into beautiful assemblages of meaningful disarray, both elaborating on and occupying the space in between these poles to develop styles of radical self- and group presentation that stressed the virtues of reassembly and rearrangement.

Their approach was very much part of "the continual reconstruction of the self" that Aaron Betsky identifies as key to hippie aesthetics.[43] The Cockettes were part of a whole spectrum of activities in mid- to late 1960s San Francisco that aimed to dissolve the boundaries between art and life, concept and practice, and personal and collective experience—from the liquid gel light shows of Elias Romero to the psychedelic poster artists who embraced denaturalizing uses of color and light. At their early cabaret style shows at the Palace Theatre such as *Gone with the Showboat to Oklahoma* (1970), *Tinsel Tarts in a Hot Coma* (1971), and *Hot Greeks* (1972), the troupe sought to offer an enveloping cultural experience by encouraging audience members to attend in similar styles of drag.

The collaborative film project *Luminous Procuress* (Steven Arnold, 1971), written by Arnold and Steven Solberg, produced by Sebastian, and starring an ensemble cast of Bay Area artists, was introduced as a kind of expanded cinema that would draw on the disintegration of the audience/performer distinction characteristic of the Cockettes' stage shows, but through cinematic mediation. The film was designed to screen as part of a series created by Arnold called the "Nocturnal Dream Show" at North Beach's struggling yet opulent Chinese Palace Theatre. By the time of its premier screening, the venue had already been established as a multimedia event space and home to the Cockettes' live stage shows. The film is likewise positioned as a kind of live event through a combination of factors, most notably the foregrounding of ritualistic, magical activity through its self-reflexive mirroring of viewer/character relations (this is, above all else, a film about the relationship between watching and becoming) and its opaque yet evocative title, which suggests a mystical experience that awaits participants.

Luminous Procuress follows two male hippies in their early twenties (Steven Solberg and Ron Farrell) as they undergo a sort of underworld quest. Unlike the twin themes of drug experimentation and heterosexual coupling explored in other hippie-quest films of the period, like *The Trip* (Roger Corman, 1969) and *Easy Rider* (Dennis Hopper, 1969), *Procuress* is narratively driven by gender and sexual transformation. The young men, making their way to a modern glass and concrete home, are introduced to the Procuress (Pandora), a science-fiction high priestess with glowing pink-white hair and a rotating wardrobe of futuristic, androgynous costumes (predominantly brightly colored bodysuits designed by Scott Runyon) sitting high on a throne graced with two naked men at her feet.

Pandora guides them through a seemingly endless series of kaleidoscopically interconnected sites. This initially involves moving through darkened spaces, pausing to look through windows or from a noticeable remove at a series of tableaux that include a group of naked men (Hibiscus at the center) interlinked and softly touching one another; Cockettes posing and lounging together on multilevel platforms in front of a sky-blue backdrop (fig. 17); a clownishly made-up pope raping a nun from behind; a group of androgynous figures frolicking in a forest glen; and the Cockettes shuffling sideways across a stage like automatons being moved along a conveyer belt.

The film dramatizes the principles of Waugh's model of gay spectatorship as these protagonists are shown as third-body onlookers, projectors/viewers that shine/gaze forward on to subjects of nonnormative spectatorial pleasure. Yet as the film progresses, the relationship

FIGURE 17 On-lookers are invited to enjoy a tableau of lounging Cockettes.

between spectator and participant is diminished as shots of the protagonists viewing others are interspersed with episodes in which the protagonists become participants. The first of these is an orgy scene in which the protagonists, shown as part of a nebulous black space without background or foreground, share in touching, kissing, and fucking two women styled to be of similar appearance to the men (long dark hair, minimal makeup, naked yellow-lit white skin). Following this, the men are then shown involved with Pandora and the Cockettes in the film's centerpiece scene: a baroque mock-medieval dinner in a seemingly endless hall dissolves into a massive food fight. The film's final scene fully integrates the characters as agents of this underworld, with Pandora and the two men now part of a Frankenstein futurescape where they stand inside a large glass incubation tube, the three characters shown bringing to life an androgynous creature.

On a strictly narrative level, the film tells a story about two ostensibly straight friends who embark on a quest of sexual and gender awakening that brings them toward an ideal of androgyny, self-creation, and transformation. However, through its very active engagement with the formal properties of film, it comes to take on other meanings altogether: meanings that are rife with a vision of hippie drag that suggest ways of thinking about and reconsidering the relationship (and possible relationships) between temporality, spatiality, and sexuality. This is most marked in the film's elaboration of futurity through a mise-en-scène that is rife with a sense of the premodern, a characteristic most pronounced in the feast scene. This set piece, strongly associated with premodern life, is contemporaneously featured in a small cycle of auteur-driven European films of the 1960s and '70s that placed male-male desire into debauched fantasias of pre-Enlightenment eras: *Fellini Satyricon* (Federico Fellini, 1969), *The Canterbury Tales* (Pier Paolo Pasolini, 1972), and *Sebastiane* (Derek Jarman, 1976).

Like the earlier group-shot tableau scene that introduces the Cockettes, this sequence further presents us with a world where nature and artifice dissolve together into qualities of texture, light, and movement. Yet, the sequence marks a departure from the tableau through its more elaborate use of cinematic technique. As the scene progresses, the medium long shots and slow pans that initially suggested a panoramic sweep give way to an ever-faster succession of more quickly edited close-up and medium close-up shots. Oscillating between shots of individuals and group shots, the sequence begins to amplify a transient sense of spatiality. That is, as the sequence unfolds, space not only becomes less organized and oriented, but also elaborated as something through which objects and bodies may move without clear direction, reason, or temporal commitment.

The scene's refusal to maintain spatially or temporally oriented action inflects the scene's aesthetic gestures to past—or temporally distant—modes of being; aristocrats, statues, court jester iconography, 1940s Hollywood starlets, and mythical figures of antiquity all keep slipping from view and collapsing into ever-shifting transient formations. This typifies what Juan Suárez has referred to as ornamental modernism, an "aesthetic tendency" operative in postwar underground film that "highlighted the supremacy of the extravagant and inessential over the sparseness and structural clarity of the industrial aesthetic."[44] Through the deployment of such decorative aesthetics in *Luminous Procuress*, use value is eschewed in favor of the beautiful swaying bodily movements that combine with the mise-en-scène and editing to create a glistening kaleidoscopic perspective. I am reminded here of Parker Tyler's notion of "cine-dance," a term which he uses to describe instances in film in which the camera becomes a "collaborator with the human dancer."[45] Both cinematic technique and the choreography of bodies, in moving away from the tableau format, encourage a mode of spatial disorientation that dissolves any notion of proper placement.

The move away from a forward-facing tableau toward spatial disorientation works to—to borrow a phrase from Sarah Ahmed—"clear a path" for the viewer that creates a sort of inviting distance. Ahmed explains, "disorientation involves contact with things but a contact in which 'things' slip as a proximity that does not hold things in place, thereby creating a feeling of distance."[46] On one hand, this distance—the distance created as people, objects, and materials are elaborated in persistent motion—invites the aesthetic delight that can occur when a clear image moves toward abstraction. But this onset of disorientation bespeaks a moment when a variety of modes of being and identifying are depicted in shifting proximities to one another.

As images of "pastness" are brought into the swing and sway of the Cockettes' impromptu motion, *Luminous Procuress* elaborates the possibility of a post-gay future-past of drag embodiment. While taking the cue, to some extent, from increasingly popular paradigms of liberation and "outness," the film seems to take up these positions less as end points than as an initial process in a future to be made up along the way. In this way, the film puts into play a gay hippie aesthetic bent on the articulation of what, from today's perspective, registers as a more transgender iteration of gay potential. The model of futurism offered in the film's closing serves to mark this male quest as a decentering experience whereby a willingness to pass through unknown, indeterminate space moves one to participate in the creation of new gender forms, if not the outright implosion of gender dictates altogether.

Peter de Rome's Out Gay World

Peter de Rome was born in Juan-les-Pins, France, in the summer of 1924 before immigrating to England as a boy. In the early 1940s, he enlisted with the Royal Air Force where he worked in the entertainment division directing plays. After the war, he continued working in arts-related fields, eventually taking a job as a publicist for Hollywood producer David O. Selznick, which resulted in de Rome's emigration in 1956, this time to New York. Shortly after his arrival, de Rome became involved in the civil rights movement, taking off for a short time to Alabama and joining his friend, the actor Madeleine Sherwood, as a participant in the Keener Freedom Walk of 1964 in protest of racial segregation, an experience that he insists forever "radicalized" him.[47] During this period, de Rome lived largely between New York and various parts of the South, a trajectory that eventually led to his taking a role in gay playwright Martin Duberman's antiracist play *In White America*, staged in New Orleans in 1964.[48] Like Duberman, who would come to play a central role in the gay liberation movement as an activist and historian, de Rome's involvement in civil rights activism—on the street and in the theater—played a critical and motivating role in his later commitment to gay activism.

Shortly after his return from the South, de Rome purchased his first Super 8 mm camera during the height of their popularity as home movie–making equipment. Testing the bounds of the medium's possibilities, the first film de Rome ever shot was of himself naked in his apartment, which he "sandwiched between 'safe' material on either side" before dropping the reel off at his local Kodak developer with little expectation of ever seeing it again. When the film was returned to him fully developed and without complaint, he further tested the limits by making a short film of himself masturbating. With a second success under his belt, de Rome's camera began to assume an increasingly important role is his day-to-day life.[49]

For his next project, a short film that would come to be titled *Butch Easter* (1966), de Rome hit the streets. De Rome explains:

> It was Easter Sunday and I was sitting on the Mall in Central Park waiting to go and take a few shots of the parade on Fifth Avenue. I saw a very attractive black boy approaching and I decided to shoot a few feet. He saw me doing it, very coolly walked almost into the camera and then out again. . . . I stopped shooting for long enough to say hello. He was from South Carolina and his name was Butch. A more inappropriate name would be hard to think of, but no matter, he was an exceptionally sweet boy. I took him home and asked him if he'd mind if I continued the film. He was quite agreeable. So I mounted the camera on a tripod, attached the remote cable release and joined him in bed . . . it wasn't long before I took his clothes off, then mine, and I lay down on top of him naked . . . his response was so immediate and so eager that I shot very quickly over his stomach. The *en suite* was planned just to provide a conclusion to the story. I arrange to meet him again, but when he turns up at our rendezvous, I am not there. Slow Fade.[50]

De Rome's use of the Super 8 mm works here as an extension of cruising. Within the space of the Easter parade, his camera takes on several different roles: a device of home movie–making, a wandering mechanical eye (with zooming capabilities!) that emphasizes the cruising gaze and, ultimately, a spectacle-making tool for narrative development. When Butch takes the bait, responding to de Rome and his camera, the interactions between the director, his camera, and the young man combine to establish a playful dynamic of male-male flirtation, constructing a live representation of male-male desire prior to the point where any overtly pornographic elements come into play.

The activity of selection is part of the narrative, soliciting males who might adequately contribute to translating male-male desire into cinematic play (whether camp, sexual, political, and/or aesthetic). Butch is an ideal candidate, in that his very name provided de Rome with a vehicle for gay camp reference. The use of his name in the title situates the film for an audience versed enough in camp vernacular to catch its double-meaning as a word used to signal a characteristically masculine man by normative standards (sometimes positioned in opposition to Nelly, a word used to denote effeminacy). In modifying Easter, with a camp twist, as *Butch Easter*, the state-recognized religious holiday is subordinated to a new public of gay men, trading in the traditional and officially sanctioned for the unofficial and vernacular.

Throughout de Rome's body of work, the filmmaker, whether on screen or off, is directly framed as an agent of out gay authorship in which he is positioned as a knowledgeable, active participant in and disseminator of gay life. By 1973, when Jack Deveau's New York–based company Hand in Hand Productions began distributing de Rome's films commercially around the US, the promotional framing of his oeuvre had moved far beyond any connotative third-body paradigm. That year, *The Erotic Films of Peter de Rome*, a retrospective compilation of his work between 1969 and 1972, was released. Promotional materials, homemade by de Rome and carried by gay newspapers, framed the series as the product of an out gay authorship legible to the world at large (fig. 18).

The explicit eroticism ("X rated, all male") is flagged in the title and assigned to de Rome, unflinchingly framing the nude photos as expressive of a male-male desire he fosters and presumably shares. For each film in the compilation, a small typed-out description whets the audience's appetite, signaling their pornographic value: "an unpredictable climax," "a film to make your eyes pop," even "cascades of galactic orgasm."[51] At the same time, de Rome's authorship is placed within a discourse of out gay life. Male-male desire is signaled as a wide-ranging experience woven into real geographies: *The Second Coming* promises a "chase half-way across Europe," *Subway* offers a "true" sex film, shot on location on a New York subway. De Rome is also legitimized as a gay auteur in these transnational geographies: not only did *Hot Pants* win "First Prize for Best Short at the II Amsterdam Wet Dream Film Festival," but mainstream British film journal *Sight and Sound* has taken note of his body of work and its challenge to censorship norms.[52] Across transnational contexts, among different kinds of audiences, he has a presence as a visible (and visibly) out author.

De Rome's promotional techniques situate his films not just as images of gay life but as actively participating in gay life. The description for *Daydreams on a Crosstown Bus* declares, "you pass a face on the street, and you're off with the imagination running. It's happened to all of us . . . the instant visionary life-style syndrome." This address to an imagined collective "us" of male-desiring men in the world is expressive of de Rome's commitment to putting gay life on film. "Visionary life-style syndrome" connects the promotional image of the visionary director with the diegesis he mediates for gay viewers, peopled with characters who are constantly on the brink of crossing from a life envisioned to a life lived out. De Rome's model of gay life gains traction and power as subjects move from private imagining and envisioning to active involvement in male-male desire in discernable, everyday spaces.

In this affirmative externalization, agency and openness are central to how de Rome repurposes tropes familiar from trance filmmaking (as discussed in chapter 1).[53] His 1969 film *Double Exposure*, shot at a

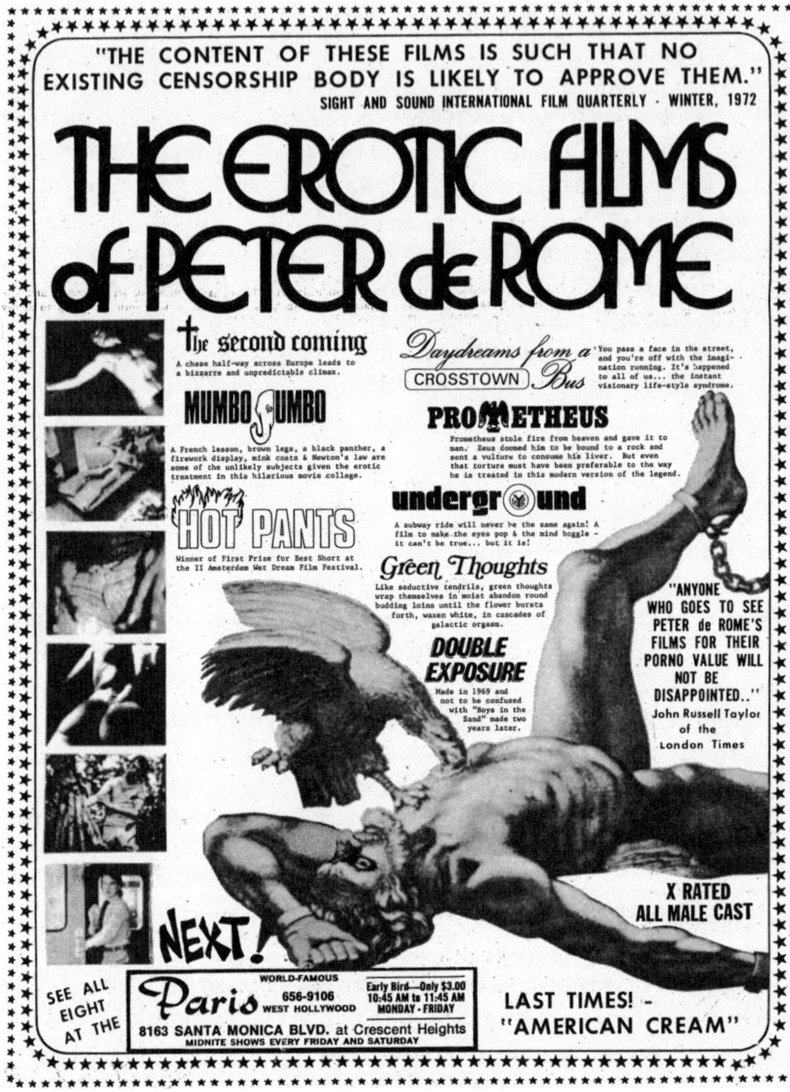

FIGURE 18 Making gay life legible under the name of Peter de Rome. Advertisement, *The Erotic Films of Peter de Rome. The Advocate* (March 13, 1974). Image courtesy of the Hall-Carpenter Archive, London School of Economics.

vacation house on Fire Island, is a striking example of how the trance film could be reconceptualized to move erotic representations of male nudes, produced by a male filmmaker, away from the homoerotic coding of the third body. As we watch the protagonist (Tom York) wander through the house, he splits into two figures. One writhes and gyrates on a sofa in the naturally lit and uncurtained home, watched by his own doppelganger. He appears, increasingly, as the erotic agent of his own openly expressed (albeit autoerotic) and clearly elaborated desire.[54] Similarly, in *Green Thoughts* (1970), the protagonist (Derek Turner) spots a naked man through an uncovered window. Delighted, he runs gleefully through London's Kew Gardens—a public botanical garden—before masturbating expressively and vigorously while surrounded by plants culled from around the world. While de Rome may use some of the suspense-building trance film tropes of wandering, wondering, and waiting, his protagonists, by film's end, expressively revel in their feeling toward men. They do so in a diurnal mise-en-scène that is the inverse of Anger's noirish nightscape in *Fireworks*. However, it is not only external space that operates in de Rome's version of out gay life, but also the careful patterning and dissolving of boundaries between internal/external and inside/outside that is one of the hallmarks of his work.

The great majority of gay films emerging around the turn of the decade still worked, to varying degrees, within previously established conventions that kept modes of spectacle and voyeurism at the forefront of gay representation. This was reproduced endlessly and redundantly in narratives structured around entering ghettoized city spaces (gay bars, apartments, selected iconic streets, bathhouses) and revealing something about the culture cloistered inside. Examples of this include gay-produced films such as *The Boys in the Band* (1970), *Some of My Best Friends Are . . .* (1971), and *Saturday Night at the Baths* (1975), as well as more mainstream films that relied heavily on "gay ghetto" themes and iconography such as *Midnight Cowboy* (1969), *The Ritz* (1976), *Norman . . . Is That You?* (1976) and, toward the end of the decade, *Looking for Mr. Goodbar* (1977) and *Cruising* (1980).[55]

De Rome's films are unique in that, instead of positioning gay characters as implicitly tethered to ghettoized and/or concealed space, they establish a relationship between models of gay activity, male-male desire, and city space that rejects ghettoized boundaries. Through elements such as editing, camera movement, and music, de Rome privileges notions of mobility across boundaries of all kinds of public and private space—in particular, spaces widely recognizable *as* public. This injection of gay representation in the public sphere—this peopling of the world with gay men—is most distilled in *Daydreams on a Crosstown Bus* (1972), a straightforward narrative vignette that depicts the fantasies of an anonymous man as he gazes out the window of a bus at another man who, upon noticing him, returns his own gaze in approval.

The mesmerizing hold of each other's gaze appears to initiate a joint, intersubjective fantasy; it is not clear whose fantasy is whose, as the film leaves open the possibility that it could be either one or even both of the men creating/experiencing these fantasies. However, this fantasy does not initially take the form of or appear as lead-in material for sexual action, but instead moves directly into the sublimely ordinary waters of two men traveling the streets, parks, and monuments of New York as a couple (fig. 19). By not doing what porn is supposed to do and getting right to the sex, de Rome brings more general issues of male-male coupling to the foreground.

While perhaps not cruising in the most conventional sense, the men in *Daydream* assert a similar renegotiation of how public space may be used by gay men and, more specifically, used *against* public space as a domain for maintaining hetero-affirmative interaction. Aaron Betsky comments that

FIGURE 19 The everyday gay life of Central Park.

> queers learned the whole idea of reinhabiting the city from the hippies. . . . It was the hippies . . . who kept the Arts and Crafts ideals of creating a better world through the revelation of material and structure in the making of the objects and spaces of everyday life. The hippies had pioneered . . . the very notion that has by now come to be known as a "lifestyle": the formalization of value systems, methods of behavior, and ways of presenting oneself that evidences itself in everything from clothing to the car one drives, and has its most stable reference point in where one lives and how one uses those spaces.[56]

This notion of reinhabiting spaces one has been discouraged from using is manifested in *Crosstown* through framing and costuming that spatialize gay coupling as simultaneously a public and private event, tying pedestrian space to a gay presence that is ordinary. The film showcases multiple images of the couple throughout the city, as part of the masses, asserting that gay life and pedestrian life are not mutually exclusive.

The organization of images results in the rhetorical assertion that city spaces of numerous kinds are also sites for gay relationship-building. First, the men are framed in close-up, walking or standing together as a couple visually matched via costuming and styling: both men have mid-length curly brown hair, wear identically designed shirts and pants in complementary colors, and are of similar height. Second, a succession of zooms reframe the environment, revealing the panoramic scale of various city spaces as well as the masses they are designed to accommodate moving through them. Last, there is a return to close-ups of the two men smiling and laughing, gazing at sights together arm in arm and pointing out things to look at to one another. Similar to the logic of rehabitation while moving beyond it, these images suggest that gay men exist in relation to and make use of any and all spaces of the city, that lifestyle can be used to assert that one's space is not just "where one lives" but anywhere and everywhere, a space of motion rather than fixity. In this context, the very notion of being on a crosstown bus ride (the site through which this fantasy takes form) works to signify mobility through numerous city spaces and the crossing of borders as a rule.

This sense of unbound movement between locations is maintained even as the film moves into sequences that are oriented around fully uncensored nudity and explicit sexual activity. The sequence dialectically decenters conventional lines between differing "value systems," "behaviors," and presentational practices associated with the distinction between public and private space, intimacy and sex. As editing is used to parallel images of the men romantically coupled and enjoying the sights of outdoor city space with images of the men nude on an apartment balcony in a similar stance, spatiality is organized to establish an alternative to that which was typically on offer in the gay film.

The imagery repeatedly resists ghettoizing structures and denies any clear distinction between inside and outside or public and private; the men engage in the same coupling activities outdoors, on the sidewalk or in the park, as they do in a domestic environment. The apartment is presented as both interior and exterior space, with the men framed in a shot taken from inside through bamboo curtains that signals a fluidity of movement between inside and outside space. Once inside, the men are shown in silhouette against floor to ceiling windows that show the surrounding cityscape, with the men sitting nude, one touching the other tenderly while watching a cat climbing around them. Nudity and tactile intimacy are presented in a light that eschews the exclusively sexual or even sensual drive typical of the erotic film, opting to frame the elements most emblematic of it (nudity, touch) as elements of domesticity, tenderness, and leisure. In other words, these images figuratively demonstrate a relaxation and dissolution of the distinction of who and what belongs where.

In its concluding images, *Daydreams* acts as a rebuttal to representations of gay social life as spatially contained and distant from the everyday. In the film's final turn, the man on the bus realizes he cannot pass up this opportunity and runs to the door, jumping off at the next stop. He is shown frantically emerging from the bus and hurrying down the street to where his comrade-in-fantasy leaned against the tree. Once there, he finds that he has missed the boat: the man has disappeared. A wide-angle shot shows the man, now standing in front the tree where the other man stood just moments ago, surrounded by a vacant expanse of concrete city space. A cut to the film's final point-of-view shot shows a wide-angle view of the tree-lined sidewalk, also depopulated, appearing to trail into infinity. The image of the empty street doesn't so much indicate a space of missed opportunity so much as space of future possibility. As the viewer is left with the perspective of the male-desiring male who looks toward the brightly lit, open-ended trajectory of the empty sidewalk, they are left with the impression that gay coupling, in all its fantastic ordinariness, lies around every corner.

Mondo Rocco and Pat Rocco's Expansive Cinema

In June 1968, when the Park Theatre introduced "A Most Unusual Film Festival," initiating what was likely the first gay film festival to be held anywhere in the world, it cobbled together an assemblage of films made over the previous ten or so years. Of these, only a small portion of films could be described as genuinely new: the program was comprised mostly of underground films, some dating back as far as the 1940s, from the likes of Anger, Smith, and Warhol. The new films that were included were physique films that also circulated as mail-order 8 mm reels for home viewing. Of these, the program contained three physique films by Pat Rocco, who, after managing three movie theaters and an ice skating rink in Moorpark, California, was beginning his career in Los Angeles as a photographer and director of plays and erotic films.[57] In most respects, these three films, *Love Is Blue, Nudist Beach Surfers,* and *Boys Out to Ball* (ca. 1968), screened as standard physique fare not unlike the work of progenitors Bob Mizer, Richard Fontaine, and Bruce of Los Angeles.

What seems most historic about the inclusion of Rocco's work in the program is simply that the director and the theater dared to advertise and host a public screening of erotic films of male nudes aimed at male spectators, given the long string of legal complications such material had met with in its nontheatrical circulation. With physique photographers and filmmakers like Bob Mizer and Herman Lynn Womack having served jail time after losing obscenity trials, the risks were very real.[58] There is no question that to do this was more than a brave act and should be understood as a form of activism—intended or not—contributing to the increased presence of male-desiring men in California's public space during the late 1960s.

Yet an important difference from other physique films and photographs began to surface in Rocco's work, one easy to overlook when focusing on the celebrated body at the center. Moving away from the secluded, private space of backyards, rooftops and home studios of the postwar physique film, Rocco began putting nude men together in discernibly less secluded, public, exterior locales. Breaking from the image of the single studio model, Rocco's films rubbed up against more popular and socially driven forms of narrative characterization.

The screening at the Park and Pat Rocco's involvement with the theater marks a crucial turning point in the historical development of gay cinema. The "Most Unusual" festival brought large audiences of gay male viewers together publicly for the first time, sometimes lined up along the block. Within a month, Park owner Shan Sayles began bankrolling new work by Rocco for inclusion in programs with highly visible promotion on the theater's marquees, in local papers such as the *Los Angeles Free Press,* and through lobby cards and brochures. With this increase in budgetary support, Rocco began developing a cinematic vision of gay life that dared to position male-desiring men as part of a wider spectrum of public space. This was remarkably apparent in the first program devoted solely to his work, "A Pat Rocco Happening," which opened at the Park in 1968. In films such as *A Very Special Friend*, *Groovy Guy*, *Boy on the Run*, and *Memories* (all 1968) characters move through outdoor locales in, around, and within driving distance of Los Angeles, including city avenues, the 101 freeway, a train yard, a barn in the wilderness, numerous residential streets, iconic buildings (City Hall, the Capitol Records headquarters), and city parks. In *Discovery* (1968), two young men are shown meeting at a popcorn stand on Main Street USA in the Disneyland theme park. They couple off and embark, arm in arm, on a series of rides before landing via boat on Treasure Island where they stroll, holding hands, eventually stripping naked, touching, and kissing as the song "When You Wish upon a Star" underscores that in a Rocco movie, "dreams you dare to dream really do come true."

Unlike the work of the Gay Girls Riding Club, James Bidgood, or George Kuchar, in which public space is often generically reinscribed through the camp pastiching of Hollywood sources, and in common with much of the work of de Rome, everyday and recognizable locations in Rocco's work reconstituted the world at large as a space of non-ironic gay romantic possibility. Sentimental orchestral music frames erotic action as a generative form of sentimental memory making.[59] In Rocco's panoramic vision of US life, gay men are inserted into the very world in which their visibility and movement is policed and repressed. Male-desiring men are shown as ubiquitous, walking the streets, driving in cars, running through train yards. These movements through space nearly always end in the joining of lovers outdoors, as fully nude men embrace in fields, parks, and the open doorways of barns.

Rocco's interest in putting gay in the world was not only part of the diegesis of the films themselves, but also an entire ethos of fellowship and community that Rocco was part of. Fundamental to this was his involvement with activism, first through the homophile movement and then as part of the gay liberation movement. By the end of the 1960s, homophile activists in Los Angeles such as Rocco and the Reverend Troy Perry were moving away from underground models of gay socialization and toward public-facing institutions as venues for the cultivation of gay life. Within this context, the Park Theatre can be understood as part of a rich and complex cultural geography mapped by the activities—social, political, and cultural—spearheaded by the homophile movement. Whether gathered on the steps of City Hall for demonstrations, in the pews of Perry's gay congregation at the Metropolitan Community Church, or beneath the footlights of a drag show staged at Joani's nightclub, homophile activists were some of the first subjects deemed nonnormative in their sex and gender interests to insist on coming together in large numbers at, within, and as part of some of the central institutions and cultural spaces of US life.

With the support of Shan Sayles and a growing number of gay-identifying young men (often recent transplants to Hollywood) who were interested in acting and performing in gay roles in film and on stage, Rocco productions became far more than isolated film projects. Instead, they were a recreational rallying point for the gestation and cultivation of gay social life, evidenced by the ways in which they often straddled a line between community engagement and entertainment entrepreneurism. Like Reverend Perry, who regularly appeared in articles and interviews in the gay press, Rocco took on a figurehead role. His work rallied people together and brought a crisp legibility to the existence of gay community activities.

The socializing function of Rocco's publicity efforts is clearly demonstrated by the creation of the group SPREE, an acronym for the "Society of Pat Rocco Enlightened Enthusiasts." Created in January 1969 by Dick Winters, Jim Kepner, and Chuck Robinson, the group met monthly for nine years, hosting a constant stream of social events in homes, bars, and other spaces in and around Los Angeles. Tickets created for

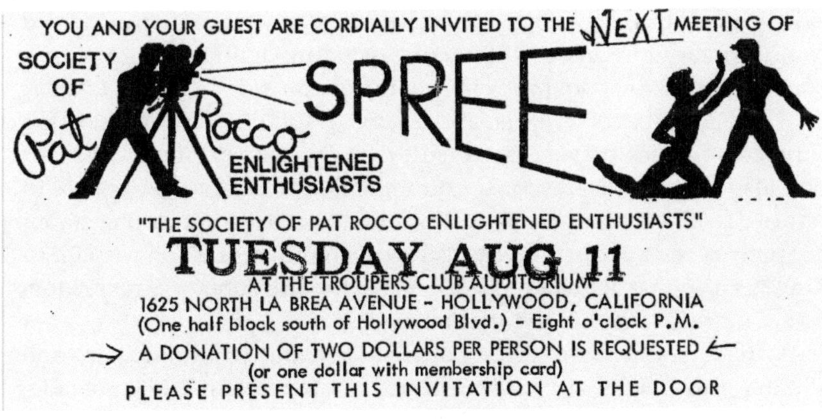

FIGURE 20 Individual author's gaze as site for social formation. Ticket, SPREE (date unknown). Image courtesy of the ONE National Gay and Lesbian Archives at the University of Southern California, Los Angeles.

its meetings and the many issues published of the *SPREE News Pictorial* show how the representation of gay life through film and photography operated as a means of building a localized yet expansion-oriented sense of gay community.

For instance, an invitation ticket for a SPREE meeting at the Troupers Club Auditorium, a rentable meeting hall run by retired actors in Hollywood, elaborates a very specific relation to filmmaking and social activity (fig. 20). In the upper-left-hand corner, a silhouette of Rocco behind the camera faces two naked silhouetted men in the upper right acting out a dramatic scene before the camera. Between the figures are lines extending out from the lens, representing the framing of the shot, placing the men as objects of Rocco's gaze. The name "SPREE" appears within these lines. The relation between artist and model(s) here is rendered as a site into which enthusiasts can insert themselves. This image aptly analogizes the working of SPREE, as members were invited to insert themselves within the expansive vision of gay-life-as-everywhere put forth in Rocco's films. Not unlike Andy Warhol's Factory, where people created works within the branded domain of the "artist" Warhol, the invitation shows a sociocultural site opened up for many under the banner of individual authorship.

This paradigm of film as a vehicle for the social expansion of gay life was amplified and reproduced through multiple issues of SPREE's periodical. Take, for example, the August 1974 issue of the publication. Despite the inclusion of the illustration of Rocco and his camera on the cover, its overriding theme is not so much film but social gathering and, in particular, a pool party attended by a "bevy of skinny dippers" held the month before (fig. 21). Inside is a double-page picture spread commemorating recent SPREE events including multiple group photos of nude men at the pool party, images of a production of *H.M.S. Pinafore* by the SPREE Theatre Players, and a photograph of Pat Rocco meeting with Los Angeles mayor Tom Bradley to discuss gay rights. The section also features notices for upcoming opportunities to participate in future gay film and stage productions such as Dick Smith's play about gay personal ads, *Room to Share*, and an upcoming workshop with Brian King inviting participants to get involved with "Super 8 Sound Movies . . . in front of or behind the camera."[60]

With an emphasis on smiling men, nudity, and activities, Rocco and SPREE's print media emphasizes notions of fellowship and camaraderie among male-desiring men and their female friends (several issues of SPREE show female participants included with mostly male groups). Film here becomes an important activity among many that functions

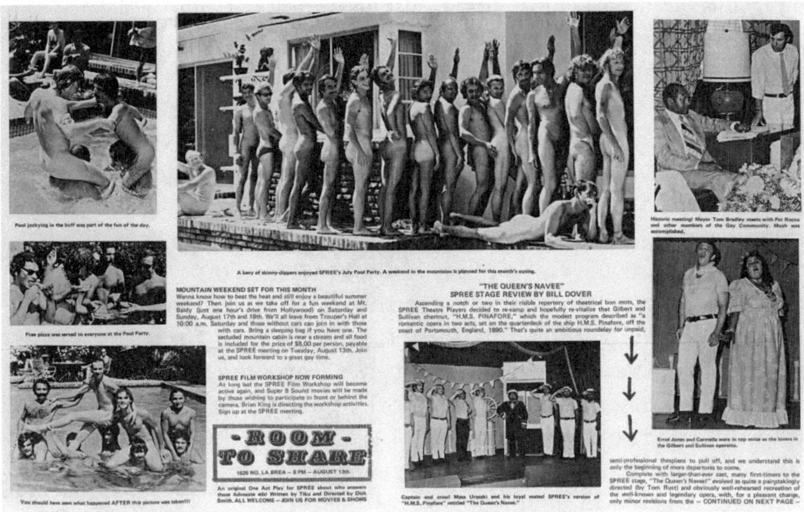

Pool jockying in the buff was part of the fun of the day.

Free pizza was served to everyone at the Pool Party.

You should have seen what happened AFTER this picture was taken!!!

A bevy of skinny-dippers enjoyed SPREE's July Pool Party. A weekend in the mountains is planned for this month's outing.

Historic meeting! Mayor Tom Bradley meets with Pat Rocco and other members of the Gay Community. Much was accomplished.

MOUNTAIN WEEKEND SET FOR THIS MONTH

Wanna know how to beat the heat and still enjoy a beautiful summer weekend? Then join us as we take off for a fun weekend at Mt. Baldy (just one hour's drive from Hollywood) on Saturday and Sunday, August 17th and 18th. We'll all leave from Trouper's Hall at 10:00 a.m. Saturday and those without cars can join in with those with cars. Bring a sleeping bag if you have one. The secluded mountain cabin is near a stream and all food is included for the price of $8.00 per person, payable at the SPREE meeting on Tuesday, August 13th. Join us, and look forward to a great gay time.

SPREE FILM WORKSHOP NOW FORMING

At long last the SPREE Film Workshop will become active again, and Super 8 Sound movies will be made by those wishing to participate in front or behind the camera. Brian King is directing the workshop activities. Sign up at the SPREE meeting.

- ROOM -
TO SHARE
1626 NO. LA BREA – 8 PM – AUGUST 13th

An original One Act Play for SPREE about who answers those Advocate ads! Written by Tiku and Directed by Dick Smith. ALL WELCOME – JOIN US FOR MOVIES & SHOWS

"THE QUEEN'S NAVEE"
SPREE STAGE REVIEW BY BILL DOVER

Ascending a notch or two in their risible repertory of theatrical bon mots, the SPREE Theatre Players decided to re-vamp and hopefully re-vitalize that Gilbert and Sullivan chestnut, "H.M.S. PINAFORE," which the modest program described as "a romantic opera in two acts, set on the quarterdeck of the ship H.M.S. Pinafore, off the coast of Portsmouth, England, 1890." That's quite an ambitious roundelay for unpaid, semi-professional thespians to pull off, and we understand this is only the beginning of more departures to come.

Complete with larger-than-ever cast, many first-timers to the SPREE stage, "The Queen's Navee!" evolved as quite a painstakingly directed (by Tom Rust) and obviously well-rehearsed recreation of the well-known and legendary opera, with, for a pleasant change, only minor revisions from the – CONTINUED ON NEXT PAGE –

Captain and crew! Masa Urasaki and his loyal mates! SPREE's version of "H.M.S. Pinafore" retitled "The Queen's Navee."

Errol Jones and Carmella were in top voice as the lovers in the Gilbert and Sullivan operetta.

FIGURE 21 SPREE as vehicle for fellowship and political activity. SPREE News Pictorial (August 1974). From the personal collection of the author.

to bring people together for an afternoon or evening event. One of the most notable things about these materials is the way in which they elaborate a vision of gay community that follows suit with other US "community-oriented" members' clubs such as the Elks or local Rotary clubs. Like these clubs, these images project fellowship and foreground activities that show members constantly being brought in to the fold of the group.

Such community-building rhetoric was central to Rocco's approach to filmmaking, especially as he moved toward the production of feature-length films. This resulted in Rocco's signature style of merging modes and genres: fiction, documentary, physique film, gay liberationist erotica. Whether in a "fiction" film such as *Someone* (1968) or documentary films such as *Marco of Rio* (1969) or *One Adventure* (1972), Rocco's films captured self-avowed gay actors and other participants in a variety of locales as unapologetically "out there in the world" and projected those images on movie screens for crowds of gay men to observe. On a pedagogical level, an important function of Rocco's films is that they "peopled" spaces that gay men had not perhaps imagined themselves as visible constituents of. Yet, the filmmaker has received little attention for his distinctive film style in part because the emphasis on the documentary elements of his films tends to obscure the way he places documentary and fiction in relation to one another. Through this practice, he articulates a liberationist vision of aggregation and expansion that would benefit from a closer exploration.

In the winter and spring of 1970, Rocco programmed a film series at the Park that played regularly in special midnight event screenings on Friday and Saturday nights. Bringing together a combination of multiple new works by the director under the title *Mondo Rocco* (a.k.a. *It's a Gay World*), the program took viewers deep into the morning hours with its kaleidoscopic vision of gay life. Like earlier Rocco work, the program foregrounded male-desiring men in multiple locations, emphasizing movement between interior and exterior space, from apartments and bars to numerous wilderness settings. Invoking the filmmaker as cultural visionary, advertisements for the program in *The Advocate* feature a full-page image of Rocco with his arms stretched around a giant globe containing shots from thirteen of the films (fig. 22). "WORLD PREMIERE," written in bold, emphasizes the program's global thematic, asserting the import of Rocco's gay world for the world at large. Like the many faux-anthropological exploitation films from which the film takes its "Mondo" title formation, the ad promises a (knowingly, playfully) spectacularized view of gay life as though from an ethnographic perspective.[61]

This emphasis on spectacularly expansive scales is directly informed by the rhetoric of "gay spirit" that, by the early 1970s, was becoming a central philosophical paradigm in gay cultural production. Encapsulated in affirmative slogans such as "gay is good" and "gay power," notions of gay spirit were coming to designate a particular kind of progressive narrative. Much of this narrative revolved around the cultivation of one's sexuality—and making rewarding sexual and romantic contact with other men—as a core feature of gay life. As David Loovis describes in his 1974 book *Gay Spirit*, making gay sexual contact exemplifies an erotics of abundance:

> Never have gay people had such opportunities for expression. . . . Sex is easily available; brilliance on every street corner, divinity in the subway, gorgeousness in the supermarket. How lucky you are to be homosexual now. Gay is good today, proud, glamorous, peaceful, graceful, *and more.*[62]

Loovis's description elaborates gay life through a psychogeographic perspective, where what the agent of gay desire seeks is locatable across multiple sites. Loovis emphasizes that this is part of a new—ostensibly postliberation—experience of abundance. Perceiving everything in

FIGURE 22 Pat Rocco's gay world. Advertisement, *Mondo Rocco, Los Angeles Advocate* (April 1970). Image courtesy of ONE National Gay and Lesbian Archives at the University of Southern California Libraries.

relation to gayness, and seeing gay life everywhere, operated, in the gay liberation years, as an important part of a counterhegemonic project that—working in a similar vein as prominent strands of black and feminist movement politics—sought to reconfigure the world through a spirit of cultural expansion. That is, as a project of renegotiating one's relation to the surrounding world, to participate in a rhetoric of gay spirit meant to see the world at large as full of gay possibility as well as to insist on and persist with this mode of perception as a means of countering the effects of heterocentrism.

The notion of gay spirit as an experience of abundance is central to how *Mondo Rocco* constructs gay life, in particular, the ways in which it sequences locations to advance a program of liberationist action premised on certain models of coming out and consciousness-raising. As a poetic mediation on the gay spirit–driven politics of consciousness-raising, the program elaborates a sense of accumulation through an overall travelogue structure that depicts gay life as a gloriously expanding phenomenon, as something that, if unblocked by the oppression caused by compulsory heterosexuality, may flourish on a universal scale. Central to this vision is the way the program oscillates between internal and external spaces, eventually snaking its way from the level of the urban and local and toward a final universalizing image that places male-male desire within the wilderness.

The program comprised *The Room*, a fiction film about two male strangers who fall in love in an apartment; *A Night at Joani's*, a documentary featuring multiple drag shows, a costume contest, and a dance party at the Los Angeles cabaret-style nightclub; *Screen Test*, a romantic interlude of two men kissing slowly and passionately in a backyard; *Groovy Guy 69*, a soft-core film about a man strolling along dirt roads, shown both naked and in a series of costumes; *Meat Market Arrest*, a documentary about a nude dancer's arrest at a gay bar; *The Prisoner*, a piece directed by SPREE member Michael Redd about a young man who, traveling through the streets of Los Angeles, has a series of encounters with men; *Hair Revisited*, a documentary of an illegal gathering for a free performance of the musical *Hair*; *The Luckiest Cat in Town*, a physique film in which four men pose separately with a cat; *Homosexuals on the March*, a documentary of three early gay rights marches featuring scores of men and women on the steps of City Hall and marching through the streets of Los Angeles; and *Kiss*, an erotic film shot in the wilderness. The sequencing is organized in three stages that move from (1) closed off and private settings in interior rooms and backyards away from public view to (2) a series of films that feature an increasing amount of public gathering to (3) the final hour of the program, which is shot exclusively outdoors.

While the program's eclecticism gives it a carnivalesque feel—as if gay life itself is an ever-unfolding series of amusements—the overall composition of the program is dominated by a through line of sequences about couples. Mediated by sentimentalizing orchestral music, these stories that revolve around the consummation of male-male desire bring this eclectic program in line with melodrama. Like the screen kiss romanticized by the swell of symphonic scoring that ends so many classic Hollywood melodramas, the program gains affective traction through the formal elevation of couples shown coming together. These moments recontextualize the film's more "observational" material about gay social life and group endeavors so that the tensions and risks inherent in building a publicly oriented gay social sphere are simultaneously sidetracked and resolved by the consummation of male-male love.

This pattern is set up from the very beginning. The first three films move from a scene of intimate domestic coupling in *The Room* to mass gay social gathering and entertainment in *A Night at Joani's*, then to two men coming together to kiss in a backyard in *Screen Test*. Bookending gay sociality in this way suggests that gay coupling is the engine behind and product of gay socialization. At the same time, the program also plays in a serial fashion like vaudeville, with each section functioning as "entertainment" in its own right, adding to the program a cumulative sense of immensity.

As the program goes on, this accumulation moves toward a melodramatic climax as films featuring crowds and assembled masses of people are linked with longer dramas of male-male consummation. This is nowhere more pronounced than in the film's final hour, as it moves from three sequences of political protest in public space to a twelve-minute film about a kiss between two men.

The protest sequence covers three different events that took place in 1969: a demonstration at City Hall and two civil rights marches. Rocco positions himself as a newscaster throughout, stopping participants in order to interview them and reporting to the camera on the particulars of each event. While the actual number of participants involved is somewhat hard to gauge (numbers look to be around a hundred people), the forty-two-minute film uses editing and mise-en-scène in conjunction with Rocco's interviews to create a sense of vast scale. Stitching together shots that pan across people gathered on steps and walking arm in arm down the street alongside conversations with individual interviewees, gay life appears as an endless stream of people who hold a range of understandings and interpretations of the historical event in which they act as participants or bystanders. Upward pans give viewers a clear sense of the array of affiliations involved with placards that read, "Gay Is Groovy," "We Stand and Smile as a Homophile," "Children of Time I'm One Too," and "The Committee for Homosexual Law Reform."

Likewise, Rocco's interviews cut between a variety of people spanning gender, race, ethnicity, age, occupation, sexual orientation, and political position. Arguably one of the film's most historically vital features in this regard is how it demonstrates the overlap between the gay liberation and homophile movements. Gay-identifying liberationists such as Al Lewis, who explains they are marching for "freedom to sex," march alongside homophiles such as Clif Laterie, who calls for "legal protection." These events are also shown as having effects that reach beyond those directly participating, with, for example, a young feminine man who, watching a march from under a storefront awning, proclaims, "I think it's great, it's the society of the gays," or a self-identifying heterosexual man, George Wayman, who asserts that "I think it's very good that people are themselves." Gay life here is characterized as expanding, bringing people into its fold and reconstituting the social field in which it exists.

Rocco's gay life creates a sense of scope as it spreads out across a kaleidoscopic number of locations, presenting gay life as a phenomenon to be found all over the world. The privileging of wilderness locales in *Mondo Rocco*'s films, and the program's persistent return to and conclusion with films that frame male-male desire within a wilderness setting, is fundamental to the film's articulation of gay life as something vast if not universal. With the sequencing moving from city life to wooded park and desert locales, the program maps an outlying territory beyond an urban Los Angeles gay life of apartments, streets, and bars, naturalizing male-male contact and erotic activity and asserting male-male desire as a natural rather than cultural phenomenon.

The program's conclusion, *Kiss*, offers its strongest endorsement of seeing gay life in vast, universalizing terms. Set to the music of an elegiac organ and interspersed with sequences of tribal drumming, the film offers an extended meditation on fear, passion, and contact, as two naked men (Gary Miller and Richard Weaver) happen upon one another in the wilderness, dropping to their knees like animals and chasing each other in circles before winding inward and facing off, and then subsequently melting into each other's arms with a passionate kiss that continues as the credits roll and the screen fades to black. Throughout, frame composition regularly returns the viewer to a panoramic view of this wilderness, reminding viewers that this act, while in one sense political (it was legally risky to make a film in 1970 with two naked men kissing at all, let alone naked out in the open), is also perfectly natural, of a piece with the grasses and forest and the wide, open sky.

In tracing the relationship between these authors and the constructions of gay life fostered by their films, it is important to consider the way gay authorship was itself defined and deployed. This was, primarily, through the way the first gay film screenings and film programs were structured around heavily promoted branded author figures.

The expansion of gay filmmaking and exhibition does not simply tell the story of a minority of people bringing themselves into visibility to each other and to society, but of the way cinema worked to articulate and bring vitality to multiple, often diffuse ideas about gay life, gay tradition, and gay futurity. During this moment, in which gay came to have the rhetorical power to bring scores of people together, this did not manifest in one unified picture of gay life, but carried the very malleability, flexibility, and sense of openness imbued in the word "gay," informing much of its socializing and politicizing force. At the same time, the historical recovery of the cinema and cinema culture of this moment of gay movement coalescence does demonstrate a few major shifts in emphasis with regard to the perspective of gay life elaborated in cinema over this period. Charting this shift in emphasis, the case studies that make up this chapter show a movement at the textual level from a more avant-garde-informed cinema invested in the aesthetic and affective coding of gay desire and possibility to more direct, denotative, pop-genre articulations of gay people in increasingly minoritarian terms that situate "gay people" as a distinct sector within the greater body of society.

Films like *Pink Narcissus* and *Luminous Procuress,* picking up on tropes familiar from postwar avant-garde trance films, pursued a gay visionary cinema that sought to imagine gay life through elaborating certain ways of seeing, feeling, and inhabiting nonnormative positions of sexuality and gender.[63] More tonal, impressionistic, and avowedly poetic than representationally clear or narratively driven, they focused on creating an emotionally immersive and psychologically stimulating experience through heavily connotative uses of image and sound.

Gay life was repeatedly rendered as a way of seeing and feeling; what the characters want or do in life is often far less important than how they work to elicit, conjure, and track transformations in certain ways of feeling and desiring. Concurrently, filmmakers such as Pat Rocco and Peter de Rome made "outness" central to the syntax of their cinema, situating gay men as a constituency with presence in the world at large. This out gay cinema emphasized male-male desire within everyday locations such as apartments, parks, city streets, and outdoor wilderness spaces. As a marketplace for more Hollywood-inspired mainstream drama became increasingly possible in the following years, the dichotomy between representational realism and dreamier, more abstract visions of gay life and possibility continued to structure much of the cinematic elaboration of gay life. At the same time, as the first wave of independent feature length dramas came on the scene in the early to mid-1970s, their investment in appealing to a wider, even mainstream, audience meant that Hollywoodian styles of representational realism, namely, in the form of character-driven protagonist-centered movies, began to take over as the dominant mode for the making of gay life on screen.

THREE

Toward a Gay Mainstream

The Boys in the Band (William Friedkin, 1970) revolves around a birthday party that takes place in an apartment located in New York's Upper East Side over the course of a single night during the summer of 1968. When the guest of honor, Harold, shows up late, the host, Michael, resentfully barks at him "You're late." Harold replies, "What I am, Michael, is a thirty-two-year-old pock-marked Jew fairy and if it takes me a while to pull myself together and if I smoke a little grass before I get up the nerve to show my face to the world it's nobody's goddamn business but my own. [pauses] And how are you this evening?"

When William Friedkin's updated version of Mart Crowley's play hit screens across the United States in the spring of 1970, following its popular two-year run as an off-Broadway production, the film became the business of many: as a "social issue" film viewed by mainstream audiences in cities and towns across the United States, as a film taken up by audiences of male-desiring men who had long awaited a major feature-length motion picture focused on their lives, and as a film reviled by many gay liberationists who felt that it was riddled with heterosexist stereotypes of gay men as effeminate, pathological, and self-hating. Likewise, *Boys* became its own sort of "business" as evidenced by the LP recording of the play (starring the original off-Broadway cast also featured in the film) released by the major record label A&M in 1969, the many productions of the play staged throughout the 1970s, and the home-movie release of the film as early as 1984 (for a time one of the only gay features made available for the home-video market, porn aside). It was also one of the first films to garner the attention of media activists and film scholars: critical responses from Vito Russo and Richard Dyer invited audiences to consider what the film's approach to representation might mean for gay viewers. This critical stance on representation also manifested in the first gay protests of any US film, when dozens of gay liberationists gathered outside the New View Theater in Los Angeles to call for a boycott of the film.[1] In other words, it wasn't long before Harold's quip, and the film's showcasing of homosexual and gay "types," seemed to be everybody's business. *The Boys in the Band* became both the first "household name" gay movie and the first in a long line of movies to be examined in terms of its capacities and limitations when it comes to representing gay people.

At a time when few cultural productions were targeted both at and beyond gay-identifying audiences, *The Boys in the Band*'s representation of male-desiring men as an ensemble of homosexual and gay types—many of which circulated within homosexual, queer, and gay subcultures—was a double-edged sword.[2] It had the potential to offer some viewers an experience of recognition, at the same time risking alienating audiences who felt either little connection to this cultural experience or that it reduced gay people to stereotypes for the entertainment of a popular audience.

However, the film is not just a presentation of types, but a dynamic elaboration of how people relate to types and what they might do with them. When Harold declares that he is "a thirty-two-year-old pockmarked Jew fairy," he is asserting not only that he fits within a certain stereotyped image of homosexuality (the fairy), but also that he has the authority, within the social contexts in which he circulates, to define himself. Harold shows us that stereotypes do not reside exclusively outside of self-definition and the possibilities of subcultural deployment.

More than this, Harold's proclamation of selfhood exceeds the realm of gay stereotyping and the presumed insularity and alienating effects of self-deprecation. Running counter to the notion of the stereotype as reductive—closing off a representation and fixing a character as a distanced spectacle for viewers to measure their normalcy against—Harold's statement opens out toward multiple points of affective entry, inviting empathy or even an intersubjective sense of identification for a range of viewers. Thus, if "what I am" or feel a connection with as a viewer is one or a combination of being Jewish, a pot smoker, self-conscious, nervous, a person with less than perfect skin, or a sex or gender dissident, or worst of all thirty-two, then Harold, through all his potentially reductive self-naming, becomes at least a potential site for connection and cross-identification.

In short, Harold, a seemingly limited stereotype, not only contains and limits but also condenses a range of immediately comprehensible positions. He repositions gayness within ethnic and demographic terms in which multiple categories of self- and group-definition intersect and are rendered to some degree equivalent. Harold's self-definition as a nested set of types not only invites audiences to consider, or at least perceive, the rhetorical and affective power of identifying and affiliating with positions of alienation and oppression, but equates doing so as a "fairy" to doing so as a "Jew."

The Boys in the Band is one example of a small but important cycle of American independent films made in the early to mid-1970s that were highly invested in portraying male-desiring men as "a people." Before the first years of the 1970s, there had been no feature-length movies made for wide theatrical release in the United States as part of categories such as gay cinema, gay film, or gay movies. Both the films of the homosexual underground made between the 1940s and '60s and the mostly short films made for screening at the first proto-gay and gay film events and programs starting in the late 1960s had a limited reach, mostly catering to audiences living in or nearby a few major cities, primarily Los Angeles, San Francisco, and New York. In 1970, however, with the waters having been tested by the work of filmmakers like James Bidgood, Peter de Rome, and Pat Rocco—filmmakers who unapologetically braved social and legal persecution to make movies about and for male-desiring men—a new crop of movies began to appear that more closely resembled the kinds of film showing on movie screens in suburban, urban neighborhood, and downtown movie theaters across the US.

A good deal had changed since Pat Rocco began screening his inexpensively produced eroto-romantic shorts in Los Angeles during the late 1960s, and films such as Rocco's *Someone* (1968), *Song of the Loon* (Andrew Herbert, 1970), *Happy Birthday, Davy* (Dick Fontaine, 1970), and *Some of My Best Friends Are . . .* (Mervyn Nelson, 1971) began to garner enough budgetary support to incorporate many of the textual and industrial features constitutive of the "major motion picture" industry, which at this juncture included Hollywood but also several newer independent and semi-independent companies. This fostered a new kind of gay movie: more time for script writing, more selective casting, more sophisticated film equipment, an increased ability to shoot on location and afford the necessary permits, larger production teams, the ability to work with larger distribution companies, and more expensive marketing campaigns all catered to the development of gay movies that more closely resembled contemporary popular film and, as such, were constructed to reach a wider audience in mainstream movie theaters across the US. In these films gay life is presented as a domain made up of specific kinds of groups, cultural experiences, problems, and solutions.

The Making of a Gay People

The notion of gay people as a distinct minority of affiliated subjects began to gain traction in the mid- to late 1960s in both popular and subcultural discourses as a variety of factors came into play. Most notably, the growing frequency of political protests by nonnormative subjects fed up with being bullied, harassed, and abused in bars, restaurants, and on the street inspired the growing organization of activist groups to such an extent that, by the end of the 1960s, the "gay movement" had come to stand as a major framework of identification and affiliation for thousands of people. Another crucial development that helped to facilitate the notion of gay people as a distinct "social unit," to employ a concept used by sociologist Erving Goffman, was the growing—though very uneven and far from wholesale—shift from a psychoanalytic discourse that interpreted male-male desire as symptom of homosexual sickness to a discourse of the social that, operating through the growing fields of sociology, social psychology, and social history, stressed the ways that certain groups are negatively impacted by social norms and regulations.[3] Between gay movement activism and sociology, the notion of gay people as a sociopolitical body became an increasingly prevalent paradigm.

Sociological literature and popular journalism put forth mediated images of gay life that stressed a mass constituency of gay people. For example, in Martin Hoffman's 1969 paperback edition of *The Gay World: Male Homosexuality and the Social Creation of Evil*, a pop-sociological study of gay life, the "gay world" is densely peopled and expansive in scale. Male-desiring men are emphatically described on the book's back cover via terms such as "life," "group," "community," "millions," "friends," and "relatives," which are employed to shore up the sense that the "gay world" is so expansive that it cannot ultimately be fully separated from the "peopling" of the world at large.[4]

"Gay people," however, also operated as a rhetorically powerful image for the expansion of gay life by activists. The cover of Don Teal's chronicle of early gay liberation activities, *The Gay Militants*, uses documentary photography in order to situate gay people as a minority "people." A panoramic image of a mass gay gathering stretches across front, side, and back. The reader can make out individual faces well enough to see that this is a cross-gender, (somewhat) cross-race, and multiethnic world while also being offered enough distance to take in this sea of people.[5] Placards that read "gay power" combine with the waving of an American flag, yoking together markers of US citizenship and patriotism with participation in out gay life.

Unlike earlier films, gay movies that worked to position gay life toward a mainstream were, to a large extent, less connotative and poetic than they were focused on representation. While films such as Pat Rocco's *Kiss* or Peter de Rome's *Daydreams on a Crosstown Bus* were short and without dialogue, prioritizing the building of a *feeling* for gay life through open-ended situations and characters that were not too firmly drawn, these new feature-length, dialogue-driven films sought to characterize gay men as individuals and/or social actors participating in the same kind of dramatic questions of coupling, employment, and family as their straight counterparts. These films foreground a "complex" view of individual lives and the problems that define and shape them.

This very complexity required a greater degree of engagement with simplified character typographies than more poetically, erotically, and/or camp-driven films. In order to work along the lines of more conventional forms of storytelling, these films produced a version of gay people that was "socialized" through the assignment of recognizable traits. Images of male-desiring men of unknown background and occupation wandering through urban locales or camping it up are here replaced with strong, socially marked images that show, for instance, outdoorsmen fishing and camping (*Song of the Loon*), feminine men decorating for a party at a gay bar (*Some of My Best Friends Are . . .*), and priests going on sabbatical to explore and actualize their desires for men (*A Very Natural Thing*). In these films, quickly discernable social types become tools through which to represent the perils, problems, and payoffs of gay life.

As Richard Dyer has argued, character typing does not only demean groups and individuals who do not comply with hegemonic norms but may also assist in elucidating the dynamics that underpin social oppression. In particular, Dyer argues that "member" types differ from other types:

> Stereotypes are linked to psychological categories, sorts of personality, within or without a cultural hegemony. Member types, on the other hand, are linked to historically and culturally specific and determined social groups or classes and their praxis.[6]

For Dyer, "social types" and "stereotypes" result in reductive forms of characterization focalized through an individual perspective of "uniqueness and inner growth [that] tend[s] to prevent people from seeing themselves in terms of class, sex group or race."[7] Member types may move in the opposite direction, fleshing out and drawing attention to how power relations and social dynamics are enacted. Indeed, member types create oppressive conditions for certain groups of people while also allowing for some sense of how groups may be moved to act together from within a shared position of subordination.

Although representations of a gay people were constructed using a range of types, the member type is prominent in all of the films explored in this chapter. Each film positions member types differently, in different spaces, to different ends. In *Song of the Loon*, the genre of the revisionist western is used to reinscribe a cowboy-and-Indian encounter as a gay love story, using a frontiersman's inclusion into Native American ways of life as a homology for coming to terms with gay life and certain practices and norms associated with it. In *Some of My Best Friends Are . . .* , member types are used, as Dyer notes about the film, "to show the operation of oppression on the lives, life-styles (and hence life-types) of gay people."[8] With its day-in-the-life portrayal of a gay bar, the film demonstrates how people of many kinds might be forced to band "together" as a "product of ghettoi[z]ation."[9] In *A Very Natural Thing*, member types are a backdrop for the protagonist's individualist journey of self-improvement through a variety of gay spaces, marking a shift away from a representation of gay people as an oppressed class toward a representation of gay life as an element that in itself may block access to various forms of personal development. These films demonstrate how the move toward the mainstream for gay film occasioned, across the decade, a growing tendency to focus on the concerns of the individual over the group. In doing so, they mark the utility of individual and group struggle as a widespread thematic and narrative hook in American independent (and semi-independent) cinema at this moment.

Authenticity, Oppression, and Liberation in the New Mainstream

As gay cinema began to crop up in more mainstream venues, what might be considered "mainstream" by the industry had come to mean something very different than it had prior to the 1969 recession faced by Hollywood. Whereas the market for mainstream film had until the mid-1960s been controlled by the majors (MGM, United Artists, Paramount, etc.), by the time of the recession, several smaller companies—referred to as mini-majors, instant majors, and independents—had become involved in the production and distribution of film on a much wider scale. With Hollywood experiencing a 34 percent drop in the number of feature films released between 1969 and 1970, these smaller companies began to fill some of the exhibition gap.[10] As a struggling Hollywood took notice of the success of a host of low-budget films coming out of small independent and semi-independent production and distribution companies, it also began to get involved with this new marketplace, leading to an overall shift in what kinds of cinema were coming to constitute the mainstream. As David A. Cook notes:

> The "Recession of 1969" and attendant corporate buy-outs . . . combined with demographic shifts in audience composition and the replacement of the Production Code by the MPAA rating system, led the majors to embrace exploitation as mainstream practice, elevating such previous B genres as science fiction and horror to A-film status, retrofitting "race cinema" as "blaxploitation," and competing with the pornography industry for "sexploitation" market share.[11]

With an eye on the changing demographics of American filmgoing and, in particular, the enormous growth of youth and counterculturally invested audiences, many films achieved box-office success through playing to the interests of these audiences while also looking to sustain a wide appeal for a general audience.

As discussed by scholars such as Cook, Noël Carroll, and Mark Betz, this model was largely developed as a working practice at Roger Corman's American International Pictures (AIP). Following the multimillion dollar success of the low-budget pseudo-independent *Easy Rider* (Dennis Hopper, 1969), the company began rerouting, streamlining, and finessing its previous experience with the low-budget mass-production of sexploitation to meet the demands of this new crossover marketplace.[12] As Cook explains:

> The AIP-Corman Strategy was to abjure the mass-audience and target market segments demographically (teenagers) in order to exploit their tastes (monster-themed science fiction, horror, hot-rods, rock and roll) with sensational low-budget material.[13]

However, AIP's output, and in particular films such *Woodstock* (Michael Wadleigh, 1970), *Joe* (John G. Avildsen, 1970), and *M.A.S.H.* (Robert Altman, 1970) far exceeded expectation; it turned out that abjuring the "mass-audience" meant, paradoxically, realizing a new youth-driven mass audience.[14] As Cook notes, the studio's "youth-cult gambit set the stage for a blurring of distinctions between mainstream and exploitation genres that would characterize the first half of the 1970s until around 1975, the distinctions themselves disappeared."[15] As summarized by Harry Benshoff and Sean Griffin, "by the end of the 1960s, exploitation, sexploitation, hardcore pornography and experimental-film practice where increasingly blurred into one another."[16]

Theater screens were crowded with stories and images of people fighting to cut loose, break out, and get free from the oppression of others: students (*The Strawberry Statement* [Stuart Hagmann, 1970], *Zabriskie Point* [Michelangelo Antonioni, 1970]), Native Americans (*Little Big Man* [Arthur Penn, 1970], *Soldier Blue* [Ralph Nelson, 1970], *A Man Called Horse* [Elliot Silverstein, 1970]), women (*Up the Sandbox* [Irving Kershner, 1972]), African Americans (*The Great White Hope* [Martin Ritt, 1970], *The Liberation of L. B. Jones* [William Wyler, 1970], *Space Is the Place* [John Coney, 1974]), and people who are blind (*Butterflies Are Free* [Milton Katselas, 1972]). Revisionist westerns such as *Lonesome Cowboys* (1968), *Easy Rider* (1969), *Five Easy Pieces* (Bob Rafelson, 1970), *McCabe and Mrs. Miller* (Robert Altman, 1971), and *Billy Jack* (Tom Laughlin, 1971) attracted young viewers by merging the outlaw individualism of traditional westerns with more contemporary elements, such as drugs, overt sexual expression, and automobiles.[17]

Gay cinema has received little attention within work on this moment in US film despite the fact that it was the development of these new industry networks that provided a funding base for the production, distribution, and exhibition of the most widely available gay films of the period. For the first time, investors could anticipate the possible success of a mainstream gay film enough to accept the financial, legal, and social risks involved. The same conglomerates and smaller companies known for a young, hip, countercultural ethos also backed many of the first widely seen gay cinematic features, with companies such as AIP, Hollywood Cinema Associates, Cinema Center Films, and New Line Cinema backing films such as *Some of My Best Friends Are . . .* , *The Boys in the Band*, *Song of the Loon*, and *A Very Natural Thing*, respectively.

These new mainstream-oriented films were distinct from gay film up to this point in that they existed both within localized subcultural networks of gay cinema as well as on a mass public scale that far exceeded the reach of gay social and cultural contexts. Moreover, much of this material was exciting for the way in which it crossed over between subcultural and wider cultural levels. Films like *Song of the Loon* and *The Boys in the Band* offered many viewers their first chance to see overt representations of male-male desire on screen. At the same time, they were already well-worn products of queer and/or homosexual subcultural networks—*Loon* as a mid-1960s pulp novel, *Boys* as a late 1960s theatrical production.

Song of the Loon

A heroic quest narrative, *Loon* tells the story of a wide-eyed twenty-something named Ephraim MacIver (Morgan Royce) as he wanders through the wilderness of the Oregon mountains, having fled the town of Astoria following the collapse of a disastrous relationship with an abusive alcoholic by the name of Montgomery (Jon Evans). He encounters a Native American called Singing Heron (John Kalfas) who bestows upon Ephraim the wisdom that he "suffers from a white man's disease . . . called jealousy"; an unavoidable consequence of his adhering to the "missionary" way of seeking to take ownership over others through monogamous coupling. This tension—between monogamy and freedom—forms the basis for Ephraim's journey of self-discovery, as a series of encounters with men, both Native American and white, reveal to him, and help him to reveal to himself, new "freer" ways of living.

Loon employs historical figures of American rusticity as a means of articulating certain aspects of gay liberation discourse popular at the moment of its production and release, such as traditional Native American iconography, naturism, and pioneerism. This section examines how the film foregrounds legitimizing notions of the natural and the authentic, working through staple elements of late 1960s/early 1970s countercultural discourse and radical gay politics: "symbolic Indianness," new masculinity, models of ethnic affiliation, and territorialization.

The novel *Song of the Loon* was first published in 1966 by Greenleaf Classics, a publishing house that mass-produced quickly written, often formulaic "pulp" material and had, by the late 1960s, developed a whole line of gay erotic fiction.[18] With little possibility of getting non-salacious stories of overt male-male desire published, authors like Richard Amory, Dirk Vanden, and Chris Davidson began to use the inattentive, or at least unconcerned, eye of those managing the pulp paperback industry as a means to develop some of their more ambitious, literary ideas. Among these novels, *Loon* proved so popular that it spawned, by the early 1970s, two sequels, *Song of Aaron* (1967) and *Listen, the Loon Sings* (1968), and even a parody novel called *Fruit of the Loon* (1968).[19] Commenting on the popularity of *Loon*, David Bergman has noted:

> In *Song of the Loon*, Amory seems socially remarkably ahead of his time—or perhaps we underestimate the awareness of pre-Stonewall gay men. Indeed the work seems more closely related to the Radica Faeries than *The Boys in the Band*. The novel ends with neither drunkenness nor suicide, but with its highly masculine heroes united in a loving, ongoing relationship in which the sexual roles are fluid and mutual.[20]

But *Loon* offered readers more than just positivity: it went beyond the demands of the pulp market to indulge in a certain level of self-conscious literary play. Combining classical form and language with the sexually overt language of contemporary pornography, *Loon* brought together in one place such unlikely elements as pastoral poetry and "boys' book" adventure scenarios and ethnography, along with explicit language (words such as "penis," "cock," "ass," and so on are sometimes repeated a dozen times within the space of just a few pages, often in scenes that involve little-to-no sexual interaction).[21] As a result, the book was not only appealing for offering positive representation, but also for selectively bringing together specific cultural forms already available to romantic and/or sexual male-male readings. *Loon* consolidates into one book the tropes of solidarity and comrade love from across a wide range of these texts, from the "serious" poetry of Walt Whitman to the enterprising male-male adventures of serials, boys' books, and Clint Eastwood films. Amory himself certainly hoped his book might be received along such lines, introducing it with a statement of intent explaining that his characters should not be read as realistic and that he has taken characters from classical pastoral fiction and "painted them a gay aesthetic red."[22] One of the more obvious ways the novel can be understood as adopting a "gay aesthetic" register is in its use of ironic camp, most notably achieved through the incongruent conflation of (high) classical poetry and (low) conventional late 1960s erotica. Consider, for example, an excerpt from one of the novel's several eroticized updates (if not outright send-ups) of pastoral poetry, which Cyrus recites aloud to Ephraim:

> In Loving struggle we'll amass
> A Store of pleasure, warming and slick,
> For winters come, but winter's pass.

Then I'll caress your lovely ass
And gently tongue and warmly lick
Lie down my love, upon the grass.

Your swollen penis will surpass.
An oaken bough, both strong and thick
For winters come, but winters pass.[23]

The casual movement between a language of pastoralism and the anatomically invested, repetitious language of pulp-porn carries a strong sense of travesty, a self-reflexive de-authentication. It both builds on and diverges from the wider tradition of American homoeroticism from Whitman to Thoreau or, even later, to Gore Vidal, placing genitally focused, almost sex manual–style sex acts above the elements of romance and intimacy—the erotics of camaraderie—that can be found in these authors' works.

Considered in the context of the joining of these two seemingly incongruous styles—pastoralism and contemporary porn—*Loon* is an interesting example of camp for the way in which it offers what Jonathan Dollimore has described as the "pleasure of unreality" that is produced as part of the "knowing" cultural relativity of camp.[24] In other words, *Loon* is, at least in part, pleasurable because it is so generically familiar in its investment in canonical homoeroticism while also being so utterly incompatible with canonical homoeroticism due its highly self-conscious and culturally relative use of contemporary gay sex tropes (exaggerated masculinity, an emphasis on active-passive dichotomy, explicit language). Even more, this incongruity amplifies, and perhaps even mocks, the natural/unnatural dichotomy, embedding "unnatural" gay sex, paradoxically, in the hypernatural, legitimating language of the pastoral.

Amory's bending of the pastoral mode is evocative of what David Shuttleton has described as a whole lineage of "rural camp"—the "artificial pastoral" novels of Ronald Firbank, the flower photographs of Robert Mapplethorpe, the rustic aestheticism of Derek Jarman's film *The Garden* (1990)—all of which Shuttleton argues contain "ironic inflections of an in-authenticating pastoral."[25] In addition, Amory's repeated collapsing of the boundaries between the typically separated imagery of the homoerotic physicality of the idealized posing male and detailed sex acts between men shares a great deal in common with the rural camp dialectics of artists such as Tom of Finland and George Quaintance, both of whose artwork combined heavily exaggerated hypermasculine physicality with a plethora of male-male sex acts, often in easily recognizable pastoral settings.[26] In combination with these works, *Loon* demonstrates how writers and artists were beginning to play with genre and medium in an effort to articulate male-male desire within vernacular terms, terms that would soon come to be characterized as specifically gay.

The film version, produced and distributed by the sexploitation company Hollywood Cinema Association, was the first gay feature-length film aimed at achieving success as a widely distributed theatrical release. As Michael Bronski has chronicled, "it was the first independently produced, non-pornographic gay male feature to be granted mainstream theatrical release . . . [and] was booked into theatres in many large American cities and found audiences eager to see how the beloved novel played on screen."[27] However, in doing so, the adaptation radically resituated *Loon* away from generic playfulness and camp vernacular toward a legitimizing tone of earnest authenticity.

The intent to cross over into the mainstream marketplace was implicit in the film's advertising campaign, which asked readers of a wide variety of magazines and newspapers across the nation, "Have you ever wondered about a love story between two men?" The film's primary promotional image presents the film within a universalizing register: an earth-toned painting of a bearded white man kneeling down to gently rest his hand on the back of a flute-playing Indian boy before a mountain vista. The message is that *Loon* is a tasteful epic, promising to provide an anatomy of love between men within a spectacular American cinematic tradition (fig. 23).

The adaptation confirmed this approach by paring down and simplifying the novel's language, removing or rewriting material that was "poetic" or erotic in a way that might encourage a camp reception. Instead the movie stressed the representation of male-male desire as part of American frontier masculinity, something moral and intrinsically "natural." As part of this process of adaptation, the visual spectacle of western frontier settings was privileged at the expense of character and story development, placing male-male desire within interrelated discourses of the natural, universal, primitive, actual, authentic, and banal. It is perhaps not surprising that Amory found the film adaptation to be a grossly misguided poaching of his novel and publicly declared, following the film's release, that "the movie version of *Loon* is not a truly gay statement at all, but a rather distorted, exploitative put-down and I disclaim any responsibility for the whole mess." Amory's chief complaint was that the film traded in the "poetic distance from real-

FIGURE 23 A universal "love story between two men." Poster, *Song of the Loon* (1970). Author's own collection.

ity" upon which the novel relied, opting instead to concentrate on the natural spectacle of the film's rugged mountain country, authentically "old west," shooting location.[28]

Magazine advertisements and posters promoted it as a vehicle for a masculinized, nature-bound version of male-male desire through a combination of film stills and narrative descriptions. Pictures of the famously rugged Trinity Alps sit alongside a short synopsis of the film that promises the spectacle of "masculine kissing" among the "rugged grandeur of Northern California's Trinity Alps and the Big Pines National Reserve." The promotion stakes its claim to authenticity in an American context by emphasizing the film's status as an "on location" shoot in an iconic landscape while also asserting the film as a credible, legitimate endeavor by extending "special appreciation . . . to the U.S. forestry service for their cooperation and assistance."[29]

This shift toward authenticity, however, does more than simply decamp the novel. It also resituates the story's figurative, allegorical, and poetic elements away from a conventionally queer-resonant vernacular of homoerotic fantasy, placing them within the service of a countercultural ethos informed by pop psychology. The film advances a version of the *Loon* story that is congruent with contemporary developments in gay liberation discourses in a way that speaks directly to a growing interest in the representation of male-male desire within countercultural, pseudonationalist terms.

Symbolic Indianness, New Masculinity, and Gay Liberation

While *Loon*'s use of the generic tropes of the western—such as outlawism, pioneerism, and manifest destiny—are often quite conventional, the film is unique in that acts of encounter are always heavily psychologized within a gay discourse that functions as the key agent for bringing the male-desiring man away from the self-hating "queerness" of old and into liberated gay identity structures. At the same time, *Loon* reconfigures the frontier heroics of the western genre, in which gains in masculine potency are achieved through a mastery of the wilderness, to include a scenario in which confrontation with gay identity is just one more element that the wild frontier might sling at the adventurous soul. More particularly, however, *Loon* figures new possibilities in the institutionalization of gay cultural practice through Native American iconography in a popular, white, appropriated form via stereotypes culled from both the cowboy-and-Indian movies (especially serials) of the 1940s and '50s as well as contemporary uses of the Native American as a countercultural icon.

In his study *Playing Indian*, Phillip J. Deloria discusses some of the ways in which countercultural movements of the late 1960s and early

1970s were invested in adopting and/or appropriating symbols of Native American culture. Deloria explains:

> The notion of oppositional political culture linked to Indianness attracted the young American, many of whom had been schooled in the iconic nationalism of the Boston Tea Party. Those original rebels had used Indianness to shift the location of their identities from Britain to America. Since the early twentieth century, people had put on Indian clothes to search for authenticity in a modern America more alienating then welcoming. Now countercultural rebels became Indian to move their identities away from Americanness altogether, to leap outside national boundaries, gesturing at repudiating the nation, and to offer what seemed a clear-eyed political critique.[30]

Dressing up and adopting Indian styles became a way of expressing countercultural affiliation, associating movements such as environmentalism, spiritualism, and radical politics and philosophy with a grounding authenticity. Indian*ness* gave young white counterculturalists a way of symbolically aligning their own ideologies and politics within a dramatic historical trajectory of oppression; in doing so, they reduced Native Americans to little more than markers of victimization and rebellion, an act Deloria has (usefully) termed "symbolic Indianness."

Since a great deal of gay liberation discourse was inspired by, if not inseparable from, the broader tenets of late 1960s countercultural ideology, "symbolic Indianness" turned up within the semiotics of gay social and activist life with the same regularity in which it appeared in the antiwar and environmentalist movements. Aspects of Native American dress and styling, for instance, operated interchangeably in hippie and gay contexts, with elements such as long hair, moccasins, and traditional Indian jewelry meant to suggest an iconography of outlawism by associating the wearer with concerns of injustice and persecution. These dress codes evoked notions of a more "real" or even a freer—more American—America, one before European occupation. Within such a logic, the donning of traditional Indian clothing, jewelry, and grooming styles worked within a rebellious, confrontational semiotics that exuded "righteousness" by mixing signifiers of the primitive and the universal, allowing participants a means of aligning themselves with the most potent underdog figure imaginable while also retaining claims to an authentic contemporary "Americanness."[31]

Despite symbolic Indianness existing as a shared practice across countercultural movements, a sizable proportion of gay activists demonstrated a specific investment in positing Native American males as working outside of—and potentially in confrontation with—norms and conventions of sexuality in the contemporary West. Most prominently, Harry Hay, a founder of both the Mattachine Society and the Radical Faerie movement and an early Gay Liberation Front (GLF) activist, sought to establish an anthropological link between gay male sexuality and a whole variety of sex and gender paradigms that he argued existed, by definition, outside of white, patriarchal western norms. Inspired by the discovery of a late nineteenth-century surgeon general's account that made mention of Southwestern Native American tribes where certain men acted as the "chief passive agent in the pederastic ceremonies," Hay sought to uncover and document instances of open and accepted male-male sexual activity in Native American tribes.[32]

While Hay was exceptionally invested in using figures of Native American ancestry as models through which to develop the gay movement, similar notions of Native American men as holders of an ancestral gay consciousness appear across gay cultural production throughout the 1970s. In *Dust unto Dust* (Tom DeSimone, 1970), the film's narrator, a solitary white frontiersman, reflects that a pair of Native American men showed him the "new wonders" of loving and living the "way they were meant to" (fig. 24). The historical porn-drama *Reflections of an Indian Boy* (Dick Clark, 1972) tells the story of white settlers who learn of sensual, whole-body group sex from a group of young Indian men.[33] Magazine spreads in publications such as *Champion* and *Quorum* regularly featured erotic photoplays that depicted homoeroticism through a register of symbolic Indianness, often featuring non–Native American models in wilderness settings (fig. 25).

For counterculturalists and the counterculturally "curious" alike, then, symbolic Indianness offered not just an opportunity to identify with a figure of struggle. It also offered a way to rhetorically and affectively amplify the process of becoming aware, investing in notions of Native American mastery that reorganize teleological western paradigms of old to new and primitive to civilized. The symbolically age-old became a signifier for cutting-edge counterculturalism, structured around a belief that uncovering old (perhaps disavowed) truths would prove the most effective way to achieve new vision.

As an early 1970s manuscript titled "Notes on Gay Male Consciousness-Raising" outlines, "In consciousness-raising . . . we relate our experiences as gay males. . . . In seeing the common root of our experiences, we begin to break down our isolation from other gay males and begin to recognize our position in society as an oppressed

FIGURE 24 A white man learns the "new wonders" of erotic action from a Native American man.

class."[34] While this particular passage does not directly evoke symbolic Indianness, it sharply echoes its counterteleological mechanisms, positing avowal of what has always been there ("seeing . . . the root as proof of a current state of oppression") as something that underscores a new way of relating "experiences." As noted by Leslie Fiedler in 1969:

> Even as he ceases to be a beatnik and becomes full hippie the ultimate Westerner ceases to be White at all and turns back into the Indian, his boots becoming moccasins, his hair bound in an Indian Headband, and a string of beads around his neck—to declare that he has fallen not merely out of Europe, but out of the Europeanized West, into an aboriginal and anarchical America.[35]

Sharing this desire to locate one's origins in the truth of a past beyond the dictates of the European, early gay liberationists incorporated Indian aesthetics as an analogy between gay discourse and Native American history, helping to legitimate the former as a phenomenon by "rooting" it deeply in the past. This occurred not only though symbolic Indianness, but also through figures of the American West in general, as is evident in the prevalence of narratives of gay liberation that translate it into the psychogeographic terms of frontier experience. As

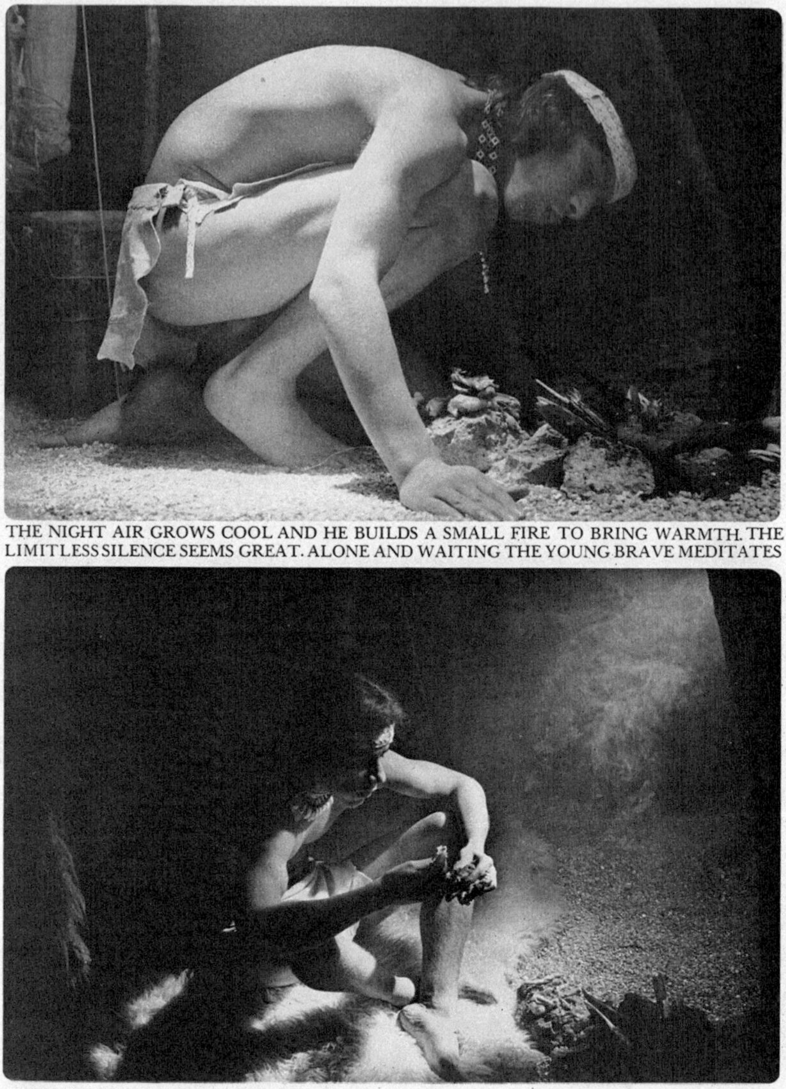

FIGURE 25 A homoerotically configured "young brave" in the wilderness at night. Photo spread, *Quorum* (date unknown). From the personal collection of the author.

Harry Hay once recalled of his experience leaving New York to go west in the 1940s, "my gay consciousness was beginning to stir. I sensed it would do better in the west."[36]

However, within *Loon*, the program for moving from a state of oppression to liberation is not just a matter of moving from New York to California, but is a confrontational process of self-actualization that is by necessity painful and, at times, isolating. Accordingly, the film figures liberation from a homophobic society and the "poisonous" internalization of this homophobia (as an inevitable outcome of a compulsory masculinity) as something that, perhaps paradoxically, can be cured through the exercising and strengthening of traditionally masculine attributes. Resonant with symbolic Indianness, survivalist traits such as courage, physical strength, and resilience; mastery of environment; and, most importantly, the ability to withstand suffering and alienation enable the men of *Loon* to transcend the vicious cycles of self-loathing and disgust that stand between them and their potential to enjoy the "new freedoms" of old.

Compared to other films of the early 1970s that sought to bring similar concerns into the mainstream, most notably *The Boys in the Band* and *Some of My Best Friends Are . . .* , *Loon* maintains a positive valuation of masculinity over and above gender play (camp, drag, swish, etc.), extending a neo-primitivist model of masculinity wherein embracing a universal manhood will assist in transcending the effects of heterosexism and homophobia, as well as the ghettoization of male-male desire. The building up of masculine attributes is a needed tonic for a homophobic world and the homophobic self bred by it. This is, in part, achieved through the film's engagement with notions of "new masculinity." As advanced by counterculturalists in the late 1960s and early 1970s, new masculinity sought to challenge norms of the pro-bureaucracy, breadwinning "organization man" of the 1950s with a new kind of masculinity that positioned androgyny and the embracing of both masculine and feminine qualities *within* each human as the way toward enlightenment.[37] Yet, as David Savran has chronicled, "new masculinity" was far from being a one-way street away from phallocentric norms. Savran suggests of the "relatively androgynous new (white) male" that

> his gender identification testifies, I believe, to a reconsolidation of the characteristics and fantasies associated with a residual, entrepreneurial masculinity combined with an avowal of certain qualities traditionally associated with femininity . . . he

> becomes one of the new "manly males" who are yet able to "reveal their emotions" . . . and "weep openly." . . . He is representative, in short, of a more radically schizoid male subjectivity, "both 'masculine' *and* 'feminine'" in which "both these 'sides'" practice a kind of guerrilla warfare one against the other, in which the masculine part of the self, feeling increasingly threatened and vulnerable, subjugates its other (within the self).[38]

Savran elucidates how the "schizoid" masculinity of the hippie can be observed in the popular media from the period in films like *Easy Rider* and *Butch Cassidy and the Sundance Kid* (George Roy Hill, 1969) and the performances of Jim Morrison. In each case, examples of masculinity are offered in which, paradoxically, manhood is achieved through a willingness to take on conventionally feminine qualities such as emotionality, sensitivity, sensuality, and so on. Savran locates the recurring trope of the hallucinogenic trip in countercultural production as the expression of a masochistic masculinity, wherein drugs are used to "regulate a free play of psychic dominance and submission and to signal a perversely heroic masculinity."[39] In other words, the white male hippie, in submitting to the control of a substance, invites the substance to have mastery over him, thus aligning himself with a passive feminized position while paradoxically also asserting his own mastery, a demonstration to his peers of his ability to "take it like a man."

As in films such as *The Trip* (Roger Corman, 1967), *Easy Rider*, and *Midnight Cowboy* (John Schlesinger, 1969), *Loon* represents male struggles related to gender and sexuality through the figure of the trip. And like these films, despite whatever confrontations with the feminine the tripping male undergoes, a successful trip is always one in which masculinity is reaffirmed through the mastering of psychedelic experience. Following a similar logic to Christian masochism, the tripper undergoes the anxieties of a destabilized reality in order to come into contact with universal truth. The tripping male seeks pacification and suffering in an endeavor to gain a greater, more encompassing sense of mastery and control.

The Trip as a Device of Gay Consciousness-Raising

In *Loon*, the formula of mastering the trip is used as dramatic model through which to situate coming out and consciousness-raising as processes of self-confrontation and discovery. While the primary purpose of Ephraim's quest appears cathartically focused on moving past the pain of losing his lover Montgomery to Calvin (Brad Fredericks), the specific way in which this plays out cinematically suggests that his preoccupation with this loss is also a stand-in for the loss of the fantasy of a stable heterosexual masculinity. More specifically, the sequence positions confrontational images of an idealized masculine physicality, and its implicit potential to overpower and control others, as a constant threat to Ephraim's well-being.

Ephraim's quest unfolds as follows: after several days of romantic bliss with Cyrus (Jon Iverson), Ephraim heads off into the woods on a spirit quest. He encounters the Indian sage Acomas (Martin Valez), who guides him to a cave where he is brought to the feet of a master sage named Running Bear (Richard Hoyt). The thumping of a single drum, rising underneath the flute music, signifies that Ephraim has entered a space of ritual. Running Bear warns Ephraim that, though within his soul "is the gentleness out of which all love is born[,] . . . if [he] allows anger to remain in his heart [he] will have succeeded in breaking [his] soul." Handing Ephraim a peace pipe, Running Bear explains that his "choice will become clear in [his] medicine dream." After ingesting a hallucinogenic substance on the master's instructions, Ephraim strips himself of his clothes and heads off on his quest.

Back in the woods, Ephraim hallucinates a variety of men, all of whom in some way compromise his masculinity by challenging his sense of safety, control, and self-worth. A key sequence sees Cyrus reaching out toward Ephraim with an ambiguous and unsettling expression on his face that suggests both love and menace; Ephraim runs in fear before being pinned to the ground by Cyrus, but their tussle soon becomes more playful. The music, fluctuating between suspenseful heavy brass tones and discordant, key-bending symphonic sounds as they swirl downward through several octaves, keeps the meaning of this action ambiguous. Is this love? Lust? Violence? Has the trip perhaps rendered the distinction between these things indistinguishable?

Finally, Ephraim is brought back into confrontation with Montgomery, first in the anthropomorphized form of a tiger, and then as a naked gunslinger. Montgomery tells him, "I'm gonna kill you, you queer" (fig. 26). Cyrus appears, kills Montgomery with an arrow, and turns into a tree, and the sequence ends with Ephraim collapsed and crying, arms stretched around the tree. His trip ends as he enthusiastically reports the transcendental effects of his trip. Running Bear declares "you have found your peace."

FIGURE 26 Montgomery threatens Ephraim on his forest trip.

For the remainder of the film, it is clear that a transition has taken place, with Ephraim now fully embracing and contributing to the dynamics of a frontier space where open relationships, interethnic encounter, and self-mastery are the law of the land. In this context, the film merges mythopoetic western frontier imagery with a pop-psychologizing rhetoric of self-enhancement that, resonant with the work of Peter de Rome and Pat Rocco, positions gay experience as a sort of consciousness-raising lifestyle upgrade. At its most rudimentary, the frontier of *Loon* holds a transformative magic through which white patriarchal possessive forms of male-male desire, once addressed (and redressed) though a fantasy gay-aboriginal coalition, come out the other side, where homoerotic beefcake is transformed into the material of gay heritage.

At the same time, the film uses symbolic Indianness to ground and authenticate gay oppression as something experienced as part of a people. In funneling gay consciousness through this figure, *Loon* participates in popular countercultural appropriations of Native American ethnicity, fashioning gay discourse in accessible terms that reinforce the film's conflation between the psychosocial dynamics of self-discovery and psychogeographical dynamics of pioneerism.

Gay-Ethnicity and Territorialization in *Loon*

As Steven Epstein has noted in his article "Gay Politics, Ethnic Identity," the late 1960s and early 1970s saw a widespread expansion and popularization of models of ethnicity, in particular an increase in various social groups not traditionally considered ethnicities—such as hippies, communalists, and lesbian separatists—incorporating such models into their political rhetoric. Outlining how this phenomenon, often referred to as "New Ethnicity," differed from traditional uses of the concept, Epstein notes how groups invested in it as a means of establishing (1) "an affective tie with the pursuit of explicitly sociopolitical goals in 'interest group form,'" (2) a placement of "ethnic-group activity firmly on the terrain of the state," and (3) an outlook that is "'Forward-looking,' seeking to expand the group's social position." In describing how "gay ethnicity" operated within this framework and was perhaps even foundational in the development of "New Ethnicity" within American society at large, Epstein clarifies that "like other ethnic groups, gay ethnicity functions typically through appeals to the professed beliefs of the dominant culture, emphasizing traditionally American values such as equality, fairness and freedom from persecution."[40]

Critical to constructing a "gay people" was the need for representation that communicated in a clear and accessible way what defines gay people as a group. Narrative models of consciousness-raising and coming out provided a "forward-looking" way to establish that a variety of people existed within a shared set of transformations and gave "gayness" a sense of ethnic legitimacy. The powerful before-and-after narrative arc of the journey from internalized self-oppression to liberation worked to bring new individuals into a state of psychological, social, and historical relation to one another through their contribution to progressive models that allowed them to measure their progress in relation to the larger group.

Within *Loon*, symbolic Indianness works as a means for elaborating such a model. In depicting Native American men as the keepers of a worldview that exists beyond the restrictions of the hetero/homo binary, who can show white queers "the way" out of the "ghetto" and into a space of liberation, *Loon* constructs gay sexuality as evidence of primordial American desires "more American than America," as part of a utopian fantasy in which the "gay people" of America join the ranks of the persecuted and, in doing so, gain ethnic legitimacy. This takes on a specific affective currency as a consequence of the way in which both male-desiring men and Native American men have been popularly characterized through an emotionalism that emphasizes suffering, sadness, and loss.

In *Loon*, Native American suffering-as-authenticity is transferred onto the male-desiring male as a means of representing the emotional conditions of his liberation as he moves out of ghettoized and closeted living and toward wholeness. Achieved through the syntax of the trip, Ephraim's new gift of authentic self-awareness helps, as Cyrus puts it, in getting "those city ways out of him" while also demonstrating that the internalization of white, heterosexual, Christian beliefs perpetuated in America's "towns and cities" are not just growth-stunting but potently lethal. This particular configuration of consciousness-raising is manifest in the anarchist leanings of a good deal of gay liberation discourse in the early 1970s. Writing in 1970, GLF activist Carl Whitman explained:

> Ghettos breed self hatred. We stagnate here, accepting the status quo. The status quo is rotten. We are all warped by our oppression, and in the isolation of the ghetto we blame ourselves rather than our oppressors. . . . To be a free territory we must govern ourselves, set up our own institutions, defend ourselves and use our own energies to improve our lives.[41]

GLF activist Marcus Overseth similarly asserted in a 1969 issue of the *San Francisco Free Press*:

> Ghetto gays . . . lose all perspective on reality. They are so busy playing the hunter or game that they can perceive no other reality, including the deeper reality of their own existence as Gay people.[42]

GLF activist Gary Alinder, in his 1969 article "Alternative Culture," argued:

> We need a thorough housecleaning. We've got to get rid of the garbage straight society stuffed in our heads. . . . For those of us who are hip, radical or just plain fed-up, a real advance in our liberation will come if we pick up the Alternative Culture Movement. . . . Alternative culture is an outgrowth of the hippie movement. It is based on the realization that straight society is wanting: their minds are repressed, their environment fouled, their food full of chemicals, their values money-oriented and competitive, their culture vapid.[43]

Each of these writers sets forth the idea of a population of gay people who will come into "their own" only after leaving behind the dominance and oppression of straight society. The individual who leaves behind the "self-hatred" and "isolation" bred through urban ghettoization may realize their potential as a member of a gay people—that is, a people with their "own energies," "institutions," and "practices."

Through its revision of the western within a transparently countercultural style and ethos, *Loon* maintains these antighetto, antiheterosexual, and at times antiurban perspectives as critically important. Ephraim's decision to stay on in the country is paralleled with a scene in which the city dwellers, Montgomery and Cyrus, are consigned to a life of shame-induced alcoholism at a tavern in town, driving home the film's positioning of the rural as "free territory" where men, in a retreat-like fashion, can shed their internalized homophobia and begin to "build a new life reflecting [their] strength and love." Such a strategy for casting off the shackles of a perverse heterosexualized society and the gay ghettoization it breeds has been characterized by Scott Herring as a "critical rusticity" that extends an "intersectional opportunity to geographically, corporeally, and aesthetically inhabit non-normative sexuality that offers new possibilities for the sexually marginalized outside the metropolis as well as within it."[44]

Returning to Savran's notion of "a residual, entrepreneurial masculinity combined with an avowal of certain qualities traditionally associated with femininity," it is interesting to note how *Song of the Loon*, along with the sort of liberationist strategies mentioned above, seeks to combine a sense of critical rusticity with entrepreneurial spirit. Just as Whitman stresses the need for a "free territory" with which to develop such institutions as "communes," "retreats," and a "political action office," *Loon* sets up a world in which "the transition from self-hate to self-love" is anachronistically portrayed in Cyrus and Ephraim's life together as pioneering frontier partners at the close of the film, albeit within the confines of "pop-genre fantasy" (fig. 27).

In the country and under the sign of pioneerism, the playful conceptual merging of "partners" and "pardners," so to speak, rhetorically situates the film within a neo-primitivist frontier past—a "real" America where male bonds implicitly slip between the erotic, romantic, and the entrepreneurial—while also using that image to construct a utopian, nonghettoized, rurally liberated version of gay male sexuality.

The collective expression of antiurban male-male desire as a liberatory practice reached its apex in the autumn of 1970, when around

FIGURE 27 A revision of the Western in which partners in business and partners in love are figured as one in the same.

one thousand primarily male "gay people" began moving from major urban centers along the western seaboard to the rugged and sparsely populated Alpine County region of California's High Sierra in order to "settle" the West on their own terms. Intending to install a completely gay government, the figure of pioneerism worked to give the settlers a sense of purpose and cohesion as a group. As reported by GLF activist and Alpine organizer Morris Night in the *San Francisco Chronicle* just as the settlement was picking up steam, "most of the people phoning in to enlist as pioneers are, to my surprise, principally middle class, and upper middle class." Closely following Epstein's dictates of new ethnicity as a model used to assert "group activity firmly on the grounds of the state" through the Alpine "stronghold," as it was called, gay radicals sought to "out-vote the locals in order to elect gay supervisors, [a] gay judge [and] . . . a gay sheriff."[45]

What each of these instances reflects are the desires of some liberationists to establish programs of gay activity on terms that existed apart from what they saw as the heterosexist, ghettoizing structures of metropolitan space. While Alpine did not succeed, and examples of a gay critical rusticity have become arguably less frequent, *Loon* remains a remarkable index of a moment when the cosmopolitanism of gay life was not taken for granted. The "alternative" rural sphere articulated in *Loon* is a space where men develop nonheterosexualized ways of interacting with one another, not so much as an act of opposition or transgression of heterosexist norms, but as a means of leaving them behind in an open-ended search for other possibilities.

The film can perhaps best be characterized as a fantasy search for gay authenticity presented in generic frontier terms. While not delivering any essentialist truth about the nature of being a gay man, the film stresses the truth-giving properties of pioneer experience as a way toward liberation. In regard to American cinematic representation as a whole, the importance the film places on movement and migration, and specifically the movement out of "ghettoized" space, stands in potent contrast to the containment of male-male desire through death in mainstream Hollywood fare. At the same time, *Loon* suggests a version of male-male desire that eschews any theatrics of gay visibility for a completely quotidian and, as such, politically challenging representation of male-male desire as implicitly out and about, running amuck in the countryside.

Some of My Best Friends Are . . .

Some of My Best Friends Are . . . , directed by Mervyn Nelson, was an independent production promoted as an American International Pictures release.[46] With a string of successful exploitation films released in the late 1960s and early 1970s (*Devil's Angels* [Daniel Haller, 1967], *The Trip*, *A Bullet for Pretty Boy* [Larry Buchanan, Maury Dexter, 1970]), AIP had become a recognizable brand for moviegoers. As with its other exploitation releases, *Friends* used a single sensational theme to draw in audiences—here, getting to see one night in a gay bar—as promotion. Like the AIP success *The Trip*, a film that follows one man's journey as he undergoes a single LSD trip, *Friends* pitches its journey into gay social life as something that will satisfy the curiosity of audiences both inexperienced and experienced in the ways of a particular subculture, inviting the former to take in the spectacle (with a patina of social awareness) and the latter to ponder the film's ability to capture their lived experience with verisimilitude.

Released on October 27, 1971, at New York's 59th Street Twin Theatres—which primarily screened a mix of exploitation and soft- and hard-core porn—the film went on to show in cities across the United

States. Reflecting the mainstream aspirations of the film, this distribution strategy included theaters more calibrated to reaching a wide audience, such as the River Oaks Theatre located in the River Oaks Shopping Center in Houston, Texas, where the film was released that same fall.[47] While there is little information to indicate how successful *Friends* was in its mainstream aspirations, reviews and advertisements for the film at the time in newspapers such as the *New York Times* and *The Nuntius* show that both mainstream and gay press outlets saw it as at least of potential interest to their readers.[48]

Some of My Best Friends Are . . . dramatizes urban gay life in the early 1970s in a way that manages to capture many of the social and historical forces shaping gay life and discourse at the highly transitional moment of the film's release. Filmed on location at New York's Zodiac Bar—an actual gay bar that was raided in March 1970 under order from the deputy inspector responsible for the raid at the Stonewall Inn the previous year—the film offers a fictional view of Christmas Eve, 1971, as experienced by a motley crew of patrons at a gay bar called the Blue Jay. Packing in a panoply of characters, the staff and patrons of the bar include (but are not limited to) a priest, a plumber, a mother, a jazz singer, a hustler, a ski instructor, a doctor, a cook, a clergyman, several businessmen, numerous hippies, an actress, a runaway youth, several college boys, and underground film phenomenon Candy Darling.

The representation of numerous types in *Friends* is used to construct, embody, and perform gay minority experience within, or perhaps even in concert with, generic (heterosexual) film conventions. The film's promotional trailer addresses both those potentially interested in the film as spectacle from a perspective of slumming and those seeking to get involved in gay world-making. The film's world-making dynamics resonate with the acceleration of mass gay migration to urban areas across the United States in the early 1970s. Formal techniques are used to establish a naturalizing representation of gay types that promotes inclusive and intersectional forms of socialization.

An orientation around the perspective of straight or "questioning" viewers is firmly established in the film's theatrical trailer. It begins with an out-of-focus view of a "don't walk" sign, then cuts to a neon bar sign before an extended tracking shot simulates the perspective of an individual moving down a long hall, through a beaded doorway, and into the sequined interior of the Blue Jay. In documentary style, the voice of a male narrator informs the uninitiated that "there's one in every city . . . one place where, for a few hours, they forget the whispers behind their backs and share the one secret that makes them different." With a cut to inside the crowded bar where patrons are drinking, smiling, and laughing, a folk-rock tune offers another perspective as the male tenor sings:

His life waits for night to fall . . .
With every glass another dream
And visions of a royal ball
He joins me in the lodge to face the mirrored walls
To find a place to rest his head
Searching . . .
Why be left alone in bed?
Let me show you to the bar

As the song continues to play, the shot of the bar patrons suddenly freezes. Overlaid text explains, "we have refrained from the customary practice of showing dramatic portions of our coming attraction due to its controversial nature and the explicit drama of its scenes." After several moments in which the words *Some of My Best Friends Are . . .* flash over the frozen image, the trailer cuts to an image of the bar patrons gathered together side by side as the camera slowly tracks by each them from right to left. Scrolling upward across the screen, another important prefacing message reads:

> The producers have attempted to portray the events with full honesty and therefore the film's content may sometimes be objectionable for viewing by younger audiences. But for those who can stand the truth . . . it is provocative adult entertainment. A penetrating insight to a world which actually exists today, it tells in one human story the many stories of its people . . . some outrageously funny . . . some shockingly grotesque and some of heart rending emotional impact.

Heavily capitalizing on notions of secrecy and exposure strongly associated with preliberation networks of male-male desire, the framing, editing, and camera movement of this trailer all work to evoke a syntax of policing, surveillance, and exposé-style reporting. Despite, if not because of, the fact that the Stonewall Inn and numerous other metropolitan bars across the US were receiving national press at the same time as a gay politics of visibility was gaining steam, representations of male-male desire in closeted and/or semicloseted contexts were also on the rise. Films such as *Friends*, *The Boys in the Band*, and *A Very Natural*

Thing all devote the great majority of their screen time to showing gay men within interior spaces such as houses, apartments, and bars. Was this emphasis on containment an invitation to slumming?

It is fairly transparent how the trailer parades the film's value to curious "straight" viewers; echoing circus dynamics, it refuses to disclose too much information, promising to reveal the "shockingly grotesque," the "outrageously funny," and the "heart rending."

At the same time, it also addresses its audience in a completely new kind of way. Whereas exposés such as *Time* magazine's 1969 "The Homosexual: Newly Visible, Newly Understood," for instance, often took an overall tone of ambivalence and a presumed sociological distance in an effort to suit a general readership, there are several ways in which *Friends* is positioned to appeal more specifically to an audience curious about gay life as a new social and cultural form, existing as one option of many in a world of lifestyle choices.[49] The trailer seeks to attract the attention of an audience who, in one way or another, wants more information about the ins and outs of gay life, whether it be for the purposes of entertainment, to broaden their perspective, or for straight-up information on what a gay bar might be like and how they work.

The trailer also works in the vein of a road map supplying key information to the "unknowing" traveler that will help them to forecast what's ahead through preparation. Its song, aptly titled "Let Me Show You to the Bar," speaks to this position of naive curiosity quite acutely, giving a sense of the cultural and physical geography of gay social life by offering lessons in how alcohol supports dreams of grandeur ("every glass another dream . . . visions of a royal ball"), how practices of looking work within bar-space ("he joins me in the lodge to face the mirrored walls"), and how the bar may operate as site of respite ("a place to rest his head").

Complementing the syntax of cultural geography set up in the trailer, the film itself engages heavily with perspectives of and feelings about gay migration at a moment when many male-desiring men and female-desiring women across the United States were relocating, en mass, to major metropolitan centers. Referring to this as the "Great Gay Migration," anthropologist Kath Weston has chronicled how the "tens of thousands" who migrated from country to city did so as part of a world-making project dependent upon processes of imagination. Weston explains:

> During the Great Gay Migration, countless individuals launched themselves into a quest for community in Benedict Anderson's sense of the term. As "members" of an

imagined community, people feel an attachment to a necessarily fictional group, be it nation, race, gender, class, or sexuality. In the process they interpret themselves *through* that attachment, so that their subjectivity becomes inseparable from a construction of "we-ness." The popular depiction of "gay people" as a constant 10% of humanity naturalized the gay community by rendering "it" susceptible to identification, quantification and spatial location.[50]

This phenomenon is of critical importance to how *Friends* formally constructs gay social life. In situating the bar as a space where both the curious outsider and those already socially "in" may be transformed by their entry into the space, the film posits a sort of point of contact where multiple positions may be brought together and naturalized while at the same time "rendering" visible the contours of a gay minority. *Friends* presents the mechanisms of gay social life as easily grasped rituals. Showing these rituals offers a wide variety of viewers a way to imagine themselves as existing within and/or capable of shaping these contours, thereby promoting a sense of possible movement between processes of imagining and making.

The film's use of a wide variety of social types offers multiple positions of identification to viewers, inciting the question "which one am I?" The film introduces and develops these characters just enough to leave open identification while also sustaining the viewer's curiosity. The questioning, curious position this elicits is markedly expressed in spatialized, cultural geographical terms though a character nicknamed "Nebraska." Having just "escaped" from the Midwest and still learning the ropes of gay life in the city, Nebraska's momentary encounter with an older man establishes his naturalization as part of gay life through the familial, as the conversation unfolds among the other patrons assembling for Christmas caroling in the background:

Older Man: Aren't you coming in too?
Younger: It's my first Christmas away from home.
Older Man: You're frightened.
Younger: [pauses] Yes. I didn't want to show it. I was more frightened outside.
Older: I was too . . . Where you in from?
Younger: Nebraska.
Older: C'mon, Nebraska, ha!
Younger: OK.

With his arm on his shoulder, the older man guides Nebraska into the circle of singing men who clear a path in, hand him sheet music, and then enfold him into the group. Moving from isolation to incorporation, the development of the episode operates as a process whereby Nebraska's migration from the rural Midwest to New York City's Greenwich Village is presented as both enabling his inclusion into and defining his role within the group. The emphasis on spatial terms is key here: the older man's invitation to the boy to come in to the circle echoes notions of coming out as coming in to gay social life. The boy's description of himself as "away from home" indicates his arrival in migratory terms. His assertion that he "was more frightened outside" indicates his naturalization into gay life, reinforced by the older man's proclamation that he was once afraid out there too. Having asserted a sharp dialectic of inside/outside—the outer world a place of danger, the bar a place of safety and comfort—the man nicknames the boy based on the state he hails from, registering it as central to his newfound participation in shaping the meaning of gay space, and his meaning within it.

The sequence shows metropolitan gay life as an alternative site for the fulfillment of needs associated with home and family, presenting the Blue Jay as not only a place of refuge—a place to "rest your weary head"—but as a sphere where specific kinds of interaction between individual and group lend the bar a sense of the familial; a sense encapsulated in the film's many socializing images of patrons decorating the bar and each other throughout the night. It follows that coming out to the Blue Jay is very much an act of homecoming. While the outside is marked by elements of coldness, heterosexism, and homophobia, the inside is presented as a remarkably warm and frenetic antidote to this.

Becoming Members: The Naturalizing Dynamics of *Friends*

Friends is unique compared to its contemporaries in the way it develops a naturalizing model for what it means to become a citizen of gay life that is both heavily conscious of the importance of gay liberation ideology while also protective of what John Grube has called "traditional gay culture."[51] In exploring this ambivalent position, it is critical to look at how the film advances a minority-based, ethnic model of gay socialization that identifies a range of specific gay types as a defining feature of a "gay culture." In his 1974 study "Urbanization and Gay Life," Joseph Harry produced early sociological data on American gay bars based on research he completed on a total of 1,980 gay bars in major cities across the United States. Through his findings, he found that large American cities, such as New York, San Francisco, and Los

Angeles, had a much higher percentage of gay bars that specialized in specific "types" of clientele. In accordance with the terminology used by gay bar guides of the period, Harry listed seven types of bars (moving from most common to least common): "Young, Dancing, Hustlers, Older, Dressy, Leather and Black."[52]

Establishing a different kind of bar, *Friends* takes up this taxonomy of highly individuated types only to collapse it into a single gay scene devoted to inclusion and integration. This works toward a model of gay sociality in which a combination of types who in everyday life may have limited interaction with one another are revalued in terms that position them against conventional heterosexuality, "traditional gay culture," and new (masculinist) strands of radical gay politics alike. Central to this is the film's situating of the two primary "straight" male characters—the bartender and piano player—as having the highest value to the group, expressed in the frequency with which all types of men seek out their advice, often on how to get by as a gay man. In one instance, an Italian American bar patron, Leo, tells the African American piano player, Larry, of his crush on a straight bar patron, commenting that, "if all goes well tonight, I just might be a swish operator." Larry, in return, offers his own hip humanist perspective on Leo to the bar, exclaiming, "Man, he's beautiful. . . . It's an object lesson, man, he's not making any excuse to anybody, he's lookin' in his own mirror and he knows where he's at."

Acting as rallying points and mascots for gay men, the hip "straights" of the Blue Jay are represented as having a certain kind of authority that enables them to recognize gay strength and assign it value. These "friends" are depicted in contrast to normative figures of WASP masculinity: the Irish American bartender, the African American piano player, the obese Jewish "den mother." These roles situate the gay patrons as the minority of minorities (or perhaps even the minorities' minority). Within this framework, the "straight" characters slip easily into familial positions in relation to the gay patrons via occupational roles; the bartender/priest takes on the role of the father, the piano player a big brother, and the cook a much-loved and adored mother.

Experiences of togetherness in the film are both inspired and facilitated by these "straight" relations and mark the Blue Jay as a special kind of bar where gay and straight don't just come together but appear almost as fans of one another. In fact, as one writer commented in a 1970 issue of the local gay Dallas paper *The Nuntius*, "the thing that seemed most amazing to us was the fact that nearly all of the bar staff were straight. We're not accustomed to this in our bars. If there is a straight in a bar in Texas, it is generally the owner. We have never seen a straight bartender, doorman, waiter, etc."[53] It is not just the "straight" characters, however, that construct the Blue Jay as a new phenomenon in gay bar dynamics but also the film's broad range of even more particular types.

Through old and young (regularly coded in terms of "young" and "dressy," with the younger dressed in hip casual wear and the older in more traditional suits, buttoned-down oxford shirts, and sweaters), the relationship between conventional age groupings and pre- and post-gay liberation experience plays out in a number of interesting ways. To provide some key examples: as an older white businessman in a suit and a hip young African American dance together, the older man shouts, "I wish my dancing were as good as my golfing," prompting the young man to yell back in affirmation that he was "really something" in their last golf match; a clergyman and a trans* woman share stories about their differing life experiences, both in and out of the bar, over a cocktail (fig. 28); a fashionable youth in a bold, billowy shirt steals a matchbook from an older, formally dressed man only to return it to him with his phone number on it, remarking, "hang up if my mom answers"; an older man explains the conventions of city life to the younger Nebraska; a younger German skier in a beatnik-style black turtleneck urges his married, formally attired boyfriend to come out;

FIGURE 28 Howard (David Drew) and Karen (Candy Darling) share stories of their life experiences.

an older man comforts a younger man after his mother follows him into the bar and publically disowns him.

Regardless of the counterculturally vindicated "gay is beautiful" ethos that operates as so much of the film's overall "voice," its representation of intergenerational experience is interesting for the way in which it sustains older aspects of gay sociality. It resists privileging youth as *the* subjects of gay liberation. As John Grube notes:

> In the traditional or "native" gay community, with basic structural units such as the mentor/protégé couple (Grube, 1986), the queen-and-entourage formation (Leznoff & Westley, 1963) and the party and dinner circles, communities were formed in which older men had privileges and duties. Older men introduced young men, for example, to their social circle, sometimes in exchange for sex, often for the glamorous social company of youth. . . . This is not true of the post-1969 *organized gay community*, which lacks an equivalent of the mentor/protégé tradition, so useful in training new leaders.[54]

The protégé/mentor unit and similar such relations, in which one participant learns the ropes of gay social life from others, appears integrated into a wide range of interactions across age, race, gender, and class: the younger discuss the benefits of coming out with the older, the older take in and shelter the younger when they are left homeless, the older gay male starts to fall for the younger trans* woman as they discover how much they have in common through a bit of bar banter.

Comparable to the mentor/protégé relationship in preliberation-era networks of male-desiring men, relations in the Blue Jay move across countless boundaries in a liberatory manner, presenting an ever-widening sphere of social interaction facilitated by the very spirit of unhindered interaction. The film's boundary crossings move not so much toward the pleasure of transgression for its own sake as they move toward a gay world-making project that is less goal oriented in any specific sense.

While Ephraim in *Loon* or even Bobby in *Pink Narcissus* fit into a countercultural transcendentalism in which their experiences of oppression lead them redemptively toward psychological and/or spiritual change, the people of the Blue Jay are less oriented toward personal discovery and much more intrigued by making and developing a shared world based on the discovery of one another. As Richard Dyer notes:

> [the film] makes free use of camera angles and composition to stress the relatedness to the specific environment . . . suggesting the possibilities of a mode of representation that does not dissolve social distinctions into psychologistic ones (whether these be individualized or social-stereotypical), but emphasises such distinctions as the basis for collective identity and historical struggle.[55]

The relatedness of the environment, while largely carried through camera angles, framing, and composition, is also supported through the film's carefully detailed mise-en-scéne. Multicolor ("disco") lighting bathes the patrons en masse within constantly changing beams of color, countless forms of decorative filigree (garland, glitter, silk sashes, ornaments, streamers, etc.) create a sense of spatial continuity linking various areas of the labyrinthine space, and art deco frescos of white clouds on black lining the walls set up a syntax of "impossible geography" that turns the bar into a fantastical "world" that appears as part of one ongoing expanse.[56] All of these elements help to establish the sense of a people who shift and move between countless social groupings while sustaining their role as part of the overall collective space of the bar.

In representing the bar as both a particular and expansive space, however, the film manages to draw attention to various forms of social interaction while at the same time emphasizing these as part of an arena where collectivity and history work to dissolve the "psychologistic" into the social. This is most evident in the bodily movement that comes to define the space, as characters are continually shown forming and reforming, moving between levels of interpersonal coupling in various booths, nooks, and corridors, hanging out in small groups and assembling as a mass. Establishing each of these formations through point-of-view shots, the film shows patrons addressing other patrons within a variety of group assemblies: gathered round the cook as she thanks them for sending gifts when she was in the hospital, scrunching together for a spontaneous burlesque number from the coat-check girl, rallied into camaraderie for the yearly tradition of crowning the waiter Christmas fairy (fig. 29).

In each of these scenarios, the patrons move in constantly shifting patterns, unconcerned with any one formation and freely existing as part of the group. Even the patrons addressing the group—whether from the stage, dance floor, or aisle—are kept within the fold through cast blocking, high-angle shots, and slow camera pans that maintain close spatial relations between group and individual. Scattered wide-angle shots that pan across the patrons from the speaker's point of view

FIGURE 29 Coming together en masse for the crowning of the Christmas fairy.

show a close proximity between the speaker and the person addressed and fill the frame from front row to back and side to side with a sea of people.

The Blue Jay operates as a synecdoche for gay life, bolstering the conceptualization of gay people as a group defined by shared experiences of oppression, certain cultural traditions, and ways of interacting. Types here are not so much utilized to heighten dramatic conflict by pitting one type against another (as happens in *The Boys in the Band*, for instance), but as a means of modeling how social relations based on affiliation and the search for common ground might contribute to an expansionist project of gay life. Staying focused at the intersection between group and individual interaction, *Friends* invites viewers to ponder how a paradigm of gay life premised on more open forms of contact may result in new social alliances.

A Very Natural Thing

At last a film comes along which separates the humor from the gayness.

CHUCK ORTLEB[57]

Starting in the summer of 1974, an advertisement began to appear in newspapers and magazines across the United States announcing "the first accurate, non-pornographic presentation of contemporary American urban gay life."[58] As an introduction to Christopher Larkin's *A Very Natural Thing*, the film's promotional campaign attempted to establish the film as a landmark moment in gay representation, promising a film that was current, tasteful, and, above all, realistic. New Line Cinema, the film's distributor, released a press kit with a letter that began by asserting its status as "the first non-exploitative gay feature film," ending with a postscript that film critic and gay activist Vito Russo "is available [through New Line] for lecture engagements."[59] Russo, who had carved out a place for himself in the gay press as an expert in the analysis of the homophobia and heterocentrism of popular film, was by this point an important figure in gay movement politics. The Russo connection asserted that *A Very Natural Thing* should be understood as a corrective to problematic filmic representations of gay people.

Premiering on June 1974 at two theaters in New York—the Cine Malibu and Cinema Village—the film went on to screen across the country at movie theaters and on college campuses. A relatively new distribution company, incorporated in 1967, New Line worked to "attract the largest audience possible" through a campaign that reduced the cost of trailers and movie posters to theaters.[60] However, it was not only at the level of advertising that the film mimicked the values of Hollywood.

Perhaps more so than any gay film prior to its release, *Natural Thing* embraces a conventional Hollywood formula structured around the pursuit of romantic love, psychological development, and individual achievement. Scholarship on the film has responded to its use of conventional film elements to produce a contemporary representation of gay life in a variety of ways. Harry M. Benshoff and Sean Griffin, for instance, describe the film as exploring "the impact of gay liberation on traditional romantic ideals."[61] Thomas Waugh, while noting the importance of these two elements, suggests that the "story builds . . . on a recognition of the inadequacy of traditional romantic patterns for gay lifestyles."[62] Where the former account sees gay liberation as impacting "traditional romantic ideals," the latter sees the film as revealing a lack of compatibility between the two systems. These differing accounts point to a slipperiness that lies at the center of the film. While in one respect the film seeks to advance the legitimacy of male-male desire in the form of conventional romantic iconography, in another it continually comes up against the representational "inadequacy" that ensues as a consequence of the attempt to funnel gay life through norms of heterosexual representation.

The film follows a man called David (Robert Joel) as he goes through several life changes, all the while attempting to figure out how to obtain a satisfying relationship. After quitting the priesthood and moving to New York, David enters into a relationship with Mark (Curt Gareth), a young businessman he meets on his first night out at a gay disco. The first half of the film is primarily concerned with demonstrating the numerous tensions produced by David's interest in a "traditional" monogamous relationship and Mark's interest in the more open, liberated dynamics he finds in bars, bathhouses, and cruising. After trying things Mark's way—testing out an orgy at a gay resort—and concluding that it is not his style, the film follows David through his turbulent breakup and a short period of being single, during which he starts to strengthen his friendships with other gay men and continues to try his hand at looser living, this time venturing out to a bathhouse. Still not feeling it, David is pleased to get into another relationship, this time with a recently divorced hip bisexual man called Jason (Bo White) whom he (and the camera) plucks out of the crowd at a gay pride march. By the film's end, it is uncertain where this new relationship will lead, but the men nonetheless profess their love for each other.

At the heart of the film lies the dissonance presented between groups and individuals, specifically the ways in which "gay people" as an entity are repeatedly shown failing to meet the needs of and as incompatible with certain kinds of gay individuals and couples, especially those who seek long-term relationships structured around a commitment to monogamy. In David's case, gay social life's failure to meet his needs as an individual is most evident in the antagonism the film sets up between romantic and sexual expression. From the start, David's interest in romantic conventions are firmly established; within days of meeting Mark, he pushes for a relationship styled on conventional film tropes and stages of heterosexual coupling recognizably culled from the recent hit *Love Story* (Arthur Hiller, 1970). Echoing a specific sequence from the film, their relationship is shown developing through a montage that cuts between images of frolicking amidst nature, late-night proclamations of love, morning-after bliss, nesting on the couch, and kiss-the-cook kitchen dynamics.

One of the first of several obstacles the film hurls at David's domestic bliss comes when David and Mark encounter another kind of domesticity in the form of an Upper West Side gay dinner party. The scene marks the first moment in the film when gay social life and friendship are shown in group terms. Introducing the group, a wide-angle shot emphasizes the sociality and connectedness among the men, showing David and Mark seated with the group at a stately dining room table within an ornate, aristocratically styled room (white linen table cloth, chandelier, polished glasses, a "hunt club" painting, etc.). Retiring to a more expansive lounge room after dinner, the men, now surrounded in interior furnishings from a wide range of periods and styles from a gilded French Gothic mantelpiece to oriental sculpture, discuss the ins and outs and pros and cons of "open" versus monogamous relationships.

Looking well practiced at matching his environs, the party's host, seated and wearing a fitted black suit, offers a bit of sociologically tinged armchair philosophy to his guests. Assuming an arch, knowing tone of paternal wisdom, he gives testament to how his relationship with his lover has evolved over time:

> I used to be hellishly jealous when we first got together. I made him throw away his old telephone numbers and his dirty magazines. [group laughter] But that doesn't change somebody's basic nature. There has to be a lot of give and take in a marriage. I know I'm a bitch and he just has to put up with it. Life is, as they say, full of compromises. At this point I could care less if he brought a different trick in here every night. But let him bring the same dewy-eyed little innocent in here twice and begin acting like he's serious about it and I'll manage to wheedle myself into that bed right between them. I've put five years of hard work into this marriage and I don't intend to let anything or anyone fuck it up for me.

This monologue sharply departs from the group-centered dynamics that characterize the great majority of 1970s gay cinema. In fact, as explored thus far, 1970s gay cinema has almost exclusively positioned male-male couples as one formation of several existing within the broader context, often liberatory, of gay group interaction. *Natural Thing* reverses this model so that gay social life is now a central force of oppression. The figures that pose a threat to the host's love life are all explicitly associated with gay sociality; the "old telephone numbers," "tricks," and "dewy-eyed little innocents" all endanger the security of his "marriage."

The host is fixed so firmly within the heavily class-coded aesthetic system of his home, his position takes on the veneer of the closet. Echoing the compositional layout and body language of classical portraiture, the mid-range, motionless shot frames him among a decadent collection of objects including oriental dolls, a figure drawing of a nude male, a hand-carved wooden chest, and a dutifully polished antique armchair in which he sits. This kind of décor was coming to be considered, within certain strains of "liberated" gay youth culture, not just as evidence of bad taste, but as antithetical to the process of liberation. Activist-writer Craig Alfred Hanson insisted:

> We tend to find the princesses' homes and apartments done in an over-decorated décor which could only be called "homo-baroque." Because of real poverty, the furnishings are more apt to be of cheap plaster, paper, or plastic then marble, velvet or crystal. I know of one old queen whose life has been devoted to collecting Wedgwood china, and another, a really ancient individual, whose dank dismal Italianate villa in the Hollywood Hills is lined with rows of musty chairs from a monastery. We cannot really expect most fairy princesses to rip down their chandeliers, smash their plaster statues of David, kick their poodle out, or flee from fairyland to reality. Most are simply too old for that. But we should expose our Princess Floradora Femadonna so that our younger brothers will not fall into the lavender cesspool and be swept down the sewers of fantasyland. . . . It is a selfish, self-serving, irrational and materialistic journey which shuns real human relations for past images and things material, and human relations are what being gay is all about.[63]

Hanson's tirade is an example of how gay liberation ideology was sometimes horrendously ageist. He "calls out" the outmoded preoccupations of some gay men while conflating this phenomenon with gender transgression. The total effect is the assertion of a barely underlying opposition that pits an imagined homosexual culture of decadence and excess against an authentic ("real human emotions") and masculinized fraternal liberation-era experience. Even more, Hanson fears the "homo-baroque" as something that could contaminate those "younger" gay men (dragging them down into a "lavender cesspool") if not exposed.

In *Natural Thing*, the dangers of fairyland seem to have corrupted gay life in a way that leaves no character un-impinged upon. In fact, the principal tension in the film ultimately comes down to the question of whether or not David will be able to escape the multiple fairylands that seem to be continually blocking his path to individual growth. Almost all of these corrupted types of "gaydom" can be observed as the after-dinner banter rolls on.

As a man named Alan sits with this new boyfriend, a discernibly younger Puerto Rican man named Miguel, various comments come flying at Miguel from across the room. Petting his leg, one man questions him as if trying to ascertain the proper taxonomy for a rare and unlikely form of house pet, remarking, "You're so quiet, you haven't said two words all evening." Alan replies that "I think Miguel is a bit overawed by his surroundings . . . besides he's kind of shy." Cut to Miguel looking despondently down at the floor as if incapable of grasping such sophisticated talk. After a voice lasciviously chimes in from another room, "Well, he shouldn't be," Miguel finally musters up the words, "Thank you, you have a very lovely apartment." Adding to the rampant ageism, classism, and jingoism that each individual contributes to the group, Mark adds a dose of homophobia when, on the way home, he comments to David, "I don't like spending my Saturday nights with a bunch of faggots."

The film eschews the opportunity to analyze these dynamics of class, race, and ethnicity within gay contexts even as it structures its representation of gay life around these elements, presenting them as obstacles that motivate, propel, and even define the heavily pop-psychologized terms of David's vision of personal development—a vision that, working at the expense of the social, sees almost any notion of mass gay sociality as oppressive.

From the "Lavender Cesspool" to the Private Beach

The next scene of gay sociality shows David attempting to make a go of Mark's way of life, accompanying him for a weekend in the gay resort town of Fire Island, New York. Unlike the dinner party, racial and ethnic diversity appear commonplace, and nonwhite and white characters alike intermingle with apparent ease as the two men are shown in the open air of a deck party. As the men approach the dance floor, they look on into an interclass, interrace, and interethnic sea of joyful dancers. The space is marked by collectivity and togetherness that stand in stark contrast to the prickly individualism of the dinner party, indicated by a shot of the two men as they pause, remove their shirts, and are brought into the crowd by one of the dancers.

The film cuts to David descending down a flight of stairs and into a barely lit basement. He discovers a diversity similar to that in evidence up on the dance floor, as a small variety of "natural"-looking men (lots of body hair, un-styled and unkempt looking hair, mostly nude) join in a session of group sex on a fluffy mohair rug. Oddly, unlike the deck party, with its assortment of skin tones and numerous fashion styles, the men in the basement appear as a mass of undifferentiated maleness threatening to consume David. The low light gives the men an overall hue, leaving the racial and ethnic makeup of the group members ambiguous. This mass is represented visually and audibly as engulfing and swallowing David and his individualism, as the dim light renders the characters' faces and other individualizing features (wrinkles, creases, gradations of color) irrecoverable to clear differentiation.

Clarifying the lecherous energies of the group, framing and character blocking work to show David frightened and peering out toward the camera as he becomes engulfed by a mass of indistinguishable brown- and olive-toned bodies. In one shot, a massive muscular back is hunched over him, lunging and ready to devour, the high angle of the shot position affectively amplifying the force of the bodies pressing down on other bodies. Numerous other shots show men ceaselessly tugging, pouncing, pushing, and squeezing. David doesn't have the patience for this particular brand of groupness. The scene cuts to a shot of him looking upset, introspective, and windswept as he and Mark peer off into the ocean in frustrated silence. The aural frenzy of funk gives way to the cleansing natural sounds of wind and surf. The gathering having created an unbridgeable gap between them, Mark and David part ways upon their return to the city.

Critically, this is one of two sequences in the film where David ascends from the dark and lecherous locations of gay sex to natural locations of white, bourgeois, heterosexual romance. The second instance finds him exploring the possibilities of group sex once again, this time in a bathhouse. Twinning this sequence with his previous descent into the realm of group encounter, David is shown wandering the labyrinthine corridors of a bathhouse so shaded that its lighting effects turn him a deep lavender as he makes way deeper into its recesses. Offering a clearer taxonomy of gay lechers, high-angle point-of-view shots show him passing by a series of men stretched out in cubbies, peering out at him, one man lunging toward him in languorous desperation. Explicitly framing this in terms of gay life, the sequence shows these men as discernable gay types: a "bottom" stretches out motionless on a bunk; another man, legs parted, stretches out his hands in the position of animal about to pounce; in an identical position a "leatherman" peers upward from under his cap.

While one might argue that such darkness is simply a conventional part of a bathhouse aesthetic, the film's particular investment in nonwhiteness as a corrosive force is made clear as David comes into the brightly lit space of the steam room. A high-angle shot looks down toward a lone African American, who peers up at David as he passes. A close-up of the man shows him gazing in hunger at David. Within moments, a panoply of men of various races and ethnicities gather around David, hungrily pawing and inspecting him. An Asian man is shown prodding at his white smooth chest in lustful admiration. The back of a head with an Afro is shown closing in on David while his head falls back, as if pulled downward by the force of the men. The orientalizing gamelan music processed through electronic echo effects—a common musical trope of the 1970s horror films—creates a menacing mood as an array of strings, aggressively strummed at random intervals, descend in discordant patterns from high to low. Ending the sequence on a startling note, a loud mechanical sound pulses loudly over blurred images of the unidentifiable men. A cut to Michael in a subway car looking zoned out in a state of post-bathhouse depression establishes that the horrible sound was simply the clatter of the moving train.

Having established that gay men in the early 1970s are stuck between two inadequate models for sustaining intimacy with a partner (old self-absorbed queens vs. young "brothers" who want sex without the hang-ups), *Natural Thing* resolves these issues with class mobility and formulaic Hollywood-style slow-motion romance. The film takes a sharp turn away from ethnically diverse gay group interaction, establishing Jason as an opportunity for a relationship based on heterosexually informed upward mobility. As David returns home with Jason to his apartment, David discovers that his new beau has bona fide heterosexual experience, authenticated by a framed family portrait of Jason with his ex-wife and child; in the portrait, the couple, in white shirts, baring their pearly whites, is drenched in white light. David affirms his discovery of Mr. Right and the two men kiss. Finally, a relationship that suits David begins to take shape. At the foundation of this intimacy lies their shared interest in themselves as individuals. At one point, for instance, David reveals the new meaning the concept of liberation has taken on for him, explaining, "I guess I have been too busy surviving and putting myself back together after Mark to take on the world's problems yet. . . . Liberating myself is the most important thing for me right now." Jason responds gently, "It's really all part of the same thing, isn't it?"

David's position is resonant with a growing trend away from the group-oriented goals of early gay liberation and the retreat toward a psychological model of self-improvement. Chronicling this phenomenon in a 1976 *Advocate* article, "The Closet as Gay Groupthink," Dean Gengle wrote:

> For the individual, the real issue is whether or not one has the courage to continue emerging from the many kinds of closets that can be built including that of the gay liberation movement itself. Identification with a group is not a necessary precondition for personal and social growth.[64]

Such notions of individualism work to recuperate David back into the white, heterosexual, bourgeois values he lapsed from in his desperation. More disconcerting, however, is the specific way in which the film's concluding scene flagrantly elevates these values as an ideal form of liberation that, through its stark visual and aural contrast to earlier scenes, positions gay collectivity and sociality as a distasteful cesspool that can be overcome with effort.

Establishing that David's mobility is clearly operating outside the kinds of gay social contexts explored earlier in the film (gay-ghetto dinner party, bathhouse, disco, etc.), the final sequence, showing David and Jason making their way down an empty road and settling in at a secluded beachside cabin, leaves no stone unturned in its assertion that gay love is at its best when dressed in the accolades of a tasteful, white, upper-class romanticism. A montage of shots unfolds to the sound of classical music: the two men coming face to face for an almost polite kiss, collapsing into the missionary position on a gleaming four-poster bed, a postcoital shot from above showing the men as they caress each other's brightly lit white hands.

As *Natural Thing* would have it, to be out in this case means, quite literally, to be outside, naked and part of the natural world, epitomized by an ending that dedicates nearly five minutes to the men's slow-motion play in the Atlantic Ocean just outside their cabin door. As Waugh notes: "It's as if the two naked figures were gamboling in some pre-social paradise. . . . It is the ultimate delusive myth of a certain middle-class core of the gay community that sexual liberation would be no problem at all if we all had our own private beach to play on."[65]

Moving onward and upward—out of the darkness of gay collectivity—the film's conclusion shows darkened images of the men's naked bodies as they run side by side toward the ocean, the image growing increasingly light as they make their way forward. In a state of baptismal jubilance, the men splash each other within sun-sprayed beads of water as the triumphant non-diegetic sound of classical strings and brass works, equally, to wash clean the residue of the black funk and orientalizing music that hung over David's previous adventures (fig. 30). The men repeatedly move apart and come together, and are shown at the close wrestling and racing down the beach in the

FIGURE 30 Liberation on the beach.

natural, tasteful, competitive joy elicited by the individual pursuit of a bright future.

From People to Gay Individuals

Between the early and mid-1970s, filmmakers and film promoters alike became increasingly interested in creating representations of gay life that hinged on socially oriented perspectives of gay people. Films like *Loon*, *Friends*, and *Natural Thing* situated their protagonists' struggles not just within the world at large, but as bound up in questions about the role of the individual in collective gay life. The contrasting strategies with which these films deal with these questions demonstrate both the degree of divergence at play in the models for gay life in circulation at this time as well some of the ways that popular cinematic conventions—in terms of genre, style, and marketing—worked to emphasize certain versions of gay life. The revisionist western, the ensemble comedy-drama, and the naturalistic bourgeois melodrama all extend different ways of seeing, thinking about, and feeling about gay life and its possibilities.

The start of the decade featured cinematic material that either offered figurative stand-ins for current gay issues, as with the Native Americans and frontiersmen of *Loon*, or films about contemporary "member types," such as the patrons of the Blue Jay bar, dealing with difficult everyday questions about secrecy, shame, and ghettoization. These films articulated the concerns of "a gay people" but did so by focusing on how various social contexts may contribute to group oppression or liberation. To the contrary, *Natural Thing* shifts the focus away from figurative models or representational member types, repositioning these characterizations so they function less as part of a social context and more as tools of psychological impact; David's encounter with gay life repeatedly brings him back to questions about the self and individual fate within an aspirational and overwhelmingly heterosexualized society. A growing marketplace for American independent films that emphasized individual, psychologistic perspectives over social and collective ones would become dominant in gay movies over the course of the rest of the decade and into the 1980s, with films such as *Saturday Night at the Baths* (David Buckley, 1975) and *Making Love* (Arthur Hiller, 1982) fashioning versions of gay life that position it as something that may stimulate or work against individualist aspirations. In these films, the sense of gay life as the context in which male-desiring men live, come together, and come into being as a people begins to drop out. However, another corner of cinema, theatrical gay hard-core, contained other possibilities for sustaining stories about gay life that, even when focused on questions of individual pleasure, often kept another eye on questions of social context and the collective possibilities of participation in gay life.

FOUR

Liberation Porn

In the late 1970s male-desiring men in the US congregated in theaters large and small, urban, suburban and rural, taking in the following sequence:

On a bright sunny day near Times Square, Clifford (Tony Rusca) makes his way down the sidewalk to his room at the Howard Johnson's motor lodge. Inside sits a coffee table littered with empty coffee cups, food wrappers, overflowing ashtrays, and a half-finished bottle of tequila, signaling a youthful hard-and-fast life. Clifford stretches out languidly on a plush brown couch as the camera pans over his stocky legs and svelte-yet-defined upper body: unadorned flesh and muscle interrupted only by the black jockey briefs that accentuate the bulge of his cock. What next? Stripping? Stroking? The introduction of a second man to the scene?

None of these. Instead, the young man exclaims to himself, "Well, Cliff, it's time to do what you gotta do," before picking up the phone and asking the operator to place a long distance call to his mother, Lucille of Gross Point, Michigan.

Close-ups of Rusca's face, giving detail to his performance of Clifford's stifled and downtrodden affect, cue us to recognize the gravity of this particular moment; these shots are cut together with medium shots that invite appreciation of his body, imbuing the moment with a strange mixture of erotic charge and dramatic tension. Lucille answers and the following conversation ensues.

Lucille: Clifford, is it actually you?

Clifford: Yes, Mother. It's me.

Lucille: I'm frantic!

Clifford: I know you are, but I'm fine, really.

Lucille: Where on earth are you, Canada?

Clifford: No, not Canada, New York City.

Lucille: The army!

Clifford: They called, huh?

Lucille: [irritated] At 7:30 a.m. . . . They called me twice. It must be serious.

Clifford: Yeah, I know being AWOL for eight weeks is serious, I know that. So how have you been?

Lucille: [adamant] Clifford, there is no point in trying to change the subject. I found your enlistment perverse, but this is even more so. You're hardly the fugitive kind . . . Don't you think we're entitled to know what made you do it?

Clifford: Well, it's difficult to explain . . .

Lucille: I want to know what happened.

Clifford: You really mean that? [Weighing it] I mean, I'll tell you.

Lucille: [getting sick of beating around the bush] Clifford!

Clifford: . . . First of all, you can tell Kathy our engagement is off.

Lucille: [relieved] Good. I find Kathy as stimulating as a bowl of oatmeal.

Clifford: . . . Listen to me. If I would have stayed in the army for one more night I would have turned gay. I ran away to save myself from myself.

Lucille: [exasperated] Clifford, that is truly bullshit.

Clifford: What are you calling bullshit?

Lucille: If you want to come out, I believe it's called, come out! Frankly, I'm relieved. I thought you'd become a Moonie.

Clifford: OK, specifically, these two MPs . . . how should I put it? Well, they got on my case. Kept inviting me out. Buying me beers. Saying things. I knew what they wanted. I didn't know what I wanted. So I ran away.

Lucille: Don't get too anguished about it, Clifford.

Clifford: [surprised, hopeful] Really?

Lucille: I think you should come out.

Clifford: [still surprised] You do?

Lucille: [assuredly] Definitely! Where's your spirit of adventure?

Clifford: [thankful] Well, I guess the truth is that I really wanted to, but something kept on stopping me.

Lucille: God knows, Clifford, it wasn't your upbringing. Be yourself, my dear, and in any case, please clear things up with the army.

Clifford: [distracted by knocking at the door]. I'll call you back?

Lucille: Promise.

Clifford: Yes, bye [Hangs up phone and gets up to answer door].

At the door stands two brawny, bearded military police in tight-fitting uniforms with helmets, aviator glasses, and black boots. Of course, it doesn't take long for most of this apparel to come off (save for some boots and a helmet), for the prog-rock soundtrack of artist Moose 100 to kick in, and for the stroking, kissing, licking, sucking, fucking, and coming to commence. Concluding this sequence from *Sex Magic* (Jack Deveau, 1977), the three men leave together. Having surpassed the formalities of their military roles and romantically and sexually consummated their relationship as a happy threesome, they walk out the door, ecstatic as they move toward a new future of outness, ease, and, surely, more sex.

All porn tells stories. Even what might seem to be a straightforward come shot is still narrative. As Richard Dyer puts it, "the desire that drives the porn narrative forward is the desire to come, to have an orgasm."[1] Yet, as *Sex Magic* demonstrates, feature-length hard-core porn stories can weave together sexual action with narrative elements that go beyond the sexual. Clifford's desire, his mother's care, the horny military police, the coming out and the coming: all of these elements exist together here as part of one story, a story that would have been impossible to accommodate in the nonpornographic movies of the 1970s (or of today) due to censorship and regulation. In the era of gay liberation and gay consciousness-raising, US gay porn makers created movies not only to turn audiences on but tune them in to the possibilities of gay liberation. While this was not the case with all gay porn of the period, scores of popular porn films provided male-desiring men with pedagogical maps and models with which to test out and experiment as they actualized their own expressions of male-male desire.[2]

Such a contention might seem preposterous, given the overt silliness of much porn plotting. However, if we look at story in porn as *merely* an empty pretext for sexual action, meant only to stimulate a viewer, we miss the way these stories function as mediations and fantasies about how life could be experienced. In the case of *Sex Magic*, for example, hooking up with the military police who arrive to arrest you is, on the face of it, ludicrous; but refusing this literalist reduction might alert us to the fact that the film is a fantastical elaboration of the reality that the military, as Allan Bérubé has shown us, has long been a context in which men have actualized male-male desire, and that this has indeed been shaped, and perhaps even generated, by the complex role and power exchanges at play within military hierarchies.[3]

Fantasy is also rarely, if ever, *merely* fantasy, but carries a utopian emphasis on possibility. Even if it is unlikely that I would cross paths with the kind of queer friendly tender-yet-tough paragons of military-culture masculinity conjured by *Sex Magic*, this does not mean that this scenario does not leave me with a sense of possibility that has meaning in the actual world. The utopian perspective of much gay porn carries a special meaning for male-desiring men who have lived and live with the (at times violent) prohibition and regulation of male-male sociosexual activity. Gay hard-core's plentitude of exciting, unlikely events echoes for male-desiring men that powerful experience that marks so many of our histories; the learned knowledge that a desire so many of us were told and are still told is impossible to actualize without punishment can in fact be actualized, lived, felt and expressed. Even the most unlikely of porn stories may carry a special affective power in echoing, often hyperbolically, the breach of this divide between the impossible and possible, and can *move* audiences—bodily, emotionally, mentally—towards the actualization of their desires through the invitation to do the important work of *imagining* such desires realized. In fact, it is this very propensity towards the hyperbolic that allows for erotically playful and comic elements to lightly open consideration of more serious, urgent concerns.

Looking at a cycle of films released between the late 1960s and the late 1970s, this chapter explores how a certain kind of porn, here referred to as liberation porn, was informed by particular currents of gay liberationist philosophy. It closely considers how utopian approaches to sociosexual experiences were central to the narrative and spatial elaboration of this body of work. Liberation porn operated in part as a world-making project that mediated and modeled ideas about and possibilities for living aimed at the large audiences of male-desiring men assembled in the booming 1970s porn theater circuit. It was a moment in porn history when genre and generic play, in line with the tradition of camp, were used to tease at the boundaries between fantasy and actuality in such a way that would alert viewers to the sensitivities of their own life experience, and to do so in the company of others.

Regardless, critics writing about porn have tended to assume that elements of plot and narrative are included for the sole purpose of sexual arousal. Daniel Harris makes this case in "The Evolution of Gay Porn," arguing that, with the loosening of censorship laws in the late 1960s and early 1970s, "plot quickly became essential to the misguided psychology of arousal basic to these films, which were premised on the naive assumption that the audience would become more excited if the sex scenes were staggered throughout the movie."[4] Regardless of how foregrounded or detailed the story may be in any given example of

1970s gay porn, the idea is that it is ultimately only present as a means to build anticipation for the sexual action.

As we have already seen, 1970s gay hard-core porn was as deeply interested in the narrative possibilities of sex as a social, cultural, and political phenomenon as it was in making explicit sex visible. Explicit sexual visuality, however, was not separate from other forms of visibility. Notions of gay visibility worked in tandem with and could be advanced through a hard-core register of what Linda Williams has termed "maximum visibility": specific formal elements such as bright "clinical" lighting, close-ups on genitalia and penetrative action, and, crucially, the visual, aural, and temporal attention given over to the come shot.[5] In many cases, in fact, these films did not minimize narrative development but instead found in the episodic structure of hard-core a means of elaborating the sociosexual dynamics of consciousness-raising.

In this, they perhaps fulfill some of the promise of "the utopian dream of the cinematic merger of the erotic and hard-core—an eros that could include graphic sex as well as a pornography that might encompass the erotic" that Williams describes in *Screening Sex*. Many of these films were in fact intensely formally ambitious in their elaborations of eros and its potential in the lives and fantasies of gay men, displaying the "subtle effects of line, color, light" that characterize, for Williams, what she calls "hard-core eroticism."[6]

The relationship between hard-core porn as industry, cinematic mode, and gay representation was far from straightforward. Gay cinema took up hard-core in a variety of complex ways, developing versions of hard-core sex within stylistic registers as diverse as the avant-garde (*Boys in the Sand* [Wakefield Poole, 1971], *L.A. Plays Itself* [Fred Halsted, 1972], *American Cream* [Rob Simple, 1972], *Sex Magic,* [Jack Deveau, 1977]), documentary (*Encounter* [Peter de Rome, 1971], *Erotikus* [Tom DeSimone, 1973], *The Boys from Riverside Drive* [Deveau, 1977]), melodrama (*Two Way Drift* [Pat Rocco, 1975], *Adam and Yves* [de Rome, 1974], *Kiss Today Goodbye* [Francis Ellie, 1976], *Navy Blue* [Ellie, 1979]), and the road film (*Drive* [Deveau, 1974], *Ballet Down the Highway* [Deveau, 1975], *Kansas City Trucking Co.* [Joe Gage, 1976]).

There is at the same time a surprising amount of continuity among the great majority of these films on two levels: (1) their dedication to establishing gay porn as a form of storytelling that sustains many of the features of underground and proto-gay short films and (2) their use of the feature-length format to posit stories about the experience of gay liberation, particularly within mass-oriented models of gay world-making. To offer one characteristic example of how the uniting

'Hot Rocco' coming

Pat Rocco told a SPREE meeting May 12 that he has made his first "hot" films.

They will be shown at the Park Theatre in a program called "Sex and the Single Gay," opening June 17, he said.

"Continental Theatres, which releases my films, challenged me to make a so-called 'hot' film that would still have a tight story line and be in good taste," Rocco said.

"We think we've done this."

FIGURE 31 Pat Rocco rises to the challenge of making "hot" films. Article, "'Hot Rocco' Coming," *The Advocate* (June 10–23, 1970). Image courtesy of the Hall-Carpenter Archives at the London School of Economics. Used with permission.

of these elements operated, a newspaper blurb (fig. 31) reporting Pat Rocco's crossover into hard-core is particularly telling.

Highlighting the desire to maintain continuity with the conventions of gay cinema up to this point while also incorporating the see-it-all allure of hard-core, the blurb promises "Sex and the Single Gay" (1970) as a program of "hot" films with "tight story line[s] and good taste." The announcement of this program at the SPREE film society maintains continuity with Rocco's established role in producing gay cinema of sociocultural import. The framing of the program suggests a familiarity and accessibility: socializing camp witticism is present in both the title, a send-up of the popular Hollywood film *Sex and the Single Girl* (Richard Quine, 1964), and the newsletter's own announcement of "'Hot Rocco' coming." Rocco himself asserts a collective, progressive narrative: this marriage of hot and tasteful elements is something "we've done."

Social solidarity, hard-cord sex, and the promise of a good story are not only parts of this advertising pitch, but are the very elements that constitute gay hard-core porn as a distinct cycle. As "hot" films with "good" stories, they take up a rhetoric of visibility—socially, sexually, and politically—not just to represent gay men and gay sex, but as a means of making gay liberatory movement legible; to impress upon the viewer a feeling for the movement of gay collective action through the careful organization of visual and aural elements. Before looking at exactly how this operates in the case studies that comprise this chapter, it will prove helpful to consider this trope across 1970s gay hard-core features as a whole.

The standard form that this takes is through the situating of gay consciousness-raising—as a social process—in a mutually enabling relationship with hard-core maximum visibility. In particular this plays out through a hard-core syntax of episodic, yet incremental, accumulating sex acts—of various positions, styles, and types—as these films rise progressively through the peaks of each new sexual encounter and the successive come shots that suggest their completion. As a tool of both affective and narrative elucidation, this syntax is extended over the length of the film so that affect and narrative promote each other as a means of advancing particular kinds of movement between formations such as public and private, individual and collective, and aloneness and togetherness.

This is achieved primarily by the way in which sexual encounters between men are spatialized through an inside/outside dialectic whereby a protagonist undergoes a transformation that is made legible though his movement between specific kinds of public, semipublic, and private spaces and how his sociosexual engagement with these places is central to the film's overall narrative momentum.

The particular terms of this pattern can be summarized as follows:

1. Being Public: The protagonist is established as existing within the public sphere, typically one that is iconographically American, often urban (New York city skyline, city streets, public monuments) or rural (the highway, the farm, the desert).
2. Encountering Gay Space: After establishing that the protagonist desires other men (often through making the viewer privy to the protagonist's fantasies), the protagonist has an encounter with another man, typically within the interior confines of an apartment, sex club bathroom, or movie theater, through which he becomes more knowledgeable, or helps someone else become more knowl-

edgeable, about the conventions of these spaces. This space is also sometimes encountered in a vision or dream.

3. Making/Sustaining Contact: The protagonist sustains contact with the men he meets, and/or seeks out further contact with new men. This often results in a predominance of phone-call sequences, where further meetings or new meetings are sought and/or arranged.
4. Togetherness: The protagonist goes back or in to a new interior space (or if he has never left the space, as is common with the movie theater or sex club plot, further in to unexplored areas) for another round, and finds himself in an orgy or consummating his desire for another man that he has longed for. This is often followed by the protagonist leaving the interior space and reentering the wider public sphere.[7]

This pattern is far from simple; there is a great deal of variability in how it is executed through the textual, extratextual, and contextual factors through which it is carried out. In liberation porn the orchestration of sexual episodes and the articulation of social movement reinforce each other.

As is evident in the above schematic, liberation porn is a deeply spatialized cinema. Yet, it is essential to keep in mind that these films' construction of space was often interwoven with the spatiality of the porn theaters and sex clubs in which they screened. In his pioneering work on the architecture of gay porn theaters, José Capino has illuminated how the on-screen spaces of gay porn echo that of porn theater design, extending an "invitation to perform the cinematic text" within the space of the theater.[8] Describing Chicago's Bijou Theater (1970–2015), Capino explains that "the spare illumination and the labyrinthine layout evoke a cinematic and liminal space consisting of a multitude of cruising environments: dark alleys, gay bars, corridors of the YMCA, public restrooms, piers and baths."[9]

In the experience of liberation porn, the narrative spaces of the film and the sociosexual spaces of the movie theater mesh to create an experience in which the lines between the action pictured in cinematic space and the actions engaged in actual space may have a homologous relationship. Just as the spaces of porn cinemas and sex clubs were (and sometimes still are) designed and essentially cinematized through the application of techniques strongly tied to filmic mise-en-scène (modulated lighting; predetermined set pathways that facilitate, support, and accentuate specific patterns of bodily movement and gesture), the films themselves echoed and reinforced the sociosexual activity occurring within these spaces. Moving forward, it is important to keep in mind, particularly as you look at the film posters and advertisements featured in this chapter, that liberation porn was marketed and elaborated as an invitation not only to watch stories resonant with one's desires, but also to actualize the desires pictured on the movie screens as part of the very process of patron participation in the sociosexual space of the porn theater. On screen and off, liberation porn sponsored a world were anticipation and actualization grew, from one seat to the next, ever closer.

Anticipatory Genres, Sociosexual Utopias: *Boys in the Sand* and *L.A. Plays Itself/Sex Garage*

As a way of establishing gay-resonant stories, gay hard-core features were not only constructed around the question of what would happen in the film's resolution and whether or not one would or could end up happy *and* gay, but also sought to create a sense of hope and anticipation around a broad range of questions to do with self (and sometimes group) fulfillment among male-desiring men. Thus, in the porn melodrama *Navy Blue*, two sailors (George Payne and Jack Wrangler), who each assume the other is straight, struggle to reveal their hidden love for one another over the course of one Christmas Eve day when they are docked in New York City. Complete with conventional melodrama underscoring, using classical songs such as "Three Frescos: II. Adagio" by Bohuslav Martinů and repurposing soundtrack scoring by Max Steiner from *The Caine Mutiny* (Edward Dmytryk, 1954), *Navy Blue* is a wistful film filled with internal monologues where the characters muse over unrequited longing and fear of coming out to one another. Bringing porn and melodrama into generic alignment, the film concludes with the sailors confessing their love to one another, fucking, and ending up tragically separated as they are redeployed to different locations. True to classic melodrama form, the couple almost makes it, but still falls victim to the hands of fate. Yet, to place male-male desire within such a popular idiom as the melodrama is to assert that this desire is deserving of both the spectacle and specificity of life as it is presented in popular movie form.

There are many other examples of such pairings between porn and other genres within gay hard-core features: notable examples include the porn-western *Dust unto Dust*, which featured songs from the soundtrack to *How the West Was Won* (John Ford/Henry Hathaway/George Marshall, 1962), historically informed costume design, and on-location desert shooting; the porn-comedy *Casey* (Donald Crane, 1971), in which a young hip blond (Cal Culver) is stalked by his critical Aunt Wanda (played by Culver in drag), who coaches him on how to make a better life for himself as a self-hating gay man (the film even boasted an original Simon and Garfunkel–style folk-rock song, "Casey," that closes out the film with the repeated lyric "Casey blew it"); and Peter de Rome's Poe-inspired porn-horror *The Destroying Angel* (1976), in which a young Catholic priest's ambivalent exploration of the possibilities of gay life results in a psychic split, producing an evil doppelganger.

These films use genre to generate questions about what liberated gay life should be and where it might take male-desiring men in a popular, accessible form, and in so doing express a range of philosophies as multifarious as gay liberation discourses themselves were, particularly in the first half of the decade. However, by the fall of 1969, when gay liberation groups began formally organizing and putting their philosophies into writing, consciousness-raising underpinned the sociopolitical and psychological progress the movement advocated for.

Over the decade, gay liberation assembled participants—including casual participants, picking up gay lib thought from the gay press—through processes of political and philosophical questioning that were utopian in bent. That is, as a movement geared toward not only a better life for gay people, but a world significantly altered by challenging the dominance of heterosexist ideology, gay liberation thought proposed processes to initiate new forms of living. This utopian impetus to create a world defined by equality, love, and freedom informed the practice of early gay liberation groups including the Gay Liberation Front, Gay Activists Alliance, and the Effeminists. Yet, having a clear answer to the question of what these new forms of living would look like was not a defining feature of liberationist discourse during this period. Take, for instance, the following propositions, the first printed as part of a pamphlet by the group Gay Flames, the second from an essay titled "The Politics of My Sex Life" by Mike Silverstein, and the third taken from the Gay Revolution Party Manifesto:

> Isn't the next big step in your liberation, now that you're open about being identified as a homosexual, to say you want make it with whoever you are attracted to, to kiss guys you feel like kissing?[10]

> All of this [gay liberation] is a hope for the future. Now there is no utopian farm, no army of lovers. There's just me sitting by myself at a typewriter, and occasionally flashing on real hope. . . . A lot of us in gay liberation understand this situation,

understand where we're at, how we got there, and what we need to do next, but we don't know what the next step is.[11]

Gay is a process of attaining mutual and equal social and sensual relationships among all human beings, which is realized only through participation in the free dynamic expression of love among people of the same-sex.[12]

Underscoring each of these statements is the sense that overt participation in gay activity is not an end point in itself, but the beginning of a process charged with a sense of anticipation. These passages share in a rhetoric that positions an emotionally enticing sense of large-scale change ("the next *big* step," "*all* of this is a hope for the future," "*all* human beings") as the product of gay sociosexual elaboration taken up on a mass scale ("kissing *whoever* you are attracted to," figuring out with "the *lot of us*" in gay liberation "what the next step is," and enacting "love among *people of the same-sex*").

Building on C. L. R James's notion of "a future in the present," José Esteban Muñoz describes this set of relations as part of a performance of "queer citizenship" that brings participants into a shared context of action-oriented hope. Muñoz argues this results in "an anticipatory illumination of a queer world" that offers "a sign of an actually existing queer reality, a kernel of political possibility within a stultifying heterosexual present."[13] Feature-length 1970s gay porn seized its unique opportunity—as the *only* corner of US film culture pushing forward into the explicit representation of male-male desire—to invite the audience to identify with and take pleasure in stories that imagined other worlds; worlds in which gay life could appear revealed and transformed within the same popular genre forms normatively constructed to naturalize heterosexuality and present it as the only appropriate mode of relationship formation.

Gay porn features utilized popular genre forms to bring legibility to a combination of gay worlds both possible and fantastical (although sometimes only seemingly so). Across these films, a sense of anticipation for a life out of sync with the "stultifying heterosexual present" was amplified by the way in which they positioned hard-core's utopian structure to work in concert with and advance affectively charged, illuminating stories about characters participating in the politics and philosophy of gay life, even if not directly referenced as such. The affective force of these stories gathered much of their emotional and erotic traction from how each one went about positioning generic figurations of romance in relation to gay hard-core's linear narratives, which stress access to and accumulation of sexual experience, stretching wholly beyond the domain of single-partner and monogamous relations, and increasingly so as the film carries on. As Richard Dyer puts it, a "predominant" trope of gay cultural production is the "utopian reconciliation of the desire for romance and promiscuity, security and freedom, making love *and* having sex."[14] From the point where gay hard-core came into being around 1970, popular genre forms offered a way, in effect, to ground gay experience within familiar forms of characterization and plot conflict.

The first gay hard-core films—films structured around uncensored penetrative sex—began screening in movies theaters in cities such as San Francisco, Los Angeles, New York, and Chicago. Featuring many of the elements that would come to define the genre, films such as *The Collector* (Tim DeSimone, 1970), *Casey*, and *Boys in the Sand* all followed a similar pattern. An hour to an hour and half in length, these films were structured around sexual vignettes, with a protagonist or protagonists moving through a series of solo scenes (or brief solo sequences) and coupled sex scenes before (typically) reaching a final group sex sequence. During this transitional phase, some of the scenes in these films featured come shots, though this had not yet settled into the standardized practice that it would within a few years' time. Out of this first relatively small cluster of films came the first gay porn "hits," the Fire Island set *Boys in the Sand* and Halsted's diptych *L.A. Plays Itself/Sex Garage* (the two were designed to play together). While these films were not hits of the same kind (Poole's film was a notable box-office success, while Halsted's film garnered a good deal of critical attention and reception as an art-porn film), they were each landmark films that ushered porn into significantly wider reception contexts and emboldened other actors, producers, and directors to contribute to the formation of the gay porn industry proper as it coalesced in the early to mid-1970s.[15]

Boys in the Sand and *L.A. Plays Itself/Sex Garage* both straddle art film, hard-core, and popular narrative filmmaking. As both of these films were taken up as labor-of-love productions without financial backing from any sector of the film industry, Poole and Halsted had the freedom to develop the kind of sex films they wanted, provided they could avoid censorship.[16] Both filmmakers moved beyond what they saw as stock presentations of sex dominating the porn market at the time. In contrast, they sought to bring together an increased attention to visual and aural aesthetics, storytelling elements, and character/star persona development, envisioning a porn industry that sought to dissolve many of the distinctions between pornographic and nonpornographic modes of filmmaking.

It turned out that there was genuine demand for movies of this sort. Each film drew large audiences in their opening cities. *Boys* opened at the 55th Street Playhouse in New York on December 29, 1971, and *L.A./Sex Garage* opened at theaters in Los Angeles in 1972. Shortly following release, each filmmaker had begun production on a second feature-length film (*Bijou* [Poole, 1972] and *Sextool* [Halsted, 1975]), been reviewed and interviewed by both the mainstream and gay press, and launched their leading men (Cal Culver/Casey Donovan and Fred Halsted) as the first widely publicized, industrially supported gay movie stars. At the start of the decade, there were no production companies set up exclusively to make gay porn features. By 1973, there were at least eight companies making films for the growing national marketplace of audiences seeking to view feature-length gay porn in traditional movie theater environments (as opposed to watching porn loops in compartmentalized peep shows or small storefront movie arcade spaces).[17] Older, soft-core and sexploitation companies, such as Shan Sayle's Los Angeles–based Signature Films, were also switching over to gay hard-core features.

Boys in the Sand and *L.A. Plays Itself/Sex Garage* established liberation porn as a new mode of gay cinema. These films wanted audiences to anticipate and participate in actions against the grain of the "stultifying heterosexual present," and as such had very different concerns and outcomes than their straight hard-core counterparts. Liberation porn was utopian in that it sought new futures, but might also, depending on a viewer's degree of participation in 1970s gay life, exist somewhere along a continuum of imagination and actualization, offering trial utopias to be experimented with.

These films exemplify liberation porn's investment in bridging the divide between the cinematic and the everyday. They mesh elements culled from a multitude of recognizable film and storytelling conventions into something like what Aaron Betsky has called "queer space." Queer space is a kind of space that, "rather than allowing you to live in the fiction of established structures . . . proposes a world of fantasy that is directly related to the body and has no definite space."[18] In very different ways, each of these films offers utopian interventions in gay life that fray at the boundaries between the fantastical and the possible, the prohibited and permissible.

Boys in the Sand

The Fire Island–set *Boys in the Sand*'s first segment, titled "Bayside," begins by following a man in his early to mid-twenties (Peter Fisk) through a winding boardwalk path to the ocean. After he strips naked and sits pensively on the isolated beach, the film transitions swiftly into a magic realist mode, as a double exposure brings into being a tall, blond-haired Californian golden boy (Casey Donovan) out on the distant horizon, slowly emerging from the water and making his way to the man on the beach.[19] What ensues is a reciprocal sexual exchange, as they trade off and engage in kissing, sensual touching, blow jobs, fucking, and coming on each other. Throughout, their sex is visually and aurally tempered by a number of filmic techniques: shadows of leaves strewn across the surface of the men's bodies, direct shots of the sun that result in sun flares pulsing across the screen, and a haunting score that carefully punctuates shifts in bodily rhythm and sexual acts with Pierre Boulez's "Nocturnes: 1. Nuages." The scene concludes with the men switching places as a medium shot shows Donovan taking a place on the beach while Fisk walks into the ocean and disappears into thin air.

Donovan becomes the film's protagonist in succeeding segments that work to expand gay life via magic realist conventions. "Poolside" begins with Donovan reading the newspaper "GAY" in front of the Fire Island post office. Noting an ad for a magical tablet in the paper, Donovan returns to his vacation house, fills out the mail-order form (in this case a male-order), and sends it off. At the pool, he throws the tablet into the water, and it produces a cloud of smoke, revealing a brawny guy with whom Donovan has more reciprocal sex, the two ending up cuddling, kissing, and horsing around on a float in the pool. In the final segment of the film, "Inside," Donovan is shown alone inside his home, watching a muscular African American telephone repairman (Tommy Moore) working on a pole outside of his window. He penetrates his ass with a dildo while fantasizing about having sex with Moore, before Moore appears to enter the home for real and engage in a long session of lightly aggressive sex with Donovan. At the film's end, Moore appears at the front door, and we are left to wonder whether the whole escapade has really happened or was just a figment of Donovan's imagination.

While the film does not conclude with group sex, as would soon be standard practice in much gay porn, it does work within a logic of aggregation, showing Donovan attaining multiple partners and multiple kinds of sexual engagement over the course of the film, from the tender and romantic to the rough and S/M-tinged. The oscillation between getting the fantasy one wants and being disoriented and potentially overwhelmed by new heights of sexual arousal is both a key part of the narrative organization of the film as well as central to its elaboration of a utopian perspective. The first two segments of the film establish this along straight-forward lines, suggesting (1) that putting one's self in a context for gay sex (nude on a Fire Island beach) may help to facilitate it and that (2) taking action to get a man, even if one is not sure what kind of man this will bring, may result in gay sex and romantic coupling. The musical score situates these processes as future oriented, with several songs culled from the 1969 space-themed symphonic prog-rock album *Astro-Sounds from Beyond the Year 2000* by the 101 Strings Orchestra.

Whereas the first two sequences—organized around the breaking down of inside/outside distinctions to construct a world in which equivalence, reciprocity, and exchange drive the action—are shot in exteriors, the final sequence constructs tensions around the question of whether the film's golden boy fantasist can gain sexual access to a working-class black man and bring his world "Inside." This vision of utopia rests on black participation as a generative force for a particular vision of gay life.

As noted in Linda Williams's reading of the film, the positioning of Moore as Donovan's fantasy object troubles any reading of the segment as simply inclusionary.[20] Multiple elements position Moore as a heavily exoticized Other who inhabits and magically invokes in the white protagonist a potent, all-absorbing eroticism, most prominently the use of the sitar music of Ravi Shankar—which was enjoying popularity in the US in the late 1960s and early 1970s—invoking the "Far East" as way to imbue the scene with a sense of mysticism. Moore's exoticism is constructed through a series of oppositions. Donovan, tied to leisure and the domestic, wanders the interior, aimlessly gazing out the window. Moore, tied to physical labor and the outdoors, undertakes repair work. Donovan, tied to a bourgeois preppie aesthetic, is clean-shaven. Moore has a Zapatista moustache (linking him to revolutionary aesthetics).[21] However, this vision of race is not only a symptom of a generalized white racist perspective: it also functions to emblematize cross-race sexual contact, and black-white interracial coupling in particular, as an experience meant to reinforce gay power via a connection to paradigms of Black Power, militancy, and revolutionary activity circulating in the early 1970s. The utopian figuration of cross-race sexual contact in "Inside" will be better understood after considering gay hard-core—and gay liberation—in relation to Black Power.

The connections between the gay liberation and Black Power movements have long been neglected in scholarship on the history of social movements. Both formed during the mid- to late 1960s in response to state violence, harassment, and discrimination. By the summer of 1969, following the momentum of political activity generated in the wake of the Stonewall riots, "gay power"—directly adapted from the term "Black Power"—was used by gay activists to call for militant gay action. "Gay is good" was fashioned from the affirmative slogan "black is beautiful." The political and rhetorical connections between these movements were outlined by Carl Whitman in his 1969 *A Gay Manifesto,* wherein he states, "In the past year there has been an awakening of gay liberation ideas and energy. How it began we don't know; maybe we were inspired by black people and their freedom movement; we learned how to stop pretending from the hip revolution. Amerika in all its ugliness has surfaced with our war and our leaders. And we are revulsed at the quality of our ghetto life."[22]

However, there was little direct interaction between these two sociopolitical formations, at least in part due to the prevalence of deeply and emphatically stated homophobic beliefs among a number of prominent Black Panther Party members.[23] Yet collaboration ensued during an extremely vital, though unfortunately brief, period from 1969 to 1970. In August 1969, the New York Gay Liberation Front declared support for the Panthers. This was followed by the founding of the group Third World Gay Revolution for people of color.[24] Black Panther cofounder Huey Newton gave a speech in August 1970—circulated in both Black Panther and gay liberation print media—titled "A Letter from Huey Newton to the Revolutionary Brothers and Sisters about the Women's Liberation and Gay Liberation Movements." In this powerful counter to homophobic ideology, Newton not only insisted that homosexuals be included in the revolutionary action of the group, but also suggested that "maybe a homosexual could be the most revolutionary."[25] Hundreds of LGBTQ+ people from across the US joined the Black Panthers for the Revolutionary Peoples' Constitutional Convention in Philadelphia, held September 5–7. The opening session of the convention began with hundreds chanting in unison "Gay, gay power to the gay, gay people! Black, black power to the black, black people! Power to the people!"[26]

While this alliance was short-lived, it nonetheless "spark[ed] excitement within gay liberation," as noted by historian Emily K. Hobson, and augmented the coalescence of "multiracial" gay group organization.[27] At the same time, the intensity and persistence of homophobia among some Panthers was not something that could be integrated with gay life. Especially problematic was a subset of the Panthers who promulgated a version of Marxist philosophy whereby homosexuality was understood as a symptom of the white bourgeois lifestyle. Conflating homosexuality with male femininity (or "effeminacy"), this philosophy buttressed an image of powerful, "authentic" black masculinity that was, in part, reified by stereotyping the white gay male as weak and feminine by contrast. According to Ronald K. Porter, Eldridge Cleaver, the party's minster of information, promoted the idea that "the black homosexual is a being whose masculinity has been destroyed and his manhood has been 'castrated' by the white man."[28]

The first gay hard-core features were produced in the wake of this negotiation between gay liberation and Black Power movements, and several films throughout the decade made suggestive use of figures of Black Power. The first Casey Donovan film, *Casey* (1971), is about the young blond's tireless search for ideal love and sexual gratification. It concludes with a scene in which a black revolutionary enters an all-white orgy and takes over, instructing the men on looser, more "loving," and affirmative styles of sex. As it becomes evident that Casey is still hung up on specific sex acts (his repeated cries of "fuck me" and "I want to suck you" are emphasized via echoing reverberation effects), the revolutionary convinces the men to run off with him and abandon Casey, left alone and naked on the floor in sexual desperation. The lesson: endless desire is a turn-off if it cannot be properly modulated by the consciousness of cool performance styles, here rendered as confrontational black agency countering gay white sexual compulsion. The film both reinforces the notion of the weak, white middle-class homosexual while, at the same time, suggesting a revolutionary black machismo that is erotically freer and less hung up. The result is a film that sexualizes black-on-white homophobia just as it paradoxically positions revolutionary black masculinity as the antidote to white gay weakness.

Several other early hard-core features are organized around images of black male sexuality that merge fetishistic, objectifying white-centered perspectives of the black male body with displays of black pleasure unmoored from the maintenance of macho, phallocentric idealizations of black manhood. In *The Night Before* (Arch Brown, 1973), for instance, a smooth, white surfer-type uses a large black dildo while he fantasizes about a black man engaging an orgy of men in a panoply of positions with little adherence to standardized roles of giving/receiving. *Adam and Yves* (Peter de Rome, 1974) envisions a utopian space in which black film culture and nonnormative sexual expression come together, as scores of men are shown moving to downstairs bathrooms at the movie house where a blaxploitation film screens and engaging in an orgy. In *A Night at the Adonis* (Jack Deveau, 1978), we see an orgy scene in a bathroom at the titular New York gay porn theater, a complex for viewing films, socializing, and having sex. Although the theater is shown to have a diverse audience (with respect to race, ethnicity, class, and age), the film makes a black man the agent of more radical forms of sexual practice; while white men pair up and move rather mechanically through hard-core sexual numbers, he moves between many partners, ending up in various dexterous positions (leaning back into a wall, lowering himself to the floor over another man). While, at one level, these films reduce black male sexual pleasure to an object of white male fantasy, the films also foreground a version of black sexual performance that is unhindered by heteromasculinist norms.

Scenes set in movie theater bathrooms are a vital reminder that porn theaters did (and still do, though there are far fewer of them) offer opportunities for cross-racial contact, as detailed by Samuel R. Delany in his study of porn theater–going in New York between theaters' height in the 1970s and their severe decline and erasure through antisex zoning laws and redevelopment practices in the 1990s. As such, it is necessary to keep in mind that, despite their objectifying, fetishizing moments, these films may not have been seen and enjoyed exclusively by white patrons. As Jennifer Nash reminds us in her critical history of race and pornography, *The Black Body in Ecstasy*, it is necessary not only to read "against the grain" of films that have problematic constructions of blackness, but also, in a reparative spirit, to examine "the multiple ways that the pornographic screen can also pleasure black spectators."[29]

The cinematic elaboration of cross-racial contact in "Inside" is in part a question of the formal composition of shot types and bodily performance. It is also informed by spatial practices facilitated by the architecture of gay sex spaces such as movie theaters, bathhouses, and sex clubs more generally (all spaces where this film has been shown, and continues to show, from time to time). Accordingly, the film's narrative orchestration and *spatialization* of sexual action has a homologous relationship to the forms of contact fostered in such spaces. In this regard, the film also brings to the fore forms of contact made possible within the expanding contexts of gay life of the period (including the context, Fire Island, which brought Donovan and Moore together the summer prior to filming).[30]

In particular, the spatiality of "Inside" features the same kind of architectural features, pathways of movements, and sites for action (including the actions of both looking and bodily contact) that structure the commercial gay sex sites of its exhibition. Within these spaces, multiple levels, pathways, openings, and thresholds between spaces (glory holes, interior "window" cut-outs, doorways, railings) make possible, or are constructed to be used for, a variety of forms of movement, encounter, contact, and visual and aural experience. Likewise, throughout "Inside" we see Donovan and Moore move through spaces that work for the erotic modulation of sexual looking and bodily contact. For example, architectural features such as small circular windows cut out on the wall in the bathroom allow for a quick survey of what's just outside on the boardwalk: a cushioned platform in the central space of the lower level that is open to view—like a stage—from all points (and from which Donovan is able to "see" Moore as he gazes from the mezzanine above).

Moments of the film both reinforce and push away from presenting Moore as objectified within this architecture. The film's depiction of Donovan fantasizing about Moore in various locations across the house is decidedly fetishistic in certain instances, most notably when he enacts the same trope utilized in *The Night Before* and inserts a black dildo while shown fantasizing alone. Conversely, not long after we first see Moore outside the house, Donovan succeeds at catching his attention by exhibiting himself naked and masturbating from a second-story window. The film cuts to shots from Moore's point of view, elaborating an interrelational experience of looking. Anticipating a dynamic that Joe Wlodarz observes in the video *O Happy Day* (Charles Lofton, 1996) (a film that inventively grapples with the historical intersection of gay power, Black Power, and porn in the 1970s), "Inside" relies on the exposition of "returned looks to emphasize the circuit of desire between subject and object and to trouble a distanced, apolitical fetishization of these images."[31]

Ultimately, "Inside" moves toward a vision of coupling that highlights the kinds of erotic reciprocity and polymorphous perversity emphasized in "Bayside" and "Poolside." Its mediation and performance of sex features very little focalization through any one character's point of view; instead, an almost constant use of two shots keeps both bodies equally in frame (fig. 32). Within these two shots, both bodies

FIGURE 32 One of the film's many two-shots that emphasizes mutuality, sensitivity, and responsiveness.

are shown as sensitive and responsive to each other and, while there is plenty of genital pleasure displayed, the film radically counters the figurative dichotomy of a phallocentric black masculinity in tension with gay white sexuality.

Taken together, *Boys in the Sand*'s three-part story of male-male desire and contact among the idyllic environs of Fire Island structures a utopian sense of anticipation through its spatialized characterization of desire and contact; it formulates space as central to the process of transforming individual experiences of desire into sociosexual interaction. It uses the hard-core mode to create a sense of anticipation for liberatory ways of being. Here, this liberation gains a socially inflected affective power from the way the narrative aligns magic realist shifts from fantasy to reality with the creation of new networks of contact. Whether in the form of public sex, a utopian vision of hardcore sexual acts resulting in a boundless spirit of play, affection, and romance, or the activation of cross-race, cross-class contact, the film affirms the sense that putting gay into action will result in an ever-expanding sphere of gay sociosexual potential, at times *imagining* toward the dissolution of boundaries between different subjectivities and social positions.

L.A. Plays Itself/Sex Garage

The film diptych *L.A. Plays Itself/Sex Garage* encompasses a kaleidoscopic variety of sexual encounters across numerous sites in Hollywood and the greater Los Angeles area. *L.A.*'s structure—made up of one gentle, reciprocal sex scene set in an idyllic wooded location near (and in) a waterfall and one rough S/M sex scene set in the interior of a home—has resulted in dystopian readings of the film that position the domestic scene as a sort of dark Sadeian rebuttal to the romantic pastoralism of the first.[32] Scholars and viewers alike have grappled with this distinct combination of pastoralism and urbanism, gentleness and violence. Richard Dyer's pioneering account considers the film in relation to underground filmmaking, seeing it as evidence of a shift toward masculinist sexuality.[33] William E. Jones reads it as an autobiographical film woven through with an account of early 1970s Hollywood street life and property development.[34] But perhaps the most valuable insight comes from David E. James, who refutes the idea that the film necessarily undermines pastoralism. As he puts it, *L.A. Plays Itself* allows "the city to play its own plural spatialities."[35]

Considering how the film as a whole emphasizes Los Angeles's "plural spatialities" (woods, streets, highways, house, auto repair shop) yields a more utopian reading. Rural, commercial, public, and domestic are brought into a dialectical relationship in which meaning is made through various pairings. The interspersed shots of highways and roads signal that all of these spaces are connected, less opposed sites than parts of an erotic mosaic, evoking the prevalent gay porn trope that Waugh has called the "erotic everywhere." This trope expresses an "appreciation for the nitty gritty of the familiar, grungy, or mundane . . . the banal environments of the locker room, the drinking place, the workplace and the contemporary urban street corner."[36]

Los Angeles is framed as a sort of tool of sexual facilitation in its own right; everyday Los Angeles here is a utopian place where "what if" fantasies are transformed into "where at" actualities. At the same time, the film's utopian image of gay life is a complex and ambivalent one, given the screen time each of these films devotes to images of rough, even potentially abusive, interactions at the intersection between sex and violence. In both the domestic sequence of *L.A.* and in the auto shop in *Sex Garage*, Halsted's lover, Joseph Yale, plays the submissive role, in the first case being tied up, whipped, kicked, and fisted by the much larger and more muscular Halsted and, in the second, being aggressively fucked by one larger man while he sucks the cock of another in a pair of women's panties. While in one sense these are "dark" scenes, made darker by the atmospheric use of low synthesizer drones bathed in space-echo effects, this does not bar them from contributing to the film's overall utopian perspective. If fact, these films are a good example of how utopian perspective, and even affirmation, do not necessarily have to privilege humanistic idealizations of goodness and pleasure that rely on the absence of pain or torment.

Engaging what might be called a minor negotiation of the utopian, in which dominant understandings of pain and pleasure are reinscribed within a logic of gay liberation, these films elaborate a highly sexualized version of Los Angeles that subordinates both assertions and relinquishings of male power to a logic of perverse pleasure that stands in contradiction to the capitalist, commercial logistics of everyday US life. This is a point made strongly in each film, as both are interjected with visual puns and juxtapositions via multiple signs, advertisements, and posters scattered around the city: for example, a Kentucky Fried Chicken sign that reads "finger lickin' good." While on one level this dialectical use of images works to make comedy out of how closely taglines and slogans may read as descriptions of sex acts, this material also works as part of the film's sexualization of everyone and everything.

This is a liberationist image of utopia because, as with nearly all other gay porn features of this period, its narrative momentum works through a logic of aggregation, in which a cumulative imaging of more sex, with more people, in more spaces works to offer models of sexual contact that can be, were, and are pursued by many male-desiring men. Sex can happen in the woods or at work, sex can involve radical performances of power and role, sex can bring numerous kinds of strangers into intimate relation, however brief or sustained. This perverse, perhaps even antihumanist, sexing of the world—perverse because it renders everything and everywhere in the name of sex, and antihumanist because it refuses to reproduce the roles on which notions of human dignity rely—poses a form of liberation through which the oppressed and ghettoized male-desiring man may claim, "this whole world is mine" and refashion it as tool for the application of his desire. Halsted's vision seems in line with the ideas of liberationist philosopher Guy Hocquenghem, who saw in transgressive, law-defying, and role-reversing acts of male-male desire a refusal of the heteropatriarchal dominance embedded in and extended through capitalist, commerce-oriented society: in particular, Hocquenghem's assertion that "the sexualization of the world heralded by the gay movement pushes capitalist decoding to the limit and corresponds to the dissolution of the human."[37]

In these Los Angeles "car culture" films, as William E. Jones describes them, vehicular movement becomes a homology that echoes cinema, with vectors of movement bringing spaces into correspondence.[38] The diptych's more transgressive performances of sex are part their own larger philosophical structure, which affirms finding correspondences and running with them. Juxtapositions of people, places, and material culture proliferate correspondences. As *Sex Garage* closes the diptych with a panoply of images of anonymous bodies—shot in medium close-ups from behind with their backsides center frame—getting into cars and onto motorcycles, the films leave audiences with a sense of the world as full of roads leading to a multiplicity of everywheres, with certainly some that will correspond to one's desired sexual modality. Halsted's is a vision of the US that sees gay sexual geographies as rerouting the everyday world in idealized utopian terms of erotic simultaneity, no matter how diffuse and individual one's experience of desire. As Halsted suggested in his voice-over in the film, "everything's for someone."

Camp, Zap, and "The Office"

Hitting screens across the United States in 1972, at the height of the hard-core porn boom, playwright Jean-Claude van Itallie's first and only porn film, *American Cream* (released under the alias Rob Simple) went considerably beyond the call of duty in terms of what might be expected from a gay fuck film of the time. Part hard-core, part Brechtian social drama, and part GI/military drag show, the film is constructed as a compilation of three separate episodes—"The Office," "Country Lads," and "Roles"—which critique popular versions of masculinity through a camp eroticism that oscillates between mocking and fetishizing tropes of phallocentric masculinity, so that both of these terms are simultaneously admired and devalued, elevated and disavowed.

"The Office" signifies a critical moment in the trajectory of the gay liberation movement in which traditional forms of camp performance were beginning to merge with radical gay activism as a means of challenging phallocentric norms. The film catches camp in transition, somewhere between Andrew Ross's description of preliberation camp as a "survivalist" means of dealing with "alienation and exclusion" (at its most basic, a means of "venting" the effects of oppression) and more overtly political configurations, such as gay activist Mike Silverstein's 1970 hailing of camp as a "guerrilla attack on the whole system of male-female roles [in] our society."[39] "The Office" uses the codified camp performance of the former in the service of the latter.

Set in a downtown Manhattan office tower on an ordinary afternoon, "The Office" uses iconographic locations and stylized costuming to establish a relationship between sex, desire, and power that is specific to American institutions in which domination, subordination, and exploitation by socially and economically privileged white males is the norm, particularly those institutions popularly known as the "military-industrial complex" (the corporation, the judicial system, the military, etc.).[40] Close analysis of how these elements operate in "The Office" demonstrates how earlier conventions of camp could be directed toward, and made to work in concert with, the contemporary concerns of radical gay discourse.

Following shots of a cluster of Manhattan skyscrapers accompanied by patriotic marching band music, the film cuts to an interior shot of a bored executive in a large corporate office. He selects a folder marked "male" from his file cabinet, sifts through the photographs of young men, and, having selected one, begins to masturbate under his desk. He has his secretary summon the boy from the photograph, who is diligently at work in a basement cubicle.

The worker is instructed to turn around and show his backside, while the executive continues to masturbate. This scene is intercut with images showing the worker posed in various costumes and uniforms (sailor, southern belle, etc.). The worker "services" the executive (oral sex, rimming, boot licking), before suddenly, as if moved to action, the worker stands up, slaps the executive's ass, rebelliously opens the file cabinet, and throws files all over the room. Noticing a reel-to-reel tape recorder on top of the file cabinet, the worker flicks it on. A militaristic voice reels off regulations such as "no colonel will suck any captain over the age of 25," "no lieutenant shall require any noncommissioned officer to bare his ass while in company uniform," and "no lieutenant will put his hand on any sergeant's balls while in training." The two men wrestle, ending with the worker lying face down on the floor while the executive aggressively fucks him. In the film's final turn of events, the worker rises up, demolishes the office, pushes the executive over his desk, and begins fucking him. This is intercut with images of President Nixon, the US Capitol building, and the White House. The soundtrack cuts from marching drums to the chorus of "Yankee Doodle Dandy." As the worker nears completion, he pulls out and ejaculates on the executive's head.

In this orchestration of sexual performance, the greatest importance lies not in the act of sex itself but in the detailed and spectacular way in which it is staged through costumes, set design, lighting, choreography, and music. With its self-conscious theatrics, the film resonates with what Steven Cohan has argued is a primary "goal" of camp: "to overly aestheticize or theatricalize" in an effort "to deliver the witty verbal or visual effect."[41] "The Office" uses such effects in order to challenge authority while in the process building group cohesion and camaraderie. This puts it in line with the activist practice of "zapping." As gay activist Arthur Evans describes, zapping involved "militant, face-to-face confrontations with homophobic persons in positions of authority" adding that zaps "had two intended audiences—our own community and the larger political world . . . in regard to our own community, zaps often used humor and theater to build up group morale and gay identity."[42] The camp-zap erotics engaged by "The Office" question dominant social structures through sustained rejection, ridicule, and mockery of male authority figures and the institutions they represent via costuming and choreography. Drawing on earlier traditions of performance, the film inverts and renegotiates the roles of executive and worker according to the dictates of ironic camp performance.

"The Office" borrows from popular tropes of the American striptease, in particular those associated with traditional burlesque stage productions that spoofed "aristocratic culture."[43] Imported to the US with the risqué acts of British performer Lydia Thompson, this conflation of class parody and sexual provocation was structured around the incongruous spectacle of women acting bawdily, manly, and "aggressive" while costumed in revealingly altered Victorian dress (tea hats, parasols).[44] Early burlesque used costuming to play with signifiers of taste, wealth, and respectability. This connection is made explicit early on in the film via an image of the worker shown dressed in Thompson-esque burlesque costuming (fig. 33). "The Office" updates the tropes of burlesque to address a gay audience increasingly concerned with the sociopolitical structure of American life. The film mobilizes and reconfigures the burlesque in order to attack the aristocracy's modern-day equivalent, "the Establishment."

Like all striptease formulas, "The Office" is set up around the curi-

FIGURE 33 Gay hard-core burlesque.

osity, tension, and excitement elicited by costuming when used, teasingly, in a ritualized dance of concealing and revealing that which is masked by the artifice of social convention. The film takes the first several minutes to establish the iconographic coding of its striptease, providing the viewer with an impressively extensive array of costuming that salaciously mixes hypermasculinity, patriotism, and homoeroticism. In this dizzying display of revealing and concealing, the viewer is given a virtual slide show of signifiers clearly designed to present the executive's male-male desire and his phallocentric power as existing in an interdependent relationship. Zapping the viewer with a montage of images, the film contrasts the sobriety of the executive's office and clothing with correlating fantasy visions revealing his internal desire.

As the executive concentrates on the image of the worker's face, a corresponding image of a jockstrap adorned with a junior rank military patch reveals the executive's phallocentric fantasy in regard to the worker. Like a junior officer and his commander, hierarchical ranking places the worker in a subordinate position to the executive. The shift to military iconography intensifies the film's phallocentric iconography, tripling signifiers of power in one image by combining tropes of athleticism (the jockstrap), the military (the patch), and hard-core pornography (the close-up, "clinically" lit crotch shot). The executive's sunglasses—masking his gaze from the viewer—along with point-of-view shots from his perspective, assert the executive's power to look where he pleases and to refuse to be fully looked at. Thus, despite the unveiling of his homoerotic fantasies, the executive's masculinity remains fully active, intact, and unpenetrated as he maintains the power of his privilege to gaze.

The patriarchal authority so firmly established in the first half of the film meets its destruction in the later half, as the worker turns on the executive. Refusing continued domination, exploitation, and pacification (to be viewed or fucked), the worker—while being fucked from behind, face down on the floor—rises out from underneath the executive and begins a complex role reversal, not just from passive to aggressive, but from sex that works according to the rules of competitive patriarchal phallocentricity to a cornucopia of polymorphously perverse sex acts. The worker renegotiates the sex narrative of the scene by introducing a gay model wherein phallocentric oppositional tropes of straight sex no longer adhere. This movement from a "hetero" to "homo" narrative structure not only endorses the deconstructive slipperiness between ideas of getting fucked and fucking but uses this slippage to boldly mock the phallocentricity of the "Establishment" by pairing images of the worker fucking the executive (Lilith style) and the Washington Monument getting fucked by the worker's superimposed ass.

The zapping power of the imagery derails normative fucking narratives (standard in both gay and straight porn alike) while ironically suggesting that the best way to "fuck the establishment" is to literally fuck the establishment with liberated gay sex. As Richard Meyer has chronicled, this sort of ideology is congruent with the "fervent" antiwar ideology prevalent in the gay liberation movement and embodied in popular slogans like "Soldiers: Make each other, not war" and "Suck Cock to beat the draft."[45] The use of irony in these zapping subversions produces what Richard Terdiman has described as a "counterdiscourse" where irony functions "to project an alternative through which any element of the here-and-now may be shown as contingent, and thereby subject the whole configuration of power within which it took its adversative meaning to the erosive, dialectical power of alterity."[46]

As striptease is incorporated into the modern context of hard-core, it is able to go far beyond what was legitimately possible on the burlesque stage. That is, the self-reflexive performance of male-male sex could be incorporated as an important part of the show and a key device in the film's contemporary rendition of revealing and concealing. This is evidenced by the film's strategy of keeping the men at least partially costumed at all times and throughout their various sex acts, thus sustaining the film's dialectic in regard to the relationship between social convention and sexual behavior. The viewer is never given the "authentic" sight of two men completely stripped down for the sake of sex (as is the case in most postliberation pornography) but is instead always reminded of how sex acts themselves are performances that can be prone to the reenactment, reproduction, and reification of patriarchal power structures.

Not unlike other films from the period such as *Pink Narcissus* and *The Erotic Films of Peter de Rome*, the film self-reflexively references itself as a camp production and as such elaborates on new and traditional practices of camp. As with these other films, "The Office" invokes the kind of classic camp codifications Matthew Tinkcom describes as "visual cues that serve as a (frequently playful) indictment of American masculine performance."[47] Yet, unlike classic gay camp productions that were used to smuggle nonnormative representations around the censorship code, "The Office" is able to be refreshingly self-conscious in its overt use of camp and as a result even provides something of a brief history of camp.

The self-reflexive use of what might be called the "decorative arts" of camp is clearest in the way in which everything in the film is so blatantly dressed up. From the homemade signs that line the walls of the office, to the numerous American flags that grace the desktops, the office and everyone in it has been satirically "dolled up" in ironic signification. This sense of the film as self-consciously dressed has a long history across gay and queer production. As Richard Dyer notes:

> Fashion and other style trades gave us a space to exercise a skill we have had to be very good at, namely, presentation. Surviving as a queer meant mastering appearances, knowing how to manipulate clothes, mannerism and lifestyle to be able to pass as straight and also to signal that we weren't.[48]

Like all camp, "The Office" demonstrates queer skill and mastery, but converts it from a strategy for survival to one of aggressive ironic comment, turning it outward and directing it toward the oppressive ideologies that have necessitated its existence to begin with. Commenting on the historical dynamics at play between irony and processes of worldmaking, Linda Hutcheon notes that "irony might not so much create communities as come into being because of the communal values and beliefs that already exist."[49]

The specific communal values and beliefs expressed in "The Office" emerge from a rich history of gay/queer performance, a great deal of which is referenced in the film. The most striking use of historically queer imagery appears when the worker is shown vigorously masturbating and dressed in a tutu (fig. 34). Viewed from a contemporary perspective, the image may appear as little more than a playful jab at gender norms. However, many viewers at the time (and older viewers in particular) would have spotted the image's pointed reference to one of the more famous forms of pre-Stonewall camp production: the GI drag show.

As Allan Bérubé has chronicled, during World War II the American armed forces encouraged troops to entertain one another in theatrical productions, providing them with officially produced instruction manuals for all levels of production. Bérubé explains:

> "Blueprint Specials" were soldier show handbooks published and distributed by Army Special Services Headquarters that contained soldier show scripts, music and

FIGURE 34 Hard-core masturbation in a tutu.

> lyrics; stage directions; and design for sets and costumes including drag routines. The Blueprint Special for the show *Hi, Yank!* had more than eight pages of dress patterns and illustration for soldier drag, including instructions for making a "G.I. showgirl" gown out of a salvaged blanket and for making the bodice of a ballet tutu out of a GI "T shirt dyed pink".[50]

Through extensive interviews with numerous men who performed in military theater troupes, Bérubé concludes that drag "not only lured gay men into the soldier shows but reflected their presence in military show production from the start."[51] Though this allowed gay men some space to meet one another, the world of the soldier show was a far cry from freedom as the military continued to strictly police, arrest, and discharge any performers who acted "too explicitly homosexual."[52]

With this context in mind, the appearance of GI drag costuming and music ("Yankee Doodle Dandy" was a popular musical trope in GI drag shows[53]) in "The Office" reconstitutes this particular style of drag performance within a camp-zap mode that uses the newly relaxed obscenity laws and censorship conventions of the early 1970s to attack the hypocritical regulations of the past. Consequently, the performance rejects the prohibitions of the closet by correcting the codifications of the past, as is triumphantly represented through the worker lifting up his tutu to expose his erection underneath. At the same time, unlike GI drag performance, which must contain and submerge overt homoeroticism, the worker's aggressive performance of male-male desire demonstrates a refusal to play by the rules of hetero-affirmative phallocentric sexuality. As Eric Jackson Jr. notes, "male homosexuality is not simply condemned by the dominant order, but rather sublimated within the latter's own ambivalent mythographies of phallic primacy."[54] Accordingly, "The Office" exposes the ambivalence hidden just underneath the sort of establishment masculinity represented by the executive, and in doing so, offers a paradigm for sexuality among men that seeks to erode the serious endeavor of phallocentric power with play.

However, despite the appearance that a successful camp takeover has come to save the day following the characters' role reversals, the final moments manage to complicate the film's resolution. Despite fulfilling both the hard-core requirements of the come shot and the gay liberationist goal of offering a "guerrilla attack on male-female roles," tenderness intervenes to counter the feeling that a simple reverse discourse has taken place.

The moment of its arrival in the film is critical, coming immediately after the hyperaggressive pandemonium that leads up to the come shot. Working in affective contrast to the sexually aggressive tone that propels the film toward its climax, the sudden intervention of affection resituates the film's overall rhetorical structure away from the reverse discourse that appeared to be the film's point. Whereas the film so far has used taxonomies of male-male sex acts as allegorical tropes, so that, for instance, the political terms of the worker coming out on top as a political act is expressed through the hard-core syntax of the worker coming out on top as a sexual act, the introduction of the worker's affection toward his boss, and even more the affection demonstrated between the two men, renegotiates his role as an agent of political and sexual triumph into one of solidarity.

By supplanting the come shot with affection, the film supplants the maximum visibility of the worker's individual fulfillment. As the executive thrusts his ass sensually up into the air, returning the worker's affection and appearing fully sensually engaged with his position of subordination, he appears to be reveling in his new role. The worker's affection operates as a demonstration of solidarity in response to the executive's stellar embracing of a compromised status in relation to phallocentric privilege. The executive becomes emblematic of a process of gay world-making, or perhaps an agent of counterpublic discourse, in which the active embracing of an individual's subordinate status relative to dominant discourse propels new, politically potent possibilities for association with others. The executive's power topples not simply so he can become subordinate to the worker but so that he can join the worker in a shared sentiment of gay world making. Within a project of gay world-making, a citizen's real duty is first and foremost to experience the fact of the subordinate status of gay desire in a spirit of camaraderie.

Camp Dialecticism in the films of Peter de Rome

Nearly all of Peter de Rome's films and related promotional materials exist at a similar intersection between traditional forms of camp and sexual liberation, and direct both toward the construction of a new liberation-based gay vernacular. This phenomenon is most discernable in the way de Rome takes tropes of homosexual and/or queer eroticism and gives them a thorough, modernizing camp treatment. In the homemade poster/magazine advertisement he produced for the theatrical release of *The Erotic Films of Peter de Rome*, he combined stills of erotic film imagery with a variety of hand-stenciled Letraset title designs for each individual film (fig. 18). These elements work together to emphasize camp mediation as fundamental to each film. For instance, the heading *The Second Coming* resituates numerous commonplace generic and symbolic markers within the domain of gay erotic activity through wordplay. Playing with conventions of both genre and gender, de Rome uses signifiers associated with white middle-class Christian culture—devotion, restraint, purity, beauty, the romantic—to articulate hard-core male-male sexual fantasy. It is hard to distinguish which set of values wins out—tastefulness or tastelessness, inoffensive or offensive, legitimate or illegitimate. The language demonstrates a flexible vernacular that drives toward an impressive level of camp excess and irony.

Much of de Rome's work combines and perhaps even updates this kind of self-reflexive camp register in accordance with the newer, more "liberated" concerns of lifestyle. In particular, de Rome's films are invested in establishing models for gay coupling, sexual activity, and social development through a lifestyle discourse oriented around the popular 1970s paradigm of getting loose. In his study *Getting Loose: Lifestyle Consumption in the 1970s*, Sam Binkley looks at how loosening, as a phenomenon, was shaped and promoted through a variety of new age publications and self-help manuals such as *The Catalog of Sexual Consciousness*, *Whole Earth Catalog*, and *Wellness*. Binkley writes that to "be yourself," to "do what was right for you," to "let it all hang out" was to release a primordial vitality, to become an artist of oneself and of one's identity and assume responsibility and take credit for what one made of oneself through the crafting of a distinctly loose style of life.[55] He further points out that various activities and regimens related to the body were central to the crafting of a looser life. Activities such as sex, massage, and dieting all carried with them the potential to bring the participant into contact with a looser, truer self—to help one to become less uptight. With experiences of discovery and epiphany standing as key markers of successful loosening, new methods, or at least a repackaging of older methods, for these activities were sought after and developed. Numerous organizations and independent practitioners began developing new models for getting loose. Of these, an emphasis on touch and sensory experience became a central component of consciousness-raising and self-realization as countercultural groups such as the Esalen Institute in Big Sur, California, developed new models for meditation and massage, inspiring numerous others across the United States to develop, market, and institute their own procedures and techniques, often under the umbrella term "bodywork."

As Binkley explains "countercultural body therapy was directed at emotional and spiritual bottlenecks and tangles lodged in the substance of the body itself—muscles, skin, tendons, bones, hair—often read as the locus of emotional stress, neurosis, anxiety and hang-ups."[56] Throughout the early 1970s, sexual schema for looser living circulated widely in US culture at large through the proliferation of best-selling manuals such as *The Sensuous Woman* (1969), *The Sensuous Man* (1971), and *The Joy of Sex* (1972), all of which promoted the honing and mastering of sexual technique as a means of getting and staying loose.[57]

Ambitiously bridging underground aesthetics, overt gay erotica, and classic Hollywood narrative, de Rome's films use scripting and choreography and, in particular, the "controlled" improvisation of sex scenes to demonstrate how sexual performance may be honed to yield greater awareness—more "conscious" modes of perception, more accurate and honest expressions of self-knowledge. This experience is repeatedly indicated in the recurring trope of characters for whom investing in their own desires results in highly visible expressions of jubilance. Their eruptions of uncontainable joy are markers of authentic experience.

In *Green Thoughts*, for instance, a young man discovers how erotically compelling the botanical world can be when, walking through London's Kew Gardens, the sight of lush green lawns, new spring flowers, and a variety of exotic trees leaves him so infused with sensual delight that he finds himself leaping and springing forth through fields of green, eventually gyrating into a tree trunk and masturbating among an assortment of rare foliage. In *Underground*, a young, bearded hippie breaks into a fit of laughter and aerobic movement as a businessman attentively provides him with oral sex in an actual New York City subway car (filmed on location during operating hours). In *Double Exposure*, *Daydreams on a Crosstown Bus*, and *Prometheus*, flexible, loose, outstretched bodies demonstrate a sense of fluidity while emphasizing the transgression of the appropriate physical and emotional boundaries that the bodies of men are expected to maintain.

In countless instances throughout de Rome's work, male-male desire is represented as connective, interrelational, and actively invested in public demonstration. Even in instances in which these relationships are represented more exclusively through sexual contact, the emphasis is on erotic play as a means of showing characters connecting through experiences of gay liberation as part of a larger group-oriented sociopolitical enterprise. In this context, de Rome's work is resonant with emergent philosophies of gay liberation that positioned erotic intimacy as a consequence of the rapidly expanding out gay "community" and as a sign of gay progress. As Dennis Altman declared in 1971:

> "Our salute will be a kiss" said Greta Garbo in *Ninotchka* and one of the best things about the new sense of community being developed by gay liberation is the considerable eroticism it releases, and as if in conformation of the Brown/Marcuse theories of polymorphous perversity, the seeming decline in compulsive scoring and promiscuity.[58]

As echoed in the young man's leap through the air in *Green Thoughts*, the concept of gay eroticism was implicitly bound up with, if not constituted by, the experience of "release." This release, however, was comprised of far more than the ecstatic relief brought on by the self-confrontation inherent in the coming out process. Release, in fact, offered a reifying ideology in its own right, detectable in Altman's contention that there is a correlation between the eroticism released by gay communion and the "seeming decline in compulsive scoring and promiscuity." For Altman, as well as for a great many other leaders of the emergent gay liberation movement, opposing older myths and stereotypes about male-male sexuality (anonymous, lecherous, compulsive, etc.) with new intimacy-bound models of plastic sexuality offered a means of articulating a model for the liberated gay self within a rhetoric of authenticity.

Accordingly, de Rome's films work in concert with the kind of instructional logic offered in consciousness-raising manual-style media that appeared throughout the 1970s: books such as *Gay Spirit* (1974) and *The Joy of Gay Sex* (1977).[59] In accord with Altman, these texts fix erotic release as a shedding and stripping away of layers of oppression toward the ascendancy of a truth-giving Dionysian erotics so potent as to yield forth a new communal brotherhood. As described in *Gay Spirit*:

> You've learned that if that interior of yours is in harmony with itself you'll be in harmony with other people, and that among them will be some who you will want to go to bed with. And believe me, they'll be eager to go to bed with you—and not just once! *Sensuous people possess a secret of living and loving* that is irresistible.[60]

Liberation was construed not only as a political act but also as a deeply transformative psychological event to be formalized through models and/or scripts for certain kinds of sociosexual behavior. This can be understood more broadly as part of a moment in the late 1960s and early 1970s that, as Anthony Giddens has noted, saw a "profusion of reflexive resources: therapy and self-help manuals of all kinds, television programs and magazine articles," contributing to a broader "reflexive project" of the self.[61]

De Rome's films privilege a presentation of gay sexuality that is mindful of the complexity with which male-male desire is expressed by a wide variety of men. Offering his own take on the subject, de Rome explains:

> The truth is that a large proportion of gay men have a variety of sexual experiences that would boggle the minds of the straight bourgeois. . . . I have known men—one now in his seventies—who have sex two or three times a day with different men every day of their lives. At the other end of the scale, of course, are those gay couples who settle down to marital bliss. Somewhere in the middle is where I would place myself. And incidentally where I would place a few million other homosexuals whose lifestyles have not yet been accurately documented.[62]

De Rome's description of gay life as lifestyle needs to be seen as a political strategy. When, for instance, he describes "men who settle down to marital bliss" as a lifestyle, he demonstrates a disregard for law—which prohibited legal marriage between members of the same sex—and, at the same time, describes a kind of relationship that is a fact of gay life. Lifestyle gives legitimacy to a popular experience despite delegitimizing government practices.

The closing sequence of *Mumbo Jumbo* makes a final explosive example out of lifestyle consumerism as a mode of legitimizing gay camp address. It begins with an inventively appropriated title—a close-up of an advertisement that reads "Shoot the Works" over an image of multicolored fireworks exploding in midair. Resituating these "works" within a discourse of gay counterpatriotism, the following succession of shots moves between a series of close-ups of five noticeably distinct (color, size, shape, etc.) penises being self-stroked to climax. Upon ejaculation each image cuts to a corresponding shot of a firework exploding, until in the final pairing of shots the penis producing the most airborne ejaculate is matched with numerous fireworks blasting in a grand finale.

The sweeping classical music of Richard Wagner's *Tristan un Isolde, Act: 1 Liebestod* (performed by Carl Schuricht) builds to a swelling crescendo in concert with the final triumphant explosions. Within the space of this small sequence, the film manages a camp recontextualization of a key trope of the melodrama: the sweeping musical climax over the heterosexual union of the lead characters, emphasizing their elation and emotional release. In *Mumbo Jumbo* it ironically underscores the sexual release of lone gay men. However, while these men may be shown on their own, they are far from being depicted as lonely. Instead, the melodramatic scoring, together with the editing, suggests a gay chorus of elated masturbators, so that the very music used to reinforce jubilant heterosexuality in the melodrama is here refitted to reinforce the collectivist dynamics of gay group-oriented processes of sexual liberation, further underlined by the public gathering and togetherness implicit in a mass firework display. Providing an acute example of camp's penchant for incongruity, this final moment is perhaps most striking for seeming both too absurd to be serious and too technically exacting and carefully crafted not to be.

The "Working Man" Trilogy

Through the three films that comprise what has come to be referred as the "Working Man" trilogy, *Kansas City Trucking Co.* (1976), *El Paso Wrecking Corp.* (1977), and *L.A. Tool and Die* (1979), Joe Gage established himself as a pioneering force in erotic cinema with his visualization of the sexual and romantic bonds shared by working-class truckers as they drive through the rural American Southwest, looking for sex, companionship, and love. The "Working Man" films provide a representation that, as John R. Burger notes, cuts through "gender rules and enforced silences and offers gay men a vision of free expression of their sexual desire in these locales."[63] The trilogy posits an alternative paradigm to configurations of male identity and sexuality as they were represented in both mainstream and gay cinema in the mid-1970s.

The narrative arc of the trilogy unfolds as follows; in *Kansas*, the trucker Hank (Richard Locke) schools a young married man named Joe (Steve Boyd) on the ways of both the road and male-male sex, while also enjoying the many opportunities for male-male sex that exists across the deserts, state parks, and truckers' bunkhouses of the Southwest. In *El Paso Wrecking Corp.*, Hank looks for work after he and his partner Gene (Fred Halsted) are fired from the trucking company, again moving through a world abundant with male-male sexual encounters.[64] In the final installment, *L.A. Tool and Die*, Hank is again left jobless, relocating from El Paso after the company shuts down. While the film appears at first to be another ode to sexual abundance, by the film's end it is *both* a treatise for abundant buddy sex and a romance about Hank's relationship with shell-shocked Vietnam vet Wylie (Will Seagers).

The trilogy takes its time to develop character relations, allowing scenes of sexual encounter to emerge in accord with broader concerns of story development, a certain visual spaciousness (long duration, wide shots), and an ease of pacing characteristic of New Hollywood films like *Five Easy Pieces. Kansas City* functions as a sort of pornographic mood piece, interlacing images of Hank and Joe sitting side by side in the truck cab with gorgeous noirish images of neon signs that move past them as they cut through the night. Sunrise and sunset shots, a key visual trope running across the trilogy that is texturized by the grain of the 16 mm film stock, showcase the dramatic vistas of the Southwest at different times of day, marking the slow passage of time as the two men journey onward. Like much gay hard-core, both *Kansas City* and *El Paso* culminate in orgy scenes—although again, these films make artful and narratively purposeful uses of this convention by making them almost hauntingly atmospheric set pieces tied to the environments in which they take place. In *El Paso*, for example, an orgy is followed by the group, in their capacity as workers for the Wrecking Corp., destroying the warehouse in which their orgy took place.

Gage innovatively uses sound design to create complex layerings of sound and image, with original music compositions by Al Steinman. In some of the trilogy's most inventive examples, sound functions as an immersive experience that interweaves the sound of music with the actors' sexual vocalizations. At the conclusion of *Kansas City*, a hypnotic and pulsing polyrhythmic drum composition is interlaced with the reverb-processed groans, calls, and ecstatic spoken proclamations produced by the all-male orgy, seeming almost to modulate the speed and rhythm of sexual performance. Taking sound experimentation even further, *El Paso* utilized certain theaters' multichannel systems to immerse patrons in music and vocal ecstasy—an opportunity that was emphasized on posters as a chance to "hear the sound of *HEAT*!"

Using the generic protocols of the road movie, the trilogy thematically explores homosocial contexts spread out along the highways of the US as generative sites of male-male (and male-male-female in one scene from *El Paso*) erotic contact. In doing so, these films advance, in Eve Sedgwick's formulation, a "hypothesiz[ing of] the potential unbrokenness between homosocial and homosexual."[65] That is, the trilogy imagines a utopian sphere paradoxically marked as a space of liberatory gay sexuality so complete and self-assured that there is little need for direct participation in gay movement practices. The gay sociopolitical activities so prevalent in urban gay life at this time appear almost nonexistent in the world of the Gage film. This does not mean that the trilogy should be understood as *only* fantasy or as fetishistic images of blue-collar life to be enjoyed by middle- and upper-middle-class audiences (though it certainly performed both of these functions). In refashioning the straight buddy couple trope of popular road films like *Easy Rider* and *Thunderbolt and Lightfoot* (Michael Cimino, 1974) within a register of gay eroticism, these films use sex as part of an imaginative resocializing of the rural US presented in popular genre film. The following analysis illuminates how the trilogy renegotiated the road film to produce a vision of the buddy couple that benefits from an emphasis on male-male eroticism and romance. Through an exploration of the trilogy's advertising campaign followed by a close reading that focuses on the trilogy's resolution in the final sequences of *L.A. Tool and Die,* this analysis elucidates the inventive ways in which the trilogy created a new vision of male-male coupling as something capable of being both erotically stimulating and pedagogically meaningful.

The trilogy engages with the increasingly complex national institutionalization and commercialization of gay life throughout the 1970s. The popular, commercial appeal of hard-core features made them an ideal form through which to address and possibly unite a range of viewers engaged in increasingly diverse segments of gay social, cultural, and political life. As venues for gay cultural production and social elaboration were proliferating wildly, the project of gay liberation became increasingly less clear. Stephen M. Engel points out that "in 1969, before the Stonewall riots, fifty homophile organizations existed in the United States; by 1973, there were over eight hundred gay and lesbian groups, and by the end of the decade they numbered into the thousands."[66] Arguably, gay life and discourse became increasingly focused on its own cultural development and less concerned with the critiques of culture at large that marked much of the politics of early gay liberation. At the same time, gay people came into existence as a mass public constituency in their own right. It is through its active engagement with the tension between these two movements that the "Working Man" trilogy—gay liberationist in its political ethos and unapologetically popular in its appeal—elaborates vital new paradigms for gay social and romantic life. To a new, mass gay public, the trilogy extended an invitation to reorient itself; precisely by checking in with the consciousness-raising values of early gay liberation.

The crossover appeal of the trilogy was integral to its extensive advertising campaign, which carried a streamlined unified aesthetic through all of its promotional material as part of a high-concept articulation of male-male desire. This foregrounded the promise of seeing ordinary men "get it on together," as the seductive female narrator (Maria Reina) in the trailer for *Kansas City Trucking Co.* put it. However, ordinariness in the case of these films became, paradoxically, part of their spectacular draw. Many hard-core features sought to offer "ordinary" versions of masculinity through normative familial, institutional, and occupational roles such as father, son, husband, worker, boss, teacher, coach. Gage's trilogy broke from this pattern by fleshing out this characterization, giving elaborative detail to the ordinary lives of his protagonists: creating "Gagemen," as they would come to be called in later advertisements and reviews, that didn't only signal ordinariness through dress or vocal performance, but configured them as part of a narrative-driven mise-en-scène that sought to place their stories as part of a discourse of sociosexual experience.

As part of an emergent industrial practice that has since come to be known as the "blockbuster strategy," the "crossover," in connection with a select combination of other branding elements, was used to situate the film within a register of mass appeal and national interest.[67] The high-concept blockbuster strategy was the result of a shift in industry practices on a "paradigmatic" scale following the 1975 success of the film *Jaws*.[68] David Cook identifies the key features of this strategy as the use of "strong, reproducible images, the saturation campaign, and wide spread product tie-ins."[69] Promotion across the trilogy mimicked this high-concept strategy, containing strong textual echoes of the advertising for *Jaws* (figs. 35–36). The poster for *Jaws* establishes a "strong," "reproducible" image for the film using a minimalist graphic layout (simple cleans lines, basic colors, black border) with an uncluttered pictorial style of illustration that reads quickly and easily. *Kansas City*'s poster appropriates many of these simple, sharp, and eye-catching stylistic virtues for its print and poster campaign. Both posters use a graphic logo to draw attention to the title, suggesting the professionalism, mass appeal, and accessibility of packaged, production-line goods (an aesthetic that Gage capitalized on later through the logo for his signature brand Gagemen). Cook suggests the poster for *Jaws* builds anticipation "on the basis of a single sensational image as if it were pornography."[70] The "X" graphically emphasized at the bottom of *Kansas City*'s poster alerts audiences to the film's spectacular promise of generic crossover.

For each of the films in the trilogy, this promotion was extended across an extensive array of formats—from multiple movie trailers to

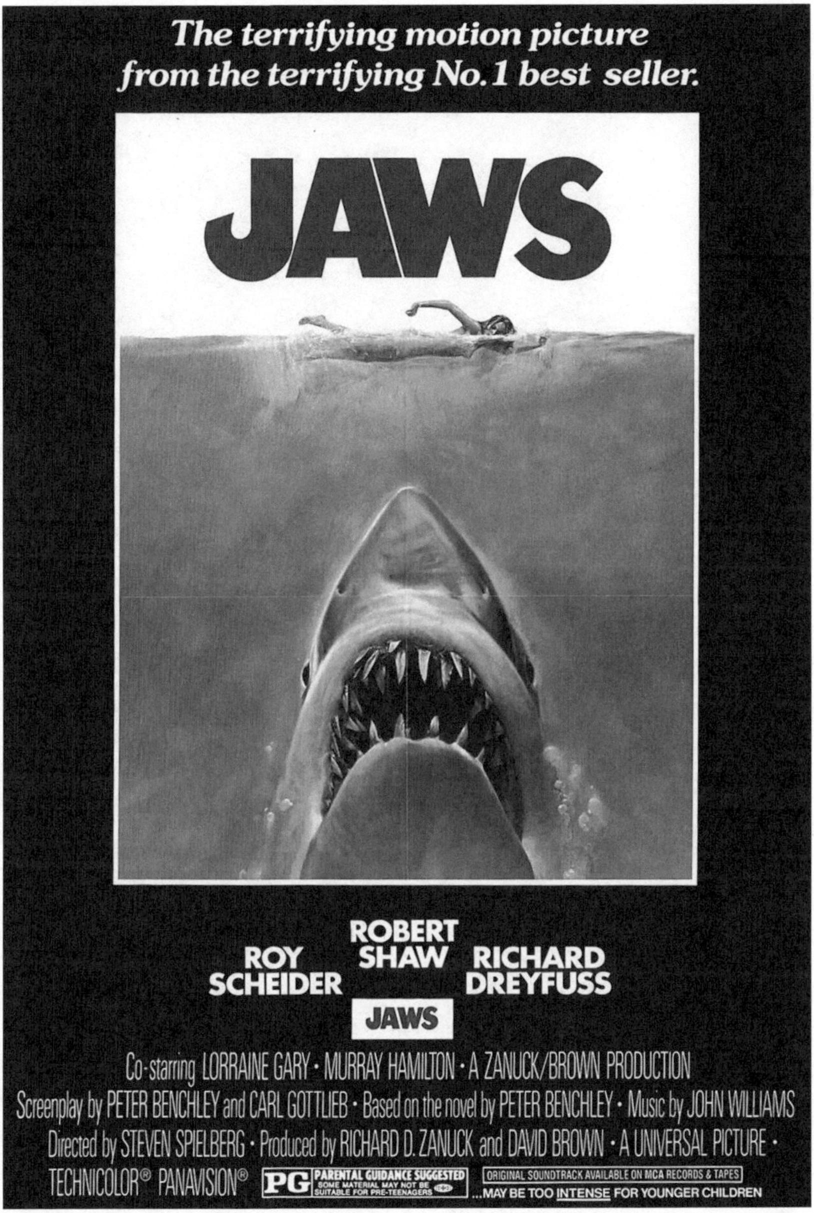

FIGURE 35 The high concept minimalism of the promotion for *Jaws*.

FIGURE 36 *Kansas City Trucking Co.* appropriates and builds on the recent promotion for *Jaws*.

star-profile interviews and novelizations in photo spreads in numerous magazines.[71] Building the event status of the film through an appeal to several different audience demographics, and referencing numerous popular 1970s genres such as the road film, the western, and the chase film, the result was a campaign that repeatedly posed the question of how these familiar elements would come together within the confines of a porn film.

The marketing sustained and promoted this tension as part of the film's event status by insisting that the harmonious cohesion of all these elements under the umbrella of porn wasn't only possible, but something porn might even be well suited for. The marketing of *El Paso Wrecking Corp.* and *L.A. Tool and Die* rested on extending porn's bountiful sex as a means of establishing other kinds of visibility *and* legibility in relation to male-male desire. Posters and magazine advertisements for *El Paso,* for instance, used the similar black-and-white aesthetic and graphic layout as for *Kansas City,* but replaced the list of cities with a list of male positionalities, including "THE STRANGER . . . [,] THE FOREMAN . . . [,] THE HUSBAND . . . [,] THE FATHER . . . [,] THE SON," the ellipses following each position suggesting endless aggregation, an unspooling of male roles, each existing in dynamic relation to the next.

Promotion and ancillary print material for *L.A. Tool and Die* continued this trope of aggregation and abundance using the same graphic listing formation: "THE CREEK . . . [,] THE SHACK . . . [,] THE HIGH SCHOOL . . . [,]" work not only settings, but as contexts for male-male desire and sociosexual contact. A photo collage of characters, showing a range of men involved in dramas modeling manhood—a welder welding, a group of men rescuing a man from an overturned car, a man throwing his head back in ecstasy—finds Hank at the center.

Not unlike Fred Halsted's topographically dense view of male-male sexuality across Los Angeles in *L.A. Plays Itself/Sex Garage,* the trilogy and its epitexts suggest a utopian field of perversities. In Gage's 1980 adaptation of *L.A. Tool and Die* in *Numbers* magazine, the text notes of a roadside bar that "the place looked jammed; people going in and out, milling about in the parking lot, getting in and out of darkened cars. 'Christ,' he thought to himself, 'Every fucking faggot in Texas must be here . . . The placed reeked with perversion.'"[72] Within this America, men move as figures for the circulation of desire through circuits of ordinariness, where bars, parking lots, and whole states become synecdoches of gay desire.[73]

These elaborations, however, are neither isolated to gay porn nor contained only within gay negotiations of popular imagery, but draw on popular working-class iconography from the period, especially that associated with all-male working-class solidarity. In his study of class in 1970s American cinema, Derek Nystrom shows how figures associated with working-class masculinity, specifically those tied to occupations conventionally regarded as all-male, came to acquire a new representational status during the period that explicitly linked them with notions of confrontation, rebellion, and militancy.[74] While these traits were far from being new elements of working-class iconography within the popular imaginary, they were beginning to operate in an entirely different manner; whereas before they had conventionally been seen as products of working-class solidarity, mobilized through collective political organization and unionization (and as such in opposition with a professional managerial class), they were increasingly framed through mainstream television and print journalism as the product of spontaneous, individually driven, reactionary, riotous behavior.

A major catalyst for this was the Hard Hat Riots of May 1970, an event Nystrom describes as the "seminal moment in the blue-collarization of Middle-Americans."[75] As narrativized in popular media from the period, the riots occurred when some two hundred thousand construction workers spontaneously erupted into the streets of New York and violently overtook a group of young antiwar protesters who were gathered near Wall Street. While in actuality the riots had been organized in advance, and were comprised of both blue-collar and white-collar men, sources such as *Life* and *Time* consistently represented the event as a spontaneous eruption of long-festering feelings of "disgust and anger with the anti-war counter-cultural left."[76] Popular media, in short, used the riots to work up a profile of the blue-collar construction worker as a new type who epitomized a total and uncontainable rebelliousness that could at any and all times erupt into collectivity, inspired not by union action or even related to matters of workers' rights, but out of individual feelings capable of spontaneous uprising; a type that "serve[d] as both a representative for an earthy, authentic brand of traditional values *and* a figure of monstrous excess."[77]

Another figure to gain currency during the early to mid-1970s as a purveyor of spontaneous, independent rebellion was the trucker, the result of a number of shutdowns that occurred in late 1973 and early 1974. In response to a number of factors, including rising fuel costs and the lowering of speed limits, in December 1973 scores of truckers began "blocking interstates in Ohio and Pennsylvania with their rigs. . . . a practice that quickly spread to a number of states" and eventually resulted in a "forty-eight hour shut down the following week," with a final shutdown in early 1974 lasting for an entire "week and half" and resulting in thousands out of work and economic disturbance on a national scale.[78] As the trucker shutdowns of 1973–74 were the result of actions taken by thousands of nonunion, independent "owner-operators" (drivers who drive their own trucks and contract out their services as opposed to unionized "teamsters"), the trucker also came to stand as a popular emblem of sudden, uncontrollable revolt.

The popular image of both the trucker and the hard-hat worker mixed private emotion with public reaction; media accounts of these events positioned them as key tropes in a narrative of working-class solidarity that comes not directly from group thought and discussion (as with a union) but is the product of certain affective relations between individuals where independently oriented sentiment swells to the point of action and sparks a mass-affective recognition, and in turn inspires a mass reaction of sudden collective mobilization. However, in the case of the trucker, it is important to note that the trope of the individual erupting into mass action was amplified by what Nystrom describes as "the paradox [of] collective solidaristic actions of men whose reputation was one of fierce independence."[79]

Just as it did in cultural production at large, from the early 1970s this popularization of the trucker and, to some extent, the construction worker became an increasingly visible part of gay cultural production. Key to this phenomenon is the way in which these figures work to express a syntax of male-male desire that pivots on a sense of affective movement between the levels of the individual and the collective. To give a few examples culled from popular gay advertisements of the period: "Digger Dan," a collectable mail-order figurine advertised to *Advocate* readers in October 1975, stands as a particularly apt example of the sociosexual, affective dynamics expressed through the "figure" of a hard-hat worker, with the copy describing that his "bold eyes" and "sweat stained body" make him "a tribute to the MEN OF AMERICA." Likewise, an ad for the 1975 play *Naked Highway: A Machodrama* features a sketch of a brawny and shirtless beefcake-style man towering over a highway that trails off into an expanse of American desert. Marking a high point in the popularity of gay trucker imagery, a 1975 special issue of *The Advocate* devoted to the topic of work gave the trucker center stage; its cover was graced with a pen-and-ink drawing of an inviting trucker leaning on the open door of his truck cab and a multipage exploration of the lives of gay truckers as the feature article (fig. 37). San Francisco's Bulldog Baths ran an ad in the December 1979 issue of *Blueboy*, featuring a burly trucker in work boots and "Bulldog"

FIGURE 37 The gay press showcases trucker life as lived among male-desiring men. Cover, *The Advocate* (September 10, 1975). Image courtesy of the Hall-Carpenter Archive, London School of Economics. Used with permission.

army cap posing on the wheel well of his truck. Interested readers were invited to send off for a heavy-stock poster enlargement of the image.[80]

All of these images are marked by values of intensity, eroticism, independence, solidarity, and affiliation. Brought together within a collectivizing syntax of rabble-rousing intensity, the elements that comprise these images relay between the independent buddy dynamics of the trucker—as a figure both out for himself and with an eye on others—and a dynamics of gay eroticism based in the advancement of ever-widening networks of male-male desire. In some ways the trucker might also be considered in these instances to be operating as a sort of rallying point for the expansion of these networks—a symbol of how numerous intersections and crossovers may be traversed, rerouted, or even blocked, to promote male-male desire as a movement of "intensity" across emotional, sexual, romantic, and geographic levels.

However, in the mid- to late 1970s, the trucker also draws much of his intensity from his particular relationship to public and private space. As an occupant of the interstate highway, the trucker exists within a unique set of spatial and temporal relations; by the very nature of his work, he is situated simultaneously within the almost hyperpublic mass space of the US interstate highway and the intensely private, physically elevated space of the truck cab. Analogous to—and surely, at times, synonymous with—the psychogeographic dynamics of many public networks of male-male desire, truckers have the interesting ability to see one another within and as part of an experience of public space that is shaped by both their separation from it and their shared role within it—constantly coming into contact with one another *as* truckers as a result of their particular and shared set of relations (often invisible to others) between public and private and individual and group. In this sense, both the intensity of the trucker as a figure of political momentum (of spontaneous uprising) and as rallying point for male-male desire embodies a buddy dynamic wherein the sustained movement and crossover between levels of individual and collective results in new possibilities of social formations, and in many instances formations whose presence is ubiquitous without being obvious.

The Liberatory Movement of *L.A. Tool and Die*

Completing the trilogy, *L.A. Tool and Die* most fully explores the narrative possibilities of the buddy couple by directing this figure toward the representation of gay love. Bringing together the staple tropes of classic Hollywood romance with the hard-core sexual representation of 1970s gay porn, the film explores intermingling dilemmas of unrequited love and unrequited sex as it follows Hank through a new series of adventures. Whereas previously his adventures were made possible through an interwoven abundance of work and sex, *L.A.* is marked from the start by a strong sense that both of these things are getting harder to come by. With the introduction of the theme of love into the narrative in combination with the new centrality of themes such as unemployment, bereavement, and social welfare, the film is marked by a sense that times are changing both for Hank personally and within the broader terms of US life.

Three particular areas are of primary concern here: (1) the trilogy's continued use of the trucker as a figure of independence and collective action, (2) the way in which numerous generic elements are placed in tension *and* in tandem with one another to promote specific kinds of cross-class, cross-race, and cross-ethnic collectivizing sexual activities, and (3) the way in which the film offers a conclusion to the trilogy that tailors hard-core sexual representation to promote liberatory gay eroticism.

To offer a brief summary of where the film picks up: with the El Paso Wrecking Corp. having gone out of business, Hank is left unemployed. His job site, now in a state of abandonment and disarray, has become a hideout for a band of hypermasculine and hypersexual chronic masturbators. Unimpressed and in need of employment, Hank, despite a warm invitation, opts out of the orgy and hits the road in search for work. Stopping off at a gay disco on the outskirts of town, he becomes instantly smitten with a handsome forever-in-blue-jeans type named Wylie. Setting up a melodrama of unrequited love, Hank, rushing after Wylie—to a score of sweeping strings—catches up with him in the parking lot only to discover that Wylie, also unemployed, is only a passerby on his way to find work further west. Based on the assumption that Hank is probably only after sex anyway, Wylie relays that he is really not that into "sport fucking." Parting ways, each man is shown announcing his regret to himself; Hank on his way back inside the disco mournfully declaring that "that was the one"; Wylie, now on the road, angrily hitting his fist against his steering wheel and exclaiming "dammit, Wylie, you're a fool!" in self-lacerating regret.

Learning through hearsay that Wylie is headed to look for work at a welding factory called L.A. Tool and Die, Hank hits the road. Cutting between the men at different points as they journey west, the film takes the time to further develop each character's individual concerns, revealing though a flashback sequence that Wylie is shell-shocked and mourning the loss of his lover that died in his arms on the battlefields of Vietnam. Conversely, Hank is shown scoring the kind of sex that suits him best when, during a dust storm, he pulls over to find a minivan of men engaged in a session of whole-body, polymorphously perverse group sex.

In the latter half of the film, Hank and Wylie are reunited and spend their days in buddy-style bonding with one another as they laugh, give each other welding tips, and share lunch breaks shoulder to shoulder at the L.A. Tool and Die. Following the reunion at the factory, their relationship gets considerably more complex as Hank invites Wylie to come spend a weekend with him on a rural land trust he has been paying off with the aim of starting a farm, but which he has yet to see. Wylie, taking Hank up on the offer, goes to meet him at the land trust office the next day only to discover him in the office bathroom engaged in a circle jerk. Giving up his anti–sport fucking outlook Wylie eventually joins in. The men, post–group sex, feeling uplifted and hopeful about their future together, are shown driving out to the property through the sun drenched countryside. Upon arrival they discover that Hank's land is nothing more than barren desert. Hank has an emotional breakdown admitting that he actually quit his job with the plan of starting the farm. From here, the two men, drinking whiskey by candlelight in the back of Hank's van, engage in a sexual encounter comprised of a seemingly endless cycle of every hard-core position. A cut to the next day finds Hank, nailing a for-sale sign into the ground and striking the underground tributary of a natural spring: the film's final image shows the property now cultivated, an expansive orange grove under blue skies.

The overall narrative structure of the film is organized around the question of whether or not Hank and Wylie will end up together, and if so, what their relationship will be like. Suspense is amplified around this question through cutting between each protagonist's journey, building anticipation for the point at which their geographical and narrative trajectories will meet. This intercutting lays out a series of dualisms connecting male-male desire, individuality and collectivity. Hank and Wylie are set up, oppositionally, in the first half of the film. On one side of this dualism is Hank: confident, fiercely independent, and unattached, a lover of buddy sex with an appreciation for fraternal solidarity. On the other side of this line is Wylie: downtrodden, shell-shocked, and lonesome, one grieving half of a couple and, at least initially, not interested in group sex in the least.

This dualism, marking Hank's experience of male-male desire as socially and publicly oriented, and Wylie's as private and monogamous, is sharply formalized within particular generic terms. This is most recognizable in each character's musical themes. Disco, funk, honky-tonk, and fusion—in a word, body music—link Hank to spaces of collective physicality (discos, dance parties, tea dances, etc.), musical ensembles, and, cinematically, to action, blaxploitation and hard-core porn, while wistful cellos, harmonica solos, and lushly orchestrated ballads associate Wylie with introspection, solo performance, and classic Hollywood genres: the romance and the western. Abrupt shifts in musical styles are synchronized with editing to sharply contrast Wylie's individuality with Hank's sociality: Wylie driving alone with a ballad on the stereo cuts to Hank in a busy disco; Wylie crying alone at the beach at sunset with the sound of a wistful harmonica cuts to Hank having group van sex to the sound of honky-tonk music (the compositional structure of the honky-tonk, with individual players "trading off" solos, echoes the routine trading-off of partners and sex acts common to the practice of group sex).

Having established Hank as a sexually skilled team player and Wylie as a hopeless lone romantic, the latter half of the film wastes little time in bringing these dualities into a potentially explosive collision. The film moves from Wylie and Hank's newfound companionship at the factory toward the possibility of their future together on the farm, only to interrupt this budding-couple trajectory by bringing it into contact with the hard-core, all-male values of the men's room at the land office. The formal organization of cinematic elements and the choreography of character movement work to bring affective legibility to a buddy-system dynamic through which individuals and couples alike have value as agents in a collective project of male-male desire. Hank is shown alone in a corridor outside the land office as he waits for Wylie to arrive; an intermittent and heterogeneous stream of men gradually funnel into the men's room: a Latino custodian with a bucket and a mop flashes him a cruisey look; a debonair African American in executive attire and smoking slims catches Hank's eye as he comes out from the door behind him; a golden-haired hard-hat construction worker leaves just enough slack in his stride for Hank to get a good look as he passes.

The sequence repeatedly shows: (a) Hank catching sight of each man, (b) each man making his way toward the bathroom, and (c) Hank shown with his head turned toward the door as he watches each man enter. This pattern establishes a visual syntax of accumulation where, one by one, like coins passed into a machine, the currency of all-male desire grows exponentially as each man joins the others. Explicitly directing this momentum toward a collectivizing social dynamic, a cut to the interior of the bathroom shows the men shedding the previously clear demarcation of occupational roles as they undress one another and move into a network of intermingled bodies.

In concert with the framing, camera movement, and chorography of the actors' movement, the generic dualisms set in place earlier begin to reemerge as Hank's return to the groove of group activity is emphasized through a non-diegetic rise in the volume of funk music. Just as the hard-core momentum of the orgy approaches the explosive climax of group ejaculation and narrative release, the genre is split wide open, subsumed by melodrama, as the music gives way to the swell of weeping violins and Wylie arrives and discovers that Hank has turned his attention elsewhere. Shown eye to eye through a pattern of shot-reverse-shot, the two men look as much like two boxers in separate corners ready to destroy one another as they do two lovers on the verge of a lusty pounce.

Instead of one genre giving way, as it initially seems will happen when the funk is abruptly cut off by the strings, the tension is elongated for a full three minutes by sustaining the sound of the strings in a low melody. The hypnotic repetition of the sound begins to build as Wylie moves from the sidelines into the group and, suddenly, marking the inclusive buddy dynamic of this movement, the funk is turned back up in the sound mix around the melody of the violin part, the two coming into harmony with one another. The music is then brought into harmony with the hard-core sexual action: the frenzy of simultaneous group ejaculation is musically reinforced by rhythm and strings alike swelling toward a climax and leading to a series of shots: Hank and Wylie framed individually as each ejaculates; the two men ejaculating together side by side as part of the group; paired close-ups of each man as he throws his head back, eyes closed in the ecstasy of release. Marking the moment of transformation, the sound of chimes signal an epiphany, paired with a shot of Wylie as his eyes move from tightly shut to wide open. The two men walk out of the bathroom lackadaisically putting themselves back together (buttoning up pants, tucking in shirts). The next cut opens the following sequence with the image of the open road.

Functioning as the fulcrum point of the story, the bathroom sequence draws attention to specific vectors of movement between levels of individuality, coupling, and collectivism. The momentum toward the come shot propels the moment forward, from Hank taking notice of the bathroom to the group climax. Yet, the particular way in which maximum visibility is managed through framing, editing, and music pushes its effects far beyond concerns of sexual display. Shots of genital ejaculation are interspersed between medium and close-up shots of Hank and Wylie in individual, couple, and group formations. The sequence reroutes hard-core visibility away from the act of individual sexual completion so that its affective movement comes to characterize the consciousness-raising interclass, interrace, and interethnic buddy dynamics of this group.

Liberatory Gay Eroticism

L.A. Tool and Die concludes the "Working Man Trilogy" with a climactic (or perhaps more accurately counterclimactic) hard-core episode and "morning after" sequence that makes legible Hank and Wylie's status as buddies, coworkers, and lovers as they work in accord with one another to produce a liberatory gay outcome. The final sex scene unfolds with Wylie and Hank at Hank's property having settled into the van, ready to consummate their budding love; bathed in shadows and warm yellow light, they light a candle and rise up into each other's arms for a kiss (fig. 38). There follows a montage of dissolving, fading, and over-

FIGURE 38 Hank and Wylie rising for a kiss.

lapping images, the camera gently tracing the contours of Hank and Wylie's bodies as they fuck, caress, finger, suck, jerk, and hold and kiss one another in endless combinations.

The sense of fluidity and connectivity established by dissolves and gently panning camera movement is reinforced by dim, yellow lighting that, in coordination with the movement of the men's bodies, yields a changing combination of shadows and light, constantly shifting which parts of their bodies are most visible at what points, refusing to privilege any one character or body part. A steady 4/4 folk-rock ballad structured around a male voice joyfully humming continually circles around, the ascending melody sounding as if it is about to shift key, only to glide its way back down again to the original note and start the climb up again. Like the "outro" section common in Top 40 radio music, where instead of coming to a definite end a song sustains a melody on into its slow fade, the melody both repeats and endlessly develops giving it a quality of the never-ending, denying any sense of resolution.

The sequence nonetheless moves to fulfill its hard-core status by offering not one but a succession of four mutually experienced come shots. Yet, like the song's structure, these climaxes are not structured around the satisfaction of completion, resolution, and closure but instead continue to dissolve as simply one part of a repertoire of sex acts capable of arrangement and rearrangement into a variety of movements. The sequence refuses closure, leaving the viewer with a series of images that converge one into the next, as a come shot dissolves to Hank reaching down to hold and kiss Wylie, to a closer shot of this moment to another closer and noticeably brighter (less "mood-lit") shot of this moment, and closer into a view of Wylie's profile before a series of cross-fades merges their male-male encounter with the gradual sight of a spectacular desert sunrise.

The sequence results in a cinematic elaboration that figures a version of male-male intimacy through which sex acts of a wide and even predictable variety may be orchestrated into a mutual project of libidinally expansive experience. The episode situates ejaculatory pleasure within expansive and utopian terms where the "fall" of one ejaculation may be little more than a precondition for the rise of another, echoed in the choreography of the sex acts themselves, as they move in revolving patterns of reciprocity and mutuality (Wylie fucks Hank, Hank fucks Wylie, etc.). At the same time, the sequence refuses to represent sex in line with hard-core's chief trope of maximum visibility, offering the spectacle of the come shot yet keeping the lighting so low that it's uncertain at times who is who and what is what. It is not just in this instant that the viewer is denied the privilege of clinically inspecting the mechanics of sex through a lens of anatomical crudeness. Throughout the scene, the key acts that make up the repertoire of hardcore's vision of sex are not themselves rejected, but supplanted by a visual syntax that strives to make eroticism out of them.

This is achieved by subordinating the visibility of sex to the legibility of male-male intimacy. It refuses to fragment eroticism into discernable and reducible constituent parts that add up to some notion of what qualifies as sex. The viewer instead is given lines of camera movement that refuse to individuate the characters and music that refuses a logic of climactic finality, reward, and completion. The viewer is invited to see sexual acts as types of movement existing within a greater dynamic of shared erotic investment. This is rendered most legible by two moments of fucking that establish pleasure as occurring before showing where it comes from—first, with an image of Hank laying on his back in ecstasy that dissolves to an image of Hank being penetrated by Wylie, and, second, in a spirit of mutuality, an image that shows Wylie throwing his head back in ecstasy dissolving to a shot of Hank penetrating him.

This legibility, however, is not only about representing male-male desire in a more fluid and erotic way, but also about making the social and political contours of gay discourse legible and, in doing so, indexing the continued importance of gay liberation practices of consciousness-raising nearly a decade after their inception and at a moment when, as historians, theorists, and critics alike have noted, when early gay "movement" values were falling out of fashion.[81] Sexuality, eroticism, and work are developed over the course of the film's narrative, and this development is anchored in a specific set of socioeconomic concerns that position these elements in dynamic relation with one another. The film's representation of sex-as-erotic-expansion goes far beyond the function of providing narrative closure, rewarding Hank and Wylie for the labors of their sociosexual cultivation. The eroticizing representational register discussed above refuses, at least initially, the organization of these elements within a system of closure and climax.

The film's representation of work and sex and its interest in *work-as-sex* and *sex-as-work* is critical here. The film's narrative is propelled forward by its representation of work and sex as interrelated elements that work for or against, enabling or disabling liberatory gay eroticism. A motivational poster shown in the factory sequence just prior to

Hank and Wylie throwing in the towel and hitting the road will clarify. In large blocks of text around a photograph of speeding race cars the poster warns "LOST TIME CAN BE LOST FOREVER . . . Let's not waste it—every minute counts!" Ironically, rather than inspiring better work practice at the factory, it works to forecast the consciousness-raising discovery made by Hank and Wylie at the film's end. That is, Hank and Wylie discover that the best way to cultivate and sustain the fruit of their labors—both as lovers, buddies, and farmers—is to take this up as an invitation; not just to "lose" time "forever," but more particularly to live "off the clock" of the daily grind. Thus, not unlike their use of stock hard-core sex acts, the buddies find the truth of their desire in characteristically restrictive forms and use the inventiveness and resilience of the 1970s rabble-rousing trucker to "go their own way" with it.

Most importantly, though, is how their decision to go "off the clock" brought them into contact with new ways of living; with more time on their hands, both Wylie's romanticism and Hank's hard-core penchant for "sport fucking" could be applied in new, more expansive ways. Here, the film echoes the liberatory potential of certain forms of polymorphously perverse activity. Informed by a combination of Marxist and Freudian theory, Herbert Marcuse posited that industrial capitalism promoted a form of alienated labor wherein the worker came to the false belief that he must live a separation between labor and pleasure as a consequence of a naturally occurring scarcity of goods that is, in actuality, imposed by the dominant class. This separation promoted in the worker a "false consciousness" that hinges on the polarization of pleasure with labor productivity, with the former only to be experienced as the reward for work. For Marcuse, this had extreme consequences for the organization of sex in relation to labor; sex must be sublimated to the "false" needs of labor that reroutes libidinal energy into economic productivity as a matter of survival. Describing the mechanics of this phenomenon, Marcuse explains:

> Men do not live their own lives but perform pre-established functions, while they work, they do not fulfil their own need and faculties but work in *alienation*. Work has now become *general* and so have the restrictions placed upon the libido; labor time, which is the largest part of the individual's life time, is painful time, for alienated labor is absence of gratification, negation of the pleasure principle. Libido is diverted for socially useful performance in which the individual works for himself only in so far as he works for the apparatus, engaged in activities that mostly do not coincide with his faculties and desires.[82]

Both story and hard-core performance (at levels of acting and film form) in *L.A. Tool and Die* seem to almost lampoon the problem of alienated labor as libidinal extraction and drain while earnestly investing in the question of getting beyond labor's obstruction of pleasure and plentitude. The film's narrative elaboration of sex is placed in homologous relation to the fulfillment of hard-core porn's industrially mandated generic protocols (seeing everything, genital focus, the closing come shot). In the film's final sequence, libido does not appear blocked by the apparatus of industrial labor but is rather given space for expansion by a noncompliant, counter-hard-core performance of seemingly hard-core sex.

Just as Hank and Wylie refuse to fulfill their preestablished function within the factory, opting instead to pursue self-employment through their agricultural venture, both these characters and the film refuse to fulfill the hard-core mode, to produce any finalizing climactic proof of an individual's singular experience of sexual pleasure—to fulfill what Richard Dyer has called "the goal of pornographic narrative."[83] Instead, running counter to the terms of normative productivity, the film demotes hard-core sex to a representation of libidinal expansion, so that instead of demonstrating pleasure in a final moment of ejaculatory expulsion and exhaustion—turning desire out *as* proof of visibly complete satisfaction—the film sustains the acts of hard-core sex only to dissolve them in temporal and spatial syntax of erotic expansion and accumulation.

The film, of course, does not function as a coherent exemplar of Marcusian theory: it is, after all, still tied at both at narrative and industrial levels to a variety of apparatuses (the porn industry, the state of California, the capitalist economy). However, it would be a mistake to dismiss its engagement with such ideas as merely inconsequential play. In this film's persistent stressing of the value of cultivation, and cultivation that is pursued in defiance of the normative economic, sociosexual, and cultural standards of US life in the 1970s, the film's insistence on keeping relations between sex and work in play potently allegorizes and facilitates a feeling for liberation.

These actors may be narratively working toward romance and erotic expansion, just as they are industrially working to sell movies, but in both instances they are also doing more than this. In a world that considers male-male desire excessive, a hedonistic overload of pleasure, the film's negotiation and even intensification of porn tropes to weave a story about cultivation and process acutely aligns with the project of gay liberation. While the film cannot escape the apparatuses it works within and as part of, it can and does use the tools that come from them to feel out other possibilities.

There are historically specific ways in which the film's elaboration of sex and work as interrelated contributes to the consciousness-raising, world-making politics of gay liberation. Summarizing some of the key tenets of the movement, Carl Whitman notes the importance of using collective expressions of male-male desire to "step outside the straight man's myths and institutions, to suspend the limited ways we deal with each other and experiment with new ways of relating."[84] Such a movement of collective bonding is reinforced by the overall affective and narrative movement of *L.A. Tool and Die* as it moves each protagonist closer and closer into states of intersubjectivity, only allowing them to achieve this intersubjectivity after each man willingly undergoes a shift into new kinds of collectivizing experience, Hank through quitting his job and going for it with Wylie, and Wylie through joining the team, so to speak, and enjoying the expanded relation of group sex.

The "morning after" scene demonstrates the overall collectivist spirit that underpins the trilogy. Momentarily back in romance mode, a lush symphonic score accompanies as Wylie heads out for a morning walk. Through his pensive manner, the viewer is made aware that he is still troubled by his experience in Vietnam; the non-diegetic sounds of bombs exploding and his lover's final words repeat, funneled through the sounds of echo effects that signal his impactful recall of past harms; the voice of his lost love repeats "don't forget me, man . . . just let somebody else inside . . . promise me." Reminiscent of the rapid shift in generic mood from fusion to classical music earlier in the men's room orgy scene, the soundtrack comes to an abrupt halt, broken by the loud metallic clanking sound of a hammer striking down repeatedly. Wylie's downcast expression turns to a confident smile as he looks on to discover Hank pounding a homemade for-sale sign into the ground. Sounding resolved and relaxed—having moved past the upset of his discovery of being ripped off by the land office—Hank reports that he might as well try and get his money back. Then, miraculously, water comes erupting out of the ground, first a small fountain, but then picking up force and momentum, showering the men and the surrounding landscape. Ecstatic, they begin shouting, leaping, embracing, and twirling. This moment of triumph is sustained for several minutes through a montage of dissolves, before a final cross-fade reveals Hank and Wylie's life a little later with an image of the men overlaid with an image of an irrigation pipe, and then a slow camera zoom moving from a close-up to a panoramic view, revealing the land, now filled with orange trees, stretching off into blue sky (fig. 39).

The final scene marks this abundance as a consequence of Hank and Wylie's disinvestment in an economy structured around alienated labor and their investment in an economy structured around the integration of work and pleasure. This is a direct consequence of the fact that the men refuse to comply with a value system that is predicated upon a false threat of annihilation as the outcome of an imagined scarcity; that pivots on the belief that they will *always* need more than what they have if they are ever to survive as independent, self-sufficient individuals.

While not necessarily transcendent in value, by the film's end it becomes clear that there is one crossover that can be said to characterize the trilogy as a whole: the oscillation from individuality to collectivity *and* the repeated framing of this movement as part of shift from conditions of scarcity to one of abundance. This sense of abundance is everywhere reinforced in the primary elements that comprise and shape the dramatic action of the film, so that what begins as a story

FIGURE 39 Hank and Wylie's newfound land of abundance.

whose elements are men, the road, and sex, by its end weaves together elements as varied as romance; war; homesteading; working-class solidarity; cross-country travel; bar brawling; sea gazing; stone skipping; unbounded male-male intimacy in bars, gas stations, battlefields, bathrooms, truck cabs, public parks, forests, deserts, abandoned houses, storerooms, offices, convertibles (including participants who are old, young, female, black, Latino, security guards, prostitutes, backpackers); and so on. These elements work not simply as a backdrop or pretext for sex but, as has been explored here, play a central role in *how* these character's relationships are developed as constituent elements within a complex social geography.

The world of abundance that Hank and Wylie come to know is not a new world manifested through the joint venture of two individuals, a consequence of elements coming into a state of concord through matrimony. The world they come into appears not as a sphere that they create, but rather *the* world, as in the world at large. These final moments illustrate an erotics of male-male desire that is deeply resonant with strategies of gay consciousness-raising and its particular emphasis on process over and above outcome. As one consciousness-raising group wrote in a 1970 manifesto, "we have been finding new ways of relating to one another . . . providing support for one another in our attempts to change our role-oriented behavior . . . gays need not be isolated; strength comes from the fusion of consciousness."[85] With no clearly articulated aim in sight, the language here consistently articulates consciousness-raising through a sense of movement with little sense of destination, stressing process-oriented terms such as finding, relating, providing, attempting, supporting, and fusing. Placed in relation to the world-making, collectivizing aims of gay liberation *as a social process*, these terms reinforce a feeling of connectivity and movement, a feeling that, if it can be reduced to a single outcome, is no more or no less than that of fellowship.

Hank and Wylie's relationship is precisely one of this kind. That is, within a mode of fellowship, where relations are constituted and experienced through shared processes of association and activity, Hank and Wylie pursue an experience of harmony that pivots on the way in which the individual and collective are organized in relation to one another. The sweeping parabolic trajectory of the story as it moves from the indentured world they leave behind at the factory and into the agrarian future that lies before them, paired with their concomitant shift from various kinds of sexual isolation into shared erotic fulfillment, works sharply to illustrate a model of liberation. As Marcuse has argued, libidinal energy, once unrestricted by a system of alienated labor, can be self-directed toward "culture-building" projects. Arguing for the importance of what he calls a "supra-individual process on common ground," he suggests that the "unrepressed force" of the libido "can promote the formation of culture only under the conditions which relate associated individuals to each other in the cultivation of the environment."[86]

Within the hard-core buddy dynamics of the trilogy, such a project of liberation plays out through a register of gay consciousness-raising as Hank and Wylie cultivate their relationship and come to know each other more fully on the common ground of their desire for men, their shared economic and occupational circumstance, and their (initial) shared reluctance to experiment with new ways of living—in other words, by making and desiring something out of their associations. This is, arguably, what gay world-making is really about, not the erection of a new sphere that protectively and/or defensively ropes off, draws lines, and demarcates, creating new institutions to exist within, but a series of relations capable of moving through, making, and remaking the world at large. As Dennis Altman noted just a few years into the gay liberation movement:

> It may indeed be profitable to regard liberation as process rather than an attainable goal, to regard men like Marcuse . . . as providing us with aims for which we strive. Liberation does not mean the end to struggle, but it does alter the ends for and the means by which we struggle.[87]

The "Working Man" trilogy embodies this sense of how struggle as a process, but even more, as a movement, is at its most generative when approached without a specific end in sight. The film's emphasis on circulatory processes of regeneration—whether in the sight of the spring rerouted into an irrigation system or a hard-core climax rerouted into romance—demonstrates how a regard for cultivation as a process in and of itself may bring about a recognition of the abundance of the world.

Conclusion

By 1979, the independent film culture that had been born in the late 1960s with the steep decline of Hollywood's dominance was now, itself, swiftly entering a state of decline. The "blockbuster syndrome" initiated by *Jaws* in 1975 changed not only what kind of movies got made but how many and how they were distributed. Studios managed their financial risk by making fewer movies, then ramping them up to event status with an onslaught of television advertising, cross-promotion, and saturation booking. The formula was successful enough to turn around Hollywood's fortunes.[1] Movie theaters like the Park that, earlier in the decade, had offered spaces for independent film culture to thrive were now returning to mainstream movie fare.[2] The late 1960s through the late 1970s proved to be an anomaly: a confluence of factors—the Hollywood recession, the socioeconomic crisis faced by many urban centers, the radical challenging of obscenity law—came together to occasion an opening, however brief, for a rich, substantial, and deeply eclectic world of cinema.

Reflecting on the intersection of cinema and gay life explored in this book, it is tempting to see a story of failure and foreclosure: forms of cinema and social experience that just couldn't make it in the face of big-budget cultural production, gentrification, and the harnessing of LGBTQ+ life to the demographic logic of US consumerism. It would be a mistake, however, to construct a "golden age" narrative about a lost revolution. This book does not endeavor to retrieve aspects of this past in order to argue that what we need is a "return." Rather, the reconsideration of artifacts undertaken here has taken place alongside a continued circulation of at least some of the films, one that has only increased in recent years. These old films continue to make contact with audiences who have been around since the start while also engaging new, younger audiences. There is something persistent in their cinematic elaborations, something that continues to speak and that keeps people showing up and even fostering new forms of cultural production and social contact.

There have been four sites of cultural production and participation that have helped to keep these films circulating. First, there is a circuit of large-scale national and international LGBTQ+ film festivals. Festivals such as Mix New York, BFI Flare, Fringe London, Frameline, and others have continued to accommodate archival and historical material. Second, event screenings organized by museums, art galleries, university cinemas, and performance spaces both large and small have played a large role in these films being more widely seen. Third, there is the emergence of event-centered queer cinema microcultures in major cities around the world. London-based Sam Ashby's "Little Joe" and Los Angeles–based Bradford Nordeen's "Dirty Looks" operate both in their home cities and in traveling road-show formats. Similarly, curator-researcher-writers such as William E. Jones, Stuart Comer, and M. M. Serra, to name a few, keep hard-to-see titles in view (e.g., Serra presented Charles Henri Ford's rarely seen *Johnny Minotaur* for the Denver Film Society). Finally, there has been the vital growth of queer cinema studies within academia in recent years.

Twenty years ago much of this body of work risked falling out of existence. Some of it certainly has, and some of it is still at risk, but the cinematic elaborations of gay life made between the mid-1940s and late 1970s are, as we speak, returning to life in university classrooms, film institutes, museums, and numerous special event spaces and sites. Within a month of my writing this, in fact, "Dirty Looks" will be rescreening films shown at the first-ever Park film program as part of special program of summer event screenings in Los Angeles.

These forms of circulation raise new questions. Did the sociosexual spaces imagined and created through the elaboration of gay cinema and its relatively low budgets and admission prices perhaps encourage a certain kind of looseness—a contingent, uncertain kind of togetherness—that is harder to come by today? What is the difference between dutifully attending a required screening as part of a university course, turning up to a special one-off screening of a rare, bucket-list movie, or ending up in the wrong (but maybe right!) place at some random time?

It is easy to be cynical about the cultural capital that accrues around these films as art objects—or as curios and relics. David Church, surveying the taste for vintage pornography, notes the potential for "cultish revival" and attracting "slummers." Here, "tactile signifiers of pastness call back to the days when adult cinema seemed more 'rebellious' because of its semi-licit status as an excitingly naughty sexual commodity." Thornier or more challenging aspects of the films are overlooked. However, he goes on to observe how "latterday revivalism also appears invested in a more earnest memorialization of sexual pioneers," spurring reevaluation and new cultural production.[3] Church's thoughtful accounting of the ways current audiences make sense—and culture—out of artifacts is instructive.

There are a number of recent works that engage with the material explored in *Coming Together,* much of which seeks to expand its potential beyond the parameters of male-male desire. For example, according to filmmakers A. L. Steiner and A. K. Burns, who made the film *Community Action Center* (2010), "we were deeply inspired by sixties and seventies gay porn-romance-liberation films like those of Fred Halsted, James Bidgood, Jack Smith and Joe Gage. We were also heavily influenced by feminist film and video artists such as Maya Deren, Lynda Benglis, Yoko Ono, Valie Export, Ulrike Ottinger, Carolee Schneemann, Barbara Hammer and many others."[4] The result is a film that pastiches iconic gay male imagery while renegotiating it and denaturalizing it through a feminist revaluation of erotic world-making. Nathan Schiff's 2008 film *Abracadaver!* both incorporates Peter de Rome as an actor, playing the leader of a homoerotic cult of magicians, and emulates common tropes in de Rome's films such as images of wandering and ritual initiation. William E. Jones's 2006 video work *V.O.*, which the director describes as a "mash-up," orchestrates images culled from gay hard-core cinema in order to create "a new narrative space [that] pays tribute to a former era of gay life and cinephilia."[5] Playing with duration, the film highlights affective dimensions of gay hard-core that become apparent when recontextualized.

As I was writing this conclusion, reflecting on lost horizons of experience and forms of contact, I came across an image online, showing a sandwich board outside Alley Cat Books and Gallery in San Francisco promoting a screening of *Pink Narcissus* (fig. 40). The world of *Pink Narcissus* awaits viewers free of charge. The sign invites us to think about

FIGURE 40 Street promotion for a special screening of *Pink Narcissus*. Photograph by Irwin Swirnoff. Used with permission.

the ways *Pink Narcissus* now participates in new forms of elaboration. No longer framed as "a homosexual's visual fantasy," instead it is clearly marked as a queer film. Encountering the board, a stranger might make a note to come back for the screening at 7 p.m., or they might look up "my gaze/yr gaze"—a phrase suggesting cinema as a site of exchange and equivalency—and discover that the screening is one of a series, placing the film in an eclectic transnational and transhistorical constellation of queer cinema from early 1960s British realism (*A Taste of Honey* [Tony Richardson, 1961]) to twenty-first-century American independent film (*By Hook or by Crook* [Harry Dodge, Silas Howard, 2001]).

They might even read an interview with organizer Irwin Swirnoff discussing the gentrification of the Bay Area, the closure of its last lesbian bar, and the need to create free community spaces.[6] While many of the forms of sociality and world-making elaborated here may not have existed at the time of the film's release, this does not mean *Pink Narcissus* is merely an arbitrary intruder to a new context: the visionary intensity of its mediation of male-male desire and its circulation as a gay text is part of what has made it available to new considerations, new audiences, and new spaces. The sign beautifully illustrates that, nearly fifty years later, *Pink Narcissus* still carries with it the liberatory potential of coming together.

Notes

INTRODUCTION

1. Daniel Harris, *The Rise and Fall of Gay Culture* (New York: Hyperion, 1997), 117–18.
2. Stephen Paul Davies, *Out at the Movies: A History of Gay Cinema* (Harpenden: Kamera Books, 2008), 13.
3. Davies, 14.
4. Tim Dean, "Introduction: Pornography, Technology, Archive," in *Porn Archives*, ed. Tim Dean and Steven Ruszcycky (Durham, NC: Duke University Press, 2014), 11.
5. George Chauncey, *Gay New York: Gender, Urban Culture, and the Making of the Gay Male World* (New York: Harper Collins Books, 1994).
6. Chauncey, 14. Chauncey explains that "the term *gay* began to catch on in the 1930s and its primacy was consolidated during the war. By the late 1940s, younger gay men were chastising older men who still used the term *queer*, which the younger men now regarded as demeaning." Chauncey, 19.
7. Chauncey, 20–21.
8. Chauncey, 19.
9. James Kepner, K. O. Neal, Emmaline Landy, and Lyn Pederson, "Toujours gai," *Pursuit & Symposium* 1, no. 1 (March/April 1966): 3.
10. Association of Motion Pictures Producers, Inc., "The Motion Picture Production Code," March 31, 1930. Reprinted as appendix 1 in Richard Maltby, *Hollywood Cinema*, 2nd ed. (Hoboken, NJ: Blackwell Publishing, 2003), 595.
11. Ronald Gregg, "Gay Culture, Studio Publicity, and the Management of Star Discourse: The Homosexualization

of William Haines in Pre-Code Hollywood," *Quarterly Review of Film and Video*, 20, no. 2 (2003): 82. While Gregg's study focuses on how the career of William Haines exemplifies this shift through his films and the surrounding star discourse that regularly incorporated references to his status as a male-desiring man, he also explores how by 1933 numerous actors who offered audiences images of gender dissidence and sexual nonconformity including "Tallulah Bankhead, John Gilbert, Buster Keaton, Pola Negri, Edna May Oliver, Charlie Farrell and Al Jolson, among others were dropped [by MGM] from their star status." Gregg, 93.

12. For a comprehensive study of this phenomenon and its relationship to constructions of male-male desire in twentieth-century art and cultural production, see Richard Meyer, *Outlaw Representation: Censorship and Homosexuality in Twentieth-Century American Art* (Boston: Beacon Press), 2002.
13. Patricia R. Zimmermann, *Reel Families: A Social History of Amateur Film* (Bloomington: Indiana University Press, 1995), 108.
14. Zimmermann, 118.
15. Patricia White, *Uninvited: Classical Hollywood Cinema and Lesbian Representability* (Bloomington: Indiana University Press, 1999).
16. Amy Villarejo, *Lesbian Rule: Cultural Criticism and the Value of Desire* (Durham, NC: Duke University Press, 2003), 1–4.
17. For a socializing use of postwar drag, see Jim Bailey's performance as Mae West in the film program of *Mondo Rocco* (Pat Rocco, 1970), where, set at Joani's nightclub in Los Angeles, an LGBTQ+ audience responds with copious laughter to Bailey's masterful performance. In terms of trans* sociality and world-making, the historical connection between audiovisual media, communication, and collectivization is a vital area in need of historical recovery work. Several excellent articles by Quinn Miller do explore how trans* positionalities are elaborated in the case of postwar television, but it is not yet certain how such material may have been taken up as part of the vernacular culture of trans* people at the time. See Quinn Miller, "The Bob Cummings Show's Artists at 'Work': Gender Transitive Programming and Counterpublicity," *Spectator* 28, no. 1 (2008): 10–28, and "Television," *TSQ: Transgender Studies Quarterly* 1, nos. 1–2 (2014): 216–19.
18. For examples of drag references to Hollywood cinema, see Esther Newton, *Mother Camp: Female Impersonators in America*, 2nd ed. (Chicago: University of Chicago Press, 1979), 16, 87.
19. In the specific case of Barbara Hammer, the filmmaker reports, "in 1975 Terry Cannon invited me to screen at the Los Angeles Film Forum. Up until this point I had only shown in dyke coffeehouses, bars, and local cinematheques." Barbara Hammer, *Hammer! Making Movies Out of Sex and Life* (New York: The Feminist Press at the City University of New York, 2010), 75.
20. The notion of intersubjectivity as a mode of special importance within the life experience of male-desiring men is explored by Earl Jackson Jr.

in *Strategies of Deviance: Studies in Gay Male Representation* (Bloomington: Indiana University Press, 1995), 20–23.

21. For a good example of the concept of sex roles in gay liberation philosophy, see "Gay Revolution and Sex Roles" written by the groups Third World Gay Revolution and Gay Liberation Front and published in *Chicago Gay Pride*, 1971 (under the title "Statement" before it was republished in *Out of the Closets: Voices of Gay Liberation*, ed. Karla Jay and Allen Young, 2nd ed., 252–62 [New York: Pyramid Books, 1974]).
22. Eve Kosofsky Sedgwick, *Touching Feeling: Affect, Pedagogy, Performativity* (Durham, NC: Duke University Press, 2003), 150.
23. Michael Warner, *Publics and Counterpublics* (New York: Zone Books, 2002), 16.
24. Warner, 122.
25. Warner, 57.
26. As George Chauncey notes, "Gay people in the prewar years . . . did not talk of *coming out of* what we call the 'gay closet' but rather of *coming out into* what they called 'homosexual society' or the 'gay world,' a world neither so small, nor so isolated, nor, often, so hidden as 'closet' implies." Chauncey, *Gay New York*, 7.
27. Samuel R. Delany, *Shorter Views: Queer Thoughts & The Politics of the Paraliterary* (Hanover, CT: Wesleyan University Press, 1999), 91; Richard Dyer, "Coming Out as Going In: The Image of the Homosexual as a Sad Young Man," *The Matter of Images: Essays on Representation* (London: Routledge, 1993), 73–92.
28. Chauncey, *Gay New York*, 350–55.
29. Annette Kuhn, *Ratcatcher* (London: BFI Film Classics, 2008), 71.

CHAPTER ONE

1. Allan Bérubé, *Coming Out under Fire: The History of Gay Men and Women in World War Two* (New York: The Free Press, 1990), 141–43, 33.
2. Alfred Charles Kinsey, Wardell Baxter Pomeroy, Clyde Eugene Martin, and Sam Sloan, *Sexual Behavior in the Human Male* (Philadelphia: W. B. Saunders Company, 1948), 650.
3. David K. Johnson, *The Lavender Scare: The Cold War Persecution of Gays and Lesbians in the Federal Government* (Chicago: University of Chicago Press, 2004).
4. Johnson, 166.
5. Juan A. Suárez, *Bike Boys, Drag Queens and Superstars: Avant-Garde, Mass Culture, and Gay Identities in the 1960s Underground Cinema* (Bloomington: Indiana University Press, 1996), 82.
6. Martin Meeker, *Contacts Desired: Gay and Lesbian Communications and Community, 1940s–1970s* (Chicago: University of Chicago Press, 2006), 1.
7. Dian Hanson, *Bob's World: The Life and Boys of AMG's Bob Mizer* (Cologne: Taschen, 2009), 19.

8. Johnson, *The Lavender Scare*, 169–71; "International Bachelors Fraternal Orders for Peace and Social Dignity," mentioned in Online Archive of California, "Mattachine Society Project Collection," accessed May 2, 2017, http://www.oac.cdlib.org/findaid/ark:/13030/kt7w1035mz/.
9. Johnson, *The Lavender Scare*, 168.
10. Johnson, 70.
11. For a detailed history of the formation and activities of these groups, see John D'Emilio, *Sexual Politics, Sexual Communities: The Making of a Homosexual Minority in the United States, 1940–1970* (Chicago: University of Chicago Press, 1983).
12. Alice L. Hutchison, *Kenneth Anger: A Demonic Visionary* (London: Black Dog Publishing, 2001), 31.
13. Curtis Harrington, Nice Guys Don't Work in Hollywood: The Adventures of an Aesthete in the Movie Business (Chicago: Drag City Incorporated, 2013), 33; Ara Osterweil, "America Year Zero," *Artforum*, January 2017, 191–94.
14. For a history of the censorship of illicit films thematized around male-male desire between 1945 and 1969, see Thomas Waugh, *Hard to Imagine: Gay Male Eroticism in Photography and Film from Their Beginnings to Stonewall* (New York: Columbia University Press, 1996), 273–83.
15. Harry Benshoff and Sean Griffin, *Queer Images: A History of Gay and Lesbian Film in America* (Lanham, MD: Rowman and Littlefield Publishers, Inc., 2006), 36–37; Richard Dyer, *The Culture of Queers* (London: Routledge, 2002), 90–115.
16. Jeffery P. Dennis, *We Boys Together: Teenagers in Love before Girl-Craziness* (Nashville: Vanderbilt University Press, 2007), 14.
17. Dennis, 14.
18. Michael DeAngelis, *Gay Fandom and Crossover Stardom: James Dean, Mel Gibson, and Keanu Reeves* (Durham, NC: Duke University Press, 2001), 51.
19. DeAngelis, 57.
20. David James, *The Most Typical Avant-Garde: History and Geography of Minor Cinemas in Los Angeles* (Berkeley: University of California Press, 2005), 15.
21. James, 16–17.
22. Whitney Strub, *Perversion for Profit: The Politics of Pornography and the Rise of the New Right* (New York: Columbia University Press, 2011), 38.
23. *Physique Pictorial* 10, no. 4 (April 1961): 17. A later issue also mentions a 1965 screening of physique films at the One Institute (then at 3473½ Cahuenga Boulevard in Hollywood) under the comedic event title "How a Well Built Man Can Succeed in Movies," making additional mention, in what is very possibly an important moment of changing practice in the policing of explicitly homoerotic film, that this event successfully showed films of fully naked men without suffering censorship. *Physique Pictorial* 11, no. 4 (June 1965): 2.
24. P. Adams Sitney, *Visionary Film: The American Avant-Garde, 1943–2000* (New York: Oxford University Press, 2002), 18–19.

25. Robert H. V. Ollendorf, *The Juvenile Homosexual Experience and Its Effect on Adult Sexuality* (New York: The Julian Press, 1966), 106.
26. Ollendorf, 107.
27. Suárez, *Bike Boys*, 129.
28. Suárez, 31.
29. "AMG Is Going into the Movie Business," *Physique Pictorial* 7 no. 4 (Winter 1957): 1.
30. Waugh, *Hard to Imagine*, 263.
31. Stephen Vider, "'Oh Hell, May, Why Don't You People Have a Cookbook?': Camp Humor and Gay Domesticity," *American Quarterly* 65, no. 4 (December 2013), 881.
32. *People of the State of California vs. Robert H. Mizer*, 1954, Municipal Court of Los Angeles, case no. 23722.
33. *Donald Thirkill vs. Physique Pictorial, et al.*, 1955, Superior Court of the State of California, case no. 642228.
34. Waugh, *Hard to Imagine*, 141–42.
35. *Physique Pictorial* 10, no. 1 (June 1960).
36. *Physique Pictorial* 5, no. 2 (Summer 1955): 15.
37. It is worth noting that a fantasy slave auction was also used as the centerpiece event of a fund-raiser emceed by gay filmmaker Pat Rocco at the Mark IV Bathhouse on April 10, 1976, an event that resulted in the large-scale deployment of police and the arrest of several participants as a consequence of the LAPD's inability to understand that this was not a genuine auctioning of male slaves. See "Police Raid at Slave Auction," *Drummer* 1, no. 6 (May/June 1976): 12–14; Judy Willmore, "The Great Slave-Market Bust: A Story Only Los Angeles Could Produce," *The Advocate*, May 5, 1976, 13–14.
38. As explored in chapter 2, James Bidgood's 1971 film *Pink Narcissus* uses camp in a similar fashion, though with a much more sustained and elaborate investment in the possibilities of camp expression.
39. *Physique Pictorial* 10, no. 2 (August 1960): 2.
40. Laura Kipnis, *Bound and Gagged: Pornography and the Politics of Fantasy in America* (New York: Grove Press, 1996), 163.
41. Suárez, *Bike Boys*, 182. Emanual Levy mentions the arrest of patrons at this screening in his article "Flaming Creatures: Jack Smith's Seminal Feature," on his blog Emanuel Levy Cinema 24/7, accessed August 13, 2017, http://emanuellevy.com/comment/flaming-creatures-the-making-and-unmaking-of-jack-smiths-seminal-feature-8/.
42. Suárez, *Bike Boys*, 183.
43. Janet Staiger, "Finding Community in the Early 1960s: Underground Cinema and Sexual Politics," in *Swinging Single: Representing Sexuality in the 1960s*, ed. Hillary Radner and Moya Luckett (Minneapolis: University of Minnesota Press, 1999), 40.
44. Staiger.

45. Paul Welch, "The Gay World Takes to the City Streets," part of the feature story "Homosexuality in America," *Life*, June 26, 1964, 45–56.
46. Warner, *Publics and Counterpublics*, 58.
47. Fabio Cleto, "Introduction: Queering the Camp," in *Camp: Queer Aesthetics and the Performing Subject; A Reader*, ed. Cleto (Ann Arbor: University of Michigan Press, 1999), 1–48.
48. For an extensive oral history of theatrical divisions in World War II, see Bérubé, *Coming Out under Fire*, especially the chapter titled "GI Drag: A Gay Refuge," 67–98.
49. Richard Dyer, *Heavenly Bodies: Film Stars and Society*, 2nd ed. (London: Routledge, 2004), 176.
50. William J. Mann, *Behind the Screen: How Gays and Lesbians Shaped Hollywood* (New York: Penguin Books, 2001), 343.
51. For a discussion of the important place of *What Ever Happened to Baby Jane?* in gay cultural reception, see David Halperin, *How to Be Gay* (Cambridge: The Belknap Press of Harvard University, 2012), 140.
52. As George Chauncey notes, gay men in the postwar years increasingly "defined themselves as gay primarily on the basis of their homosexual interests rather than effeminacy, and many of them, in a break with older homosexual cultural norms, adopted a new, self-consciously 'masculine' style." Chauncey, *Gay New York*, 21.

CHAPTER TWO

1. Jim Clifford, "Marathon Suggestions for Our Relationship to the Media," October 11, 1970, Box 12, Folder 130, Foster Gunnison Jr. Archive and Special Collections, Thomas J. Dodd Research Center, University of Connecticut.
2. Lillian Faderman and Stuart Timmons, *Gay L.A.: A History of Sexual Outlaws, Power Politics, and Lipstick Lesbians* (New York: Basic Books, 2006), 1–2.
3. David Carter, *Stonewall: The Riots That Sparked the Gay Revolution*. (New York: St. Martin's Press, 2005), 109. For an extensive historical recovery of this event, see Victor Silverman and Susan Stryker, *Screaming Queens: The Riot at Compton's Cafeteria*, DVD, Frameline, San Francisco, 2010.
4. Lynn Witt, Sherry Thomas, and Eric Marcus, eds., *Out in All Directions: The Almanac of Gay and Lesbian America* (New York: Warner Books, 1995), 210.
5. Gay media event flyers, Box 11, Folder 116 and Box 14, Folder 171, Foster Gunnison Jr. Archive and Special Collections, Thomas J. Dodd Research Center, University of Connecticut.
6. Clifford, "Marathon Suggestions."
7. John Marvin, "The Great Gay Movie Boom," *Quorum* 2, no. 8 (n.d.).
8. Janet Staiger, *Authorship in Film*, ed. Staiger and David A. Gerstner (London: Routledge, 2003), 51.

9. Staiger.
10. Michel de Certeau, *The Practice of Everyday Life,* trans. Steven Rendall (Berkeley: University of California Press, 1984).
11. Staiger, *Authorship in Film,* 51.
12. Jon Lewis, *Hollywood vs. Hardcore: How the Struggle over Censorship Saved the Modern Film Industry* (New York: New York University Press, 2000), 146–47.
13. *Ginsberg v. New York,* 390 U.S. 629.
14. Lewis, *Hollywood vs. Hardcore,* 149.
15. Brochure for "Autumn at the Park," November/December 1968. From the personal collection of the author.
16. Stuart Samuels, *Midnight Movies* (New York: Macmillan Publishing Co., 1983), 10.
17. Waugh, "Cockteaser," in *Pop Out: Queer Warhol,* ed. Jennifer Doyle, Jonathan Flatley, and Jose Esteban Muñoz (Durham, NC: Duke University Press, 1996), 173.
18. Waugh, 67.
19. David A. Cook, *Lost Illusions: American Cinema in the Shadow of Watergate and Vietnam* (Berkeley: University of California Press, 2000), 3.
20. Douglas Gomery, "Motion Picture Exhibition in 1970s America," in Cook, *Lost Illusions,* 400.
21. Gomery.
22. For specific accounts in regard to each of these film categories, see Ed Guerrero, *Framing Blackness: The African-American Image in Film* (Philadelphia: Temple University Press, 1993), in particular the chapter titled "The Rise and Fall of Blaxploitation," 69–113; Eric Shaefer, "Gauging a Revolution: 16 mm Film and the Rise of the Pornographic Feature," in *Porn Studies,* ed. Linda Williams (Durham, NC: Duke University Press, 2004), 370–400; Cook, "Horror and the Mainstreaming of Exploitation" in Cook, *Lost Illusions,* 220–38.
23. Cook, "Horror and the Mainstreaming of Exploitation," 284.
24. Eddie Muller and Daniel Faris, *Grindhouse: The Forbidden World of "Adults Only" Cinema* (New York: St. Martins Griffen, 1996), 135.
25. Lewis, *Hollywood vs. Hardcore,* 168.
26. Lewis, 193.
27. Muller and Faris, *Grindhouse,* 12.
28. Gay cinema as a marketplace venture among theater owners, and in particular Shan Sayles, is discussed in Paul Alcuin Siebenand, "The Beginning of Gay Cinema in Los Angeles: The Industry and the Audience," PhD diss. (University of Southern California, June 1975), 84.
29. Advertisement for the Park-Miller, *Los Angeles Advocate,* September 1969, 21.
30. For a brief discussion of adult films released by Sher, see Shaefer, "Gauging a Revolution," 373; David James notes that Sher owned "half a dozen theatres in LA" and another "twenty-nine" nationally (James, *The Most Typical Avant-Garde,* 222); in an interview with the director Emile de Antonio,

he notes that the Art Guild Cinema extended to over "seventy theatres" in the western US alone. This contention would benefit from more research as it has implications for how vast in reach the distribution for proto-gay and gay film may have been. Gary Crowdus and Dan Georgakas, "'History Is the Theme of All My Films': An Interview with the Emile de Antonio," in *New Challenges for Documentary*, ed. Alan Rosenthal and John Corner (Manchester: Manchester University Press, 2005), 102.

31. For more on midnight movies, see J. Hoberman and Jonathan Rosenbaum, *Midnight Movies* (New York: Harper and Row, 1983).
32. Harold Bloom, *The Visionary Company*, 2nd ed. (New York: Cornell University Press, 1971), 2.
33. Greg Youmans, *Word Is Out*, Queer Film Classics (Vancouver: Arsenal Pulp Press, 2011), 108.
34. Youmans, 105.
35. Youmans, 108.
36. Ronald Gregg, "Fashion, Thrift Stores and the Space of Pleasure in the 1960s Queer Underground Film," in *Birds of Paradise: Costume as Cinematic Spectacle*, ed. Marketa Uhlirova (London: Koenig Books, 2013), 293–305, 300.
37. Parker Tyler, *Screening the Sexes: Homosexuality in the Movies* (New York: Anchor Books, 1972), 181.
38. Labrunie Ducasse, "Pink Narcissus," review in *Interview Magazine*, August 1971; reprinted by the DVD booklet for *Pink Narcissus* (London: BFI, 2007), 15–16.
39. *The Advocate*, no. 74, December 1971.
40. *The Advocate*, no. 74, December 1971.
41. *The Advocate*, no. 74, December 1971.
42. *The Advocate*, May 5, 1976, 7.
43. Aaron Betsky, *Queer Space: Architecture and Same Sex Desire* (New York: William Morrow and Company, 1997), 173.
44. Suárez, "Kenneth Anger: Clothing, Queerness, Magic," in Uhlirova, *Birds of Paradise*, 283.
45. Parker Tyler, *Sex Psyche Etcetera in the Film* (Middlesex: Penguin Books, 1971), 185.
46. Sarah Ahmed, *Queer Phenomenology* (Durham, NC: Duke University Press, 2006), 166.
47. Peter de Rome, *The Erotic World of Peter de Rome* (London: GMP, 1984), 138; the story of de Rome's involvement with the Keener Freedom Walk is also discussed in Mary Stanton, *Freedom Walk: Mississippi or Bust* (Jackson: University of Mississippi Press, 2003), 130–32.
48. De Rome, *The Erotic World of Peter de Rome*, 125.
49. De Rome, 138.
50. De Rome, 139.
51. *The Advocate*, no. 133, March 13, 1974, 35.

52. For a history of this festival, see Elena Gorfinkel, "Wet Dreams: Erotic Film Festivals of the Early 1970s and the Utopian Sexual Public Sphere," *Framework: The Journal of Cinema and Media* 47, no. 2 (2006): 59–86.
53. For more on the use of trance imagery in 1970s gay porn, see Ryan Powell, "Bijou (Wakefield Poole, 1972)," *Porn Studies* 4, no. 3 (2017): 280–88.
54. This exact location, the overall mise-en-scène, and several shot compositions used in *Double Exposure* were appropriated—sometimes to a tee—two years later in Wakefield Poole's box-office hit *Boys in the Sand* (1971), a fact that persistently bothered de Rome and which he spoke publically about throughout his life. In *The Erotic World of Peter de Rome*, the filmmaker writes that *Boys in the Sand*'s use of *The Fire Island Kids* was "probably the first case of porn plagiarism." De Rome, 142.
55. For a sustained discussion of this phenomenon, see the chapter titled "Frightening the Horses: Out of the Closets and into the Shadow" in Russo, *The Celluloid Closet: Homosexuality in the Movies* (Cambridge: Harper and Row Publishers, 1981), 125–80.
56. Betsky, *Queer Space*, 173.
57. Biography, ONE National Gay and Lesbian Archives, accessed August 2, 2017, http://www.oac.cdlib.org/findaid/ark:/13030/kt3k4025zg/admin/.
58. For a history of specific obscenity trials from 1945 to 1959, see Waugh, "Cockteaser," 273–83.
59. For more on the careful and programmatic use of music in Rocco's films, see Brian Wuest, "Defining Homosexual Love Stories: Pat Rocco, Categorization, and the Legitimation of Gay Narrative Film," *Film History* 29, no. 4 (2017): 76–78.
60. SPREE News Pictorial, August 1974.
61. See *Mondo Cane* (Paolo Cavara, Gualitero Jacopetti, Franco Prosperi, 1962), *Mondo Cane 2* (Cavara, Prosperi, 1963), *Mondo Bizarro* (R. L. Frost, 1966), and *Mondo Freudo* (Frost, 1966).
62. David Loovis, *Gay Spirit: A Guide to Becoming a Sensuous Homosexual* (New York: Strawberry Hill Publishing, 1974), 17.
63. While I am drawing here on P. Adams Sitney's conceptualization of visionary film in his work on avant-garde and experimental film, I am also seeking to explore some of the particular shades of meaning the term "visionary" might hold within the specific contexts of gay life and cultural production. For instance, whereas Sitney describes visionary film as a poetic cinema that "operates in different realms" from commercial film, with the two having "no significant influence on each other," much of gay visionary cinema is similarly invested in elaborating a poetic vision that would not be accommodated within mainstream commercial cinema while at the same time incorporating, revising, and re-encoding many of the codes and conventions found in commercial cinema. Thus, gay visionary cinema is just as often a revisionist cinema in relation to commercial cinema as it is separate and distinct from it. Sitney, *Visionary Film*, xiii.

CHAPTER THREE

1. Dyer, "Stereotyping," 37–39; Russo, *Celluloid Closet*, 175–79. This protest is explored in the documentary *Making the Boys* (Crayton Robey, 2011). It is also discussed in Matt Bell, ed., *The Boys in the Band: Flashpoints of Cinema, History and Queer Politics* (Detroit: Wayne State University Press, 2016), 12.
2. For a further exploration of the film's orchestration of homosexual versus queer types, see Ryan Powell, "Gothic Spatiality and the Limits of Gay Visibility," in Bell, 88–112. For other studies that explore the notion of types within the realm of gay culture, see Martin P. Levine, *Gay Macho: The Life and Death of the Homosexual Clone* (New York: New York University Press, 1998); Newton, *Mother Camp.*
3. Erving Goffman, *Relations in Public: Microstudies of the Public Order* (New York: Basic Books, 1971).
4. Martin Hoffman, *The Gay World: Male Homosexuality and the Social Creation of Evil* (New York: Bantam Books, 1969), back cover. For an exploration of the representation of gay life in sociological literature, see Jeffrey Escoffier, "Homosexuality and the Sociological Imagination," in *A Queer World*, ed. Martin Duberman (New York: New York University Press, 1997), 248–61.
5. Don Teal, *The Gay Militants* (New York: Stein and Day, 1971), cover sleeve.
6. Richard Dyer, "Stereotyping," in *Gays and Film*, ed. Richard Dyer (London: British Film Institute, 1977), 37.
7. Dyer, 36.
8. Dyer, 28.
9. Dyer, 38.
10. Cook, *Lost Illusions*, 2.
11. Cook, 3–4.
12. Noël Carroll, "The Future of Allusion: Hollywood in the Seventies (and Beyond)," *October* 20 (Spring 1982): 57–59; Mark Betz, "Art, Exploitation, Underground," in *Defining Cult Movies*, ed. Mark Jancovich, Antonio Lázaro Reboll, Julian Stringer, and Andy Wills (Manchester: Manchester University Press, 2003), 217–18.
13. Cook, *Lost Illusions*, 191.
14. Cook, 171.
15. Cook, 171.
16. Harry Benshoff and Sean Griffin, *Queer Images: A History of Gay and Lesbian Film in America* (Oxford: Rowman and Littlefield Publishers, 2006), 134.
17. Barbara Klinger, "The Road to Dystopia: Landscaping the Nation in *Easy Rider*," in *The Road Movie Book*, ed. Steven Cohan and Ina Rae Hark (London: Routledge, 1997), 179–204.
18. Susan Stryker, *Queer Pulp: Perverted Passions from the Golden Age of the Paperback* (San Francisco: Chronicle Books, 2001), 117.

19. Richard Amory, *Aaron's Song* (San Diego: Greenleaf, 1967), and *Listen, the Loon Sings* (San Diego: Greenleaf, 1968); Ricardo Armory, *Fruit of the Loon* (San Diego: Greenleaf, 1968).
20. David Bergman, "The Cultural Work of Sixties Gay Pulp Fiction," in *The Queer Sixties*, ed. Patricia Juliana Smith (New York: Routledge, 1999), 32.
21. Bergman, 29. Bergman has described the book as "part boy's book folksiness and oracular high-mindedness."
22. Michael Bronski, introduction to *Song of the Loon*, by Richard Amory (Vancouver: Arsenal Pulp Press, 2005), 10.
23. Amory, *Song of the Loon* (Vancouver: Arsenal Pulp Press, 2005; orig. published San Diego: Greenleaf, 1966), 78.
24. Jonathan Dollimore, *Sexual Dissidence: Augustine to Wilde, Freud to Foucault* (Oxford: Oxford University Press, 1991), 312.
25. David Shuttleton, "The Queer Politics of Gay Pastoral," in *De-Centering Sexualities: Politics and Representations beyond the Metropolis*, ed. Richard Phillips, Diane Watt, and David Shuttleton (London: Routledge, 2000), 131–32.
26. Tom Waugh, *Out/Lines: Underground Gay Graphics from Before Stonewall* (Vancouver: Arsenal Pulp Press, 2002), 35–37; Felix Lance Falkon with Thomas Waugh, *Gay Art: A Historic Collection* (Vancouver: Arsenal Pulp Press, 2006), 98–104; Micha Ramakers, *Dirty Pictures: Tom of Finland, Masculinity and Homosexuality* (New York: St. Martin's Press, 2000), 118–20.
27. Bronski, introduction to *Song of the Loon*, 11.
28. Amory, "Song of the Loon 'Becomes a Looney Tune,'" *Vector Magazine*, July 1970, reprinted in *Song of the Loon* (Vancouver: Arsenal Pulp Press, 2005), 221, 220.
29. Poster republished in *Little Joe: A Magazine about Queers and Cinema, Mostly*, no. 1 (2010), 66–67.
30. Phillip J. Deloria, *Playing Indian* (New Haven, CT, and London: Yale University Press, 1998), 161.
31. Deloria, 156.
32. Quoted in Stuart Timmons, *The Trouble with Harry Hay: Founder of the Modern Gay Movement* (Boston: Alyson Publications, 1990), 196.
33. The film is featured as a cover story in *The Advocate*, no. 88, June 21, 1972, 21.
34. Anonymous, "Notes on Gay-Male Consciousness-Raising," reprinted in Jay and Young, *Out of the Closets*, 295.
35. Leslie Fiedler, *The Return of the Vanishing American* (London: Cape, 1968), 25.
36. Quoted in Timmons, *The Trouble with Harry Hay*, 114.
37. David Savran, *Taking It Like A Man: White Masculinity, Masochism, and Contemporary American Culture* (Princeton, NJ: Princeton University Press, 1998), 125–26.
38. Savran, 125–26.
39. Savran, 127.

40. Steven Epstein, "Gay Politics, Ethnic Identity," in *Social Perspectives in Lesbian and Gay Studies: A Reader*, ed. Peter M. Narfi and Beth E. Schneider (London: Routledge, 1998), 148.
41. Carl Whitman, "A Gay Manifesto," in *We Are Everywhere: A Historical Sourcebook of Gay and Lesbian Politics*, ed. Mark Blasius and Shane Phelan (New York: Routledge, 1997), 386–87. Originally published in *The Red Butterfly* pamphlet, 1972.
42. Marcus Overseth, "Grows Rapidly; What Kind of People?," *San Francisco Free Press*, December 7–21, 1969.
43. Gary Alinder, "Alternative Culture," *San Francisco Free Press*, no. 5., November 15–30, 1969.
44. Scott Herring, "Out of the Closets, into the Woods: *RFD, Country Women*, and the Post-Stonewall Emergence of Queer Anti-Urbanism," *American Quarterly* 59, no. 2 (June 2007): 346.
45. Quoted in Donovan Bess, "Gay Advance Guard Will Visit Alpine," *San Francisco Chronicle*, November 10, 1970, 9.
46. Though listed in advertisements, AIP was only involved in the film's distribution.
47. Advertisement for *Some of My Best Friends Are . . .* in *The Nuntius* 2, no. 11 (November 1971).
48. See Vincent Canby, "Screen: One Night in a Gay Bar," *New York Times*, October 28, 1971, http://www.nytimes.com/movie/review?res=9D05E0DE1038EF34BC4051DFB667838A669EDE; Anonymous, "Movie Review: *Some of My Best Friends Are . . .* Two Viewpoints but a Must for You/All," *The Nuntius* 2, no. 11 (November 1971), 10.
49. "The Homosexual: Newly Visible, Newly Understood," *Time*, October 31, 1969, 56–57.
50. Kath Weston, "Get Thee to a Big City," *GLQ: Gay and Lesbian Quarterly Review* 2 (1995): 257.
51. John Grube, "Native and Settlers: An Ethnographic Note on Early Interaction of Older Homosexual Men with Younger Gay Liberationists," *Journal of Homosexuality* 20, nos. 3–4 (1990): 119.
52. Joseph Harry, "Urbanization and the Gay Life," *Journal of Sex Research* 10, no. 3 (1974): 242.
53. Review of *Some of My Best Friends Are . . .* in *The Nuntius* 2, no. 11 (November 1971).
54. Grube, "Native and Settlers," 133–34.
55. Dyer, "Stereotyping," 39.
56. Lucy Fisher uses the term "impossible geography" in an analysis of stage design in the musicals of Busby Berkeley to describe their use of aesthetics to establish "a synthetic cinematic universe." *Designing Women: Cinema, Art Deco, and the Female Form* (New York: Columbia University Press, 2003), 137.
57. New Line press kit *A Very Natural Thing*, Foster Gunnison Archives, University of Connecticut, Box 46, folder 438.

58. *The Advocate*, January 11, 1978, 30.
59. New Line press kit.
60. New Line press kit.
61. Benshoff and Griffin, *Queer Images*, 171.
62. Waugh, *The Fruit Machine* (Durham, NC: Duke University Press, 2000), 21.
63. Craig Alfred Hanson, "The Fairy Princess Exposed," in Jay and Young, *Out of the Closets*, 269.
64. Dean Gengle, "The Closet as Gay Group-Think," *The Advocate*, June 30, 1976, 29.
65. Waugh, *Fruit Machine*, 22.

CHAPTER FOUR

1. Dyer, *Only Entertainment*, 2nd ed. (London: Routledge, 2002), 142.
2. And not only male-desiring men: there is a long and underexplored history to be unearthed about women interested in and/or existing within contexts of male-male desire and sociality. For a discussion of this in the context of some of Joe Gage's 1970s hard-core cinema, see Ryan Powell, "Queer Interstates: Cultural Geography and Social Contact in *Kansas City Trucking Co.* and *El Paso Wrecking Corp.*," in *Queering the Countryside: New Frontiers in Rural Queer Studies*, ed. Mary L. Gray, Colin R. Johnson, and Brian J. Gilley, 181–202 (New York: New York University Press).
3. See Bérubé, *Coming Out under Fire*.
4. Daniel Harris, *The Rise and Fall of Gay Culture* (New York: Hyperion: 1997), 113.
5. Linda Williams, *Hard Core: Power Pleasure and the Frenzy of the Visible* (Berkeley: University of California Press, 1989), 48.
6. Williams, *Screening Sex* (Durham, NC: Duke University Press), 181–82.
7. Along with the titles explored in this chapter, see *Bijou* (Wakefield Poole, 1972); *Prometheus* (Peter de Rome, 1972); *Station to Station* (Tom DeSimone, 1974); *Ballet Down the Highway, Kiss Today Goodbye, Sex Magic, The Boys from Riverside Drive, A Night at the Adonis* (Deveau, 1978); *Navy Blue, Fire Island Fever* (Deveau, 1979); *Just Blonds* (Deveau, 1980).
8. José B. Capino, "Homologies of Space: Text and Spectatorship in All-Male Adult Theaters," *Cinema Journal* 45, no. 1 (2005): 50–65.
9. Capino, "Homologies of Space," 59.
10. Konstantin Berlandt, "My Soul Vanished from Sight: A California Saga of Gay Liberation" originally printed in *Gay Flames* Pamphlet no. 10, December 1970. Reprinted Jay and Young, *Out of the Closets*, 53.
11. Jay and Young, *Out of the Closets*, 274.
12. Reprinted in Jay and Young, 342.
13. José Esteban Muñoz, *Cruising Utopia: The Then and There of Queer Futurity* (New York: New York University Press, 2009), 49.
14. Dyer, *Only Entertainment*, 146.

15. For a 1974 screening of the film, a copy of *L.A. Plays Itself/Sex Garage* was brought into the permanent collection of the Museum of Modern Art in New York.
16. Attempts to censor the representation of gay sex in the early to mid-1970s were typically carried out on a local level. A particularly well-reported case was the cover story of the January 30, 1974, issue of *The Advocate*, in the article "Raids Jar Hollywood Gays," which detailed the a citywide raid on gay filmmakers including Pat Rocco, Jaguar Productions, and the Homosexual Entertainment Guild. *The Advocate* 130:1–3.
17. Companies include American Models Guild, Eight of Clubs, Hand in Hand Films, Jaguar Productions, Joe Gage Films, Signature, Poolmar, and Zenith Films.
18. Betsky, *Queer Space*, 21.
19. The golden boy is a reoccurring gay porn type that Jeffrey Escoffier has traced back to photographer and filmmaker J. Brian. As Escoffier puts it, the type designates "lightly built and handsome young men, often blonde." Jeffrey Escoffier, *Bigger Than Life: The History of Gay Porn Cinema from Beefcake to Hardcore* (Philadelphia: Running Press, 2009), 123.
20. Williams, *Screening Sex*, 151–54.
21. For a discussion of this phenomenon, see the section "Zapata Moustache," in Kevin Clarke, *Porn: From Andy Warhol to X-Tube* (Berlin: Bruno Gmünder, 2001), 98.
22. Carl Wittman, *A Gay Manifesto* (New York: Red Butterfly, 1969).
23. Hobson, *Lavender and Red: Liberation and Solidarity in the Gay and Lesbian Left* (Oakland: University of California Press, 2016), 30–31; Ronald K. Porter, "A Rainbow in Black: The Gay Politics of the Black Panther Party," *Counterpoints* 367, "Sexualities in Education: A Reader" (2012), 364–75.
24. Hobson, *Lavender and Red*, 31.
25. Huey Newton, "A Letter from Huey," in *The Gay Liberation Book: Writings and Photographs on (Gay) Men's Liberation*, ed. Len Richmond and Gary Noguera (San Francisco: Ramparts Press, 1973), 142–45.
26. Hobson, *Lavender and Red*, 33.
27. Hobson, 33–34.
28. Porter, "A Rainbow in Black," 368.
29. Delany notes of that in porn theaters "the population was incredibly heterogeneous—white, black, Hispanic, Asian, Indian, Native American, and a variety of pacific Islanders." Samuel R. Delany, *Times Square Red, Times Square Blue* (New York: New York University Press, 1999), 15; Jennifer C. Nash, *The Black Body in Ecstasy: Reading Race, Reading Pornography* (Durham, NC: Duke University Press, 2014), 82.
30. Wakefield Poole, *Dirty Poole: The Autobiography of a Gay Porn Pioneer* (Los Angeles: Alyson Books, 2000), 154.
31. Joe Wlodarz, "Beyond the Black Macho: Queer Blaxploitation," *Velvet Light Trap* (Spring 2004), 21.

32. *L.A. Plays Itself* and *Sex Garage* were constructed to and, at least to some extent, did play together as one piece, though advertisements tended to feature only *L.A.* on the listing.
33. Richard Dyer, "Underground and After," in *Now You See It*, 2nd ed. (London: Routledge, 1990).
34. William E. Jones, *Halsted Plays Himself* (Los Angeles: Semiotext(e), 2011), 23–27.
35. James, *The Most Typical Avant-Garde*, 374
36. Waugh, *Out/Lines*, 33.
37. Guy Hocquenghem, *Homosexual Desire* (London: Allison & Busby Limited, 1978), 131.
38. William E. Jones, *Halsted Plays Himself* (Los Angeles, Semiotext(e), 2011), 33.
39. Andrew Ross, "Uses of Camp," in *Camp: Queer Aesthetics and the Performing Subject; A Reader* (Ann Arbor: University of Michigan Press, 1999), 323; Mike Silverstein, "God Save the Queen," *Gay Sunshine*, no. 3, November 1970.
40. Caroll W. Pursell, *The Military-Industrial Complex* (New York: Harper & Row Publishers, 1972).
41. Steven Cohan, *Incongruous Entertainment; Camp, Cultural Value and the MGM Musical* (Durham, NC: Duke University Press, 2005), 18.
42. Arthur Evans. "Zap: You're Alive," in *Gay Today*, August 30, 1999, accessed July 31, 2017, http://gaytoday.badpuppy.com/garchive/viewpoint/083099vi.htm.
43. Rachel Schtier, *Striptease: The Untold History of the Girlie Show* (New York: Oxford University Press, 2004), 2.
44. Kurt Gänzl, *Lydia Thompson, Queen of Burlesque* (New York: Routledge, 2002), 77–101.
45. Richard Meyer, "*Gay Power* circa 1970: Visual Strategies for Sexual Revolution," *GLQ: A Journal for Lesbian and Gay Studies* 12, no. 3 (2006): 454.
46. Richard Terdiman, *Discourse/Counter-Discourse: The Theory and Practice of Symbolic Resistance in Nineteenth Century France* (Ithaca, NY: Cornell University Press, 1985), 76.
47. Mathew Tinckom, *Working Like a Homosexual: Camp, Capital, Cinema* (Durham, NC: Duke University Press, 2002), 42.
48. Dyer, *The Culture of Queers*, 63.
49. Linda Hutcheon, *Irony's Edge: The Theory and Politics of Irony* (London: Routledge, 1994), 95.
50. Bérubé, *Coming Out under Fire*, 69.
51. Bérubé, 82.
52. Bérubé, 72.
53. Bérubé, 79.
54. Earl Jackson Jr., *Strategies of Deviance* (Bloomington: Indiana University Press, 1995), 2.
55. Sam Binkley, *Getting Loose: Lifestyle Consumption in the 1970s* (London: Duke University Press, 2007), 3–4.

56. Binkley, 212.
57. Binkley, 172; J., *The Sensuous Woman* (New York: L. Stuart, 1969); M., *The Sensuous Man* (New York: L. Stuart, 1971); Alex Comfort, *The Joy of Sex* (New York: Simon and Shuster, 1977).
58. Altman, *Homosexual: Oppression and Liberation* (London: Allen Lane, 1971), 137.
59. Charles Silverstein and Edmund White, *The Joy of Gay Sex: An Intimate Guide for Gay Men to the Pleasures of a Gay Lifestyle* (New York: Crown Publishers, 1977).
60. Loovis, *Gay Spirit*, 165.
61. Anthony Giddens, *The Transformation of Intimacy: Sexuality, Love and Eroticism in Modern Societies* (Stanford, CA: Stanford University Press, 1992), 30.
62. De Rome, *The Erotic World of Peter de Rome*, 7.
63. John R. Burger, *One-Handed Histories: The Eroto-Politics of Gay Male Video Pornography* (New York: Harrington Park Press), 40.
64. For an analysis of the use of cultural geography in the film, see Ryan Powell, "Queer Interstates: Cultural Geography and Social Contact in *Kansas City Trucking Co.* and *El Paso Wrecking Corp.*," in *Queering the Countryside: New Frontiers in Rural Queer Studies*, ed. Mary L. Gray, Colin R. Johnson, and Brian J. Gilley, 181–202 (New York: New York University Press).
65. Eve Kosofsky Sedgwick, *Between Men: English Literature and Male Homosocial Desire* (New York: Columbia University Press, 1985), 1.
66. Stephen M. Engel. *The Unfinished Revolution* (Cambridge: Cambridge University Press, 2001), 45–46.
67. Cook, *Lost Illusions*, 24.
68. Cook, section titled "*Jaws*: The Paradigmatic Event Film of the Seventies," in *Lost Illusions*, 40–41; Peter Kramer, *The New Hollywood: From Bonnie and Clyde to Star Wars* (London: Wallflower Press, 2005), 9; Thomas Schatz, "The New Hollywood," in *Film Theory Goes to the Movies: Cultural Analysis of Contemporary Film*, ed. Jim Collins, Ava Preacher Collins, and Hillary Radner (Hoboken, NJ: Taylor and Francis, 2012), 17–20.
69. Cook, *Lost Illusions*, 43.
70. Cook, 43.
71. Examples include Robert Locke, "My Brother the Porn Star: An Interview with Richard Locke," *Blueboy* 27 (December 1978); "El Paso Wrecking Company," *Mandate* 3 no. 34 (February 1978): 68–69. Kearns, "The Gage Boys Are Rolling Again with *L.A. Tool and* Die," *Drum*, no. 34 (January 1981).
72. Joe Gage, "L.A. Tool & Die," *Numbers* 33 (November 1980): 68.
73. This metaphor is directly exemplified throughout in Edmund White and Tom Lake, *States of Desire: Travels in Gay America* (New York: Dutton, 1980).
74. Derek Nystrom, *Hard Hats, Rednecks, and Macho Men: Class in 1970s American Cinema* (New York: Oxford University Press, 2009).
75. Nystrom, 29.

76. Nystrom, 30.
77. Nystrom, 35.
78. Ibid., 83.
79. Nystrom, 84.
80. Advertisement for Waynes Art, *The Advocate*, October 8, 1975, 38: advertisement for *Naked Highwayman, After Dark* 8, no. 3 (July 1975), 21; advertisement for Bulldog Baths, *Blueboy*, December 1979.
81. For discussions of the shift away from gay movement values see: Dennis Altman, *The Homsexualization of America* (Boston: Beacon Press, 1982), 108–44; David Esienbach, *Gay Power" An America Revolution* (New York: Carrol & Graff, 2006); Seymour Kleinberg, *Alienated Affection: Being Gay in America* (New York: St, Martin's Press, 1980), 143–57;
82. Herbert Marcuse, *Eros and Civilization: A Philosophical Inquiry into Freud* (London: Routledge, 1998; first published by Routledge & Kegan Paul, 1956).
83. Richard Dyer, *Only Entertainment* (London: Routledge, 2002), 144.
84. Whitman, "A Gay Manifesto," 30.
85. Young, "Out of the Closets, Into the Streets," 30.
86. Marcuse, *Eros and Civilization*, 209–10.
87. Altman, *Homosexual*, 108.

CONCLUSION

1. Cook, *Lost Illusions*, 64–65.
2. "Alvarado/Park Theatre," *Los Angeles Theatres*, https://losangelestheatres.blogspot.com/2017/03/alvarado-theatre.html, accessed June 10, 2018.
3. David Church, *Disposable Passions: Vintage Pornography and the Material Legacies of Adult Cinema* (New York: Bloomsbury, 2016), 11.
4. Quoted in Greg Youmans, "Performing Essentialism: Reassessing Barbara Hammer's Films of the 1970s," *Camera Obscura* 81 (2012): 112.
5. https://williamejones.com/portfolio/v.o, accessed June 10, 2018.
6. Sarah Hotchkiss, "Projecting the Fight against Queer Erasure, Film by Film," *KQED*, accessed June 10, 2018, https://www.kqed.org/arts/13820341/queer-film-my-gaze-yr-gaze-alley-cat-books-irwin-swirnoff.

Bibliography

Ahmed, Sarah. *Queer Phenomenology*. Durham, NC: Duke University Press, 2006.

Alinder, Gary. "Alternative Culture." *San Francisco Free Press*, November 15–30, 1969.

Altman, Dennis. *Homosexual: Oppression and Liberation*. London: Allen Lane, 1971.

———. *The Homosexualization of America*. Boston: Beacon Press, 1982.

Amory, Richard. *Listen, the Loon Sings*. San Diego: Greenleaf Classics, Inc., 1968.

———. *Song of Aaron*. San Diego: Greenleaf Classics, Inc., 1967.

———. *Song of the Loon*. Vancouver: Arsenal Pulp Press, 2005. First published 1966 by Greenleaf Classics, Inc.

Armory, Ricardo. *Fruit of the Loon*. San Diego: Greenleaf Classics, Inc., 1968.

Bell, Matt, ed. *The Boys in the Band: Flashpoints of Cinema, History, and Queer Politics*. Detroit: Wayne State University Press, 2016.

Benemann, William. *Male-Male Intimacy in Early America: Beyond Romantic Friendships*. New York: Harrington Park Press, 2006.

Benshoff, Harry, and Sean Griffin. *Queer Images: A History of Gay and Lesbian Film in America*. Lanham, MD: Rowman and Littlefield Publishers, Inc., 2006.

Bergman, David. "The Cultural Work of Sixties Gay Pulp Fiction." In *The Queer Sixties*, edited by Patricia Juliana Smith, 26–42. New York: Routledge, 1999.

Berlandt, Konstantin. "My Soul Vanished from Sight: A California Saga of Gay Liberation." In *Out of the Closets: Voices of Gay Liberation*, edited by Karla Jay and Allen Young, 38–56. 2nd ed. New York: Pyramid Books, 1974. First published December 1970 in *Gay Flames* Pamphlet, no. 10.

Bérubé, Allan. *Coming Out under Fire: The History of Gay Men and Women in World War Two*. New York: The Free Press, 1990.

Bess, Donovan. "Gay Advance Guard Will Visit Alpine." *San Francisco Chronicle*, November 10, 1970.

Betsky, Aaron. *Queer Space: Architecture and Same Sex Desire*. New York: William Morrow and Company, 1997.

Betz, Mark. "Art, Exploitation, Underground." In *Defining Cult Movies: The Cultural Politics of Oppositional Tastes*, edited by Mark Jancovich, Antonio Lázaro Reboll, Julian Stringer, and Andy Wills, 202–22. Manchester: Manchester University Press, 2003.

Binkley, Sam. *Getting Loose: Lifestyle Consumption in the 1970s*. London: Duke University Press, 2007.

Bronski, Michael. Introduction to reprinted *Song of the Loon*, by Richard Amory, 9–26. Vancouver: Arsenal Pulp Press, 2005. First published 1966 by Greenleaf Classics, Inc.

Burger, John R. *One-Handed Histories: The Eroto-Politics of Gay Male Video Pornography*. New York: Routledge, 1994.

Buscombe, Edward, ed. *The BFI Companion to the Western*. London: Palgrave Macmillan on behalf of the British Film Institute, 1996.

Canby, Vincent. "Screen: One Night in a Gay Bar." *New York Times*, October 28, 1971. Accessed July 31, 2017. http://www.nytimes.com/movie/review?res=9D05E0DE1038EF34BC4051DFB667838A669EDE.

Capino, José B. "Homologies of Space: Text and Spectatorship in All-Male Adult Theaters." *Cinema Journal* 45, no. 1 (2005): 50–65.

Carroll, Noël. "The Future of Allusion: Hollywood in the Seventies (and Beyond)." *October* 20 (Spring 1982): 51–81.

Carter, David. *Stonewall: The Riots That Sparked the Gay Revolution*. New York: St. Martin's Press, 2005.

Chauncey, George. *Gay New York: Gender, Urban Culture, and the Making of the Gay Male World, 1890–1940*. New York: Basic Books, 1994.

Church, David. *Disposable Passions: Vintage Pornography and the Material Legacies of Adult Cinema*. New York: Bloomsbury, 2016.

Clarke, Kevin. *Porn: From Andy Warhol to X-Tube*. Berlin: Bruno Gmünder, 2001.

Cleto, Fabio. "Introduction: Queering the Camp." In *Camp: Queer Aesthetics and the Performing Subject; A Reader*, edited by Fabio Cleto, 1–48. Ann Arbor: University of Michigan Press, 1999.

Clifford, Jim. "Marathon Suggestions for Our Relationship to the Media." October 11, 1970. Box 12, Folder 130, Foster Gunnison Jr. Archive and Special Collections, Thomas J. Dodd Research Center, University of Connecticut.

Cohan, Steven. *Incongruous Entertainment: Camp, Cultural Value, and the MGM Musical*. Durham, NC: Duke University Press, 2005.

Comfort, Alex. *The Joy of Sex*. New York: Simon and Schuster, 1972.

Cook, David A. *Lost Illusions: American Cinema in the Shadow of Watergate and Vietnam*. Berkeley: University of California Press, 2000.

Crowdus, Gary, and Dan Georgakas. "'History Is the Theme of All My Films': An Interview with Emile de Antonio." In *New Challenges for Documentary,* edited by Alan Rosenthal and John Corner, 94–109. 2nd ed. Manchester: Manchester University Press, 2005.

DeAngelis, Michael. *Gay Fandom and Crossover Stardom: James Dean, Mel Gibson, and Keanu Reeves.* Durham, NC: Duke University Press, 2001.

de Certeau, Michel. *The Practice of Everyday Life.* 2nd ed. Translated by Steven Rendall. Berkeley: University of California Press, 1984.

Delany, Samuel R. *Shorter Views: Queer Thoughts & The Politics of the Paraliterary.* Hanover, CT: Wesleyan University Press, 1999.

———. *Times Square Red, Times Square Blue.* New York: New York University Press, 1999.

Deloria, Phillip J. *Playing Indian.* New Haven, CT, and London: Yale University Press, 1998.

D'Emilio, John. *Sexual Politics, Sexual Communities: The Making of a Homosexual Minority in the United States, 1940–1970.* Chicago: University of Chicago, 1983.

Dennis, Jeffery P. *We Boys Together: Teenagers in Love before Girl-Craziness.* Nashville: Vanderbilt University Press, 2007.

de Rome, Peter. *The Erotic World of Peter de Rome.* London: Gay Men's Press, 1984.

Dimendberg, Edward. *Film Noir and the Space of Modernity.* Cambridge, MA: Harvard University Press, 2004.

Dollimore, Jonathan. *Sexual Dissidence: Augustine to Wilde, Freud to Foucault.* Oxford: Oxford University Press, 1991.

Donald Thirkill vs. Physique Pictorial, et al. Superior Court of the State of California, case no. 642228, 1955.

Doty, Alexander. "The Queer Aesthete, the Diva, and *The Red Shoes.*" In *Out-takes: Essays on Queer Theory and Film,* edited by Ellis Hanson, 46–71. Durham, NC: Duke University Press, 1999.

Ducasse, Labrunie. Review of "Pink Narcissus," directed by James Bidgood. *Interview Magazine,* August 1971. Reprinted in the DVD booklet for *Pink Narcissus.* London: British Film Institute, 2007.

Dyer, Richard. "Coming Out as Going In: The Image of the Homosexual as a Sad Young Man." In *The Matter of Images: Essays on Representation,* 73–92. Routledge: London, 1993.

———. *The Culture of Queers.* London: Routledge, 2002.

———. *Heavenly Bodies: Film Stars and Societies.* London: Macmillan Education Limited, 1986.

———. *Now You See It: Studies in Lesbian and Gay Film.* London: Routledge, 1990.

———. *Only Entertainment.* London: Routledge, 1992.

———. "Stereotyping." In *Gays and Film,* edited by Richard Dyer, 27–39. London: British Film Institute, 1977.

Eisenbach, David. *Gay Power: An American Revolution*. New York: Carrol and Graff, 2006.

"El Paso Wrecking Company." *Mandate* 3, no. 34 (February 1978): 68–69.

Engel, Stephen M. *The Unfinished Revolution: Social Movement Theory and the Gay and Lesbian Movement*. Cambridge: Cambridge University Press, 2001.

Epstein, Steven. "Gay Politics, Ethnic Identity: The Limits of Social Constructionism." In *Social Perspectives in Lesbian and Gay Studies: A Reader*, edited by Peter M. Narfi and Beth E. Schneider, 148–49. London: Routledge, 1998.

Escoffier, Jeffrey. *Bigger Than Life: The History of Gay Porn Cinema from Beefcake to Hardcore*. Philadelphia: Running Press, 2009.

———. "Homosexuality and the Sociological Imagination." In *A Queer World: The Center for Gay and Lesbian Studies Reader*, edited by Martin Duberman, 248–61. New York: New York University Press, 1997.

Evans, Arthur. "Zap: You're Alive." *Gay Today*, August 30, 1999. Accessed July 31, 2017. http://gaytoday.badpuppy.com/garchive/viewpoint/083099vi.htm.

Faderman, Lillian, and Stuart Timmons. *Gay L.A.: A History of Sexual Outlaws, Power Politics, and Lipstick Lesbians*. New York: Basic Books, 2006.

Falkon, Felix Lance, and Thomas Waugh. *Gay Art: A Historic Collection*. Vancouver: Arsenal Pulp Press, 2006. Revised edition. First published 1972 with Falkon as sole author.

Fielder, Leslie. *The Return of the Vanishing American*. London: Jonathan Cape, 1968.

Fisher, Lucy. *Designing Women: Cinema, Art Deco, and the Female Form*. New York: Columbia University Press, 2003.

Fuss, Diana. "Introduction: Inside/Out." In *Inside/Out: Lesbian Theories, Gay Theories*, edited by Diana Fuss, 1–10. London: Routledge, 1991.

Gage, Joe. "L.A. Tool & Die." *Numbers*, no. 33 (November 1980): 68–73.

Gänzl, Kurt. *Lydia Thompson: Queen of Burlesque*. New York: Routledge, 2002.

A Gay Male Group. "Notes on Gay Male Consciousness-Raising." In *Out of the Closets: Voices of Gay Liberation*, edited by Karla Jay and Allen Young, 293–301. 2nd ed. New York: Pyramid Books, 1974.

Gengle, Dean. "The Closet as Gay Group-Think." *The Advocate*, no. 193, June 30, 1976.

Gerassi, John. *The Boys of Boise: Furor, Vice, and Folly in an American City*. New York: Collier Books, 1966.

Gerstner, David. "The Production and Display of the Closet: Making Minnelli's 'Tea and Sympathy.'" *Film Quarterly* 50, no. 3 (Spring 1997): 13–26.

Giddens, Anthony. *The Transformation of Intimacy: Sexuality, Love and Eroticism in Modern Societies*. Stanford, CA: Stanford University Press, 1992.

Goffman, Erving. *Relations in Public: Microstudies of the Public Order*. New York: Basic Books, 1971.

Gomery, Douglas. "Motion Picture Exhibitions in 1970s America." In *Lost Illusions: American Cinema in the Shadow of Watergate and Vietnam*, edited by David A. Cook, 397–416. Berkeley: University of California Press, 2000.

Gorfinkel, Elena. "Wet Dreams: Erotic Film Festivals of the Early 1970s and the Utopian Sexual Public Sphere." *Framework: The Journal of Cinema and Media* 47, no. 2 (2006): 59–86.

Gregg, Ronald. "Fashion, Thrift Stores and the Space of Pleasure in the 1960s Queer Underground Film." In *Birds of Paradise: Costume as Cinematic Spectacle*, edited by Markheta Uhlirova, 293–305. London: Koenig Books, 2013.

———. "Gay Culture, Studio Publicity, and the Management of Star Discourse: The Homosexualization of William Haines in Pre-Code Hollywood." *Quarterly Review of Film and Video* 20, no. 2 (2003): 81–97.

Grube, John. "Native and Settlers: An Ethnographic Note on Early Interaction of Older Homosexual Men with Younger Gay Liberationists." *Journal of Homosexuality* 20, no. 3–4 (1990): 119–35.

Guerrero, Ed. *Framing Blackness: The African-American Image in Film*. Philadelphia: Temple University Press, 1993.

Hadleigh, Boze. *The Lavender Screen: The Gay and Lesbian Films—Their Stars, Makers, Characters, and Critics*. New York: Citadel Press, 1993.

Halperin, David. *How to Be Gay*. Cambridge, MA: The Belknap Press of Harvard University, 2012.

Hammer, Barbara. *Hammer! Making Movies Out of Sex and Life*. New York: The Feminist Press at the City University of New York, 2010.

Hanson, Craig Alfred. "The Fairy Princess Exposed." In *Out of the Closets: Voices of Gay Liberation*, edited by Karla Jay and Allen Young, 266–69. 2nd ed. New York: Pyramid Books, 1974.

Hanson, Dian. *Bob's World: The Life and Boys of A.M.G.'s Bob Mizer*. Cologne: Taschen, 2009.

Harrington, Curtis. *Nice Guys Don't Work in Hollywood: The Adventures of an Aesthete in the Movie Business*. Chicago: Drag City, 2013.

Harris, Daniel. *The Rise and Fall of Gay Culture*. New York: Hyperion, 1997.

Harry, Joseph. "Urbanization and the Gay Life." *Journal of Sex Research* 10, no. 3 (August 1974): 238–47.

Herring, Scott. "Out of the Closets, into the Woods: *RFD, Country Women*, and the Post-Stonewall Emergence of Queer Anti-Urbanism." *American Quarterly* 59, no. 2 (June 2007): 341–72.

Hobson, Emily K. *Lavender and Red: Liberation and Solidarity in the Gay and Lesbian Left*. Oakland: University of California Press, 2016.

Hocquenghem, Guy. *Homosexual Desire*. London: Allison and Busby Limited, 1978.

Hoffman, Martin. *The Gay World: Male Homosexuality and the Social Creation of Evil*. New York: Bantam Books, 1969.

"The Homosexual: Newly Visible, Newly Understood." *Time*, October 31, 1969.

"'Hot Rocco' Coming." *The Advocate*, no. 8, June 10, 1970.

Hutcheon, Linda. *Irony's Edge: The Theory and Politics of Irony*. London: Routledge, 1994.

Hutchison, Alice L. *Kenneth Anger: A Demonic Visionary*. London: Black Dog Publishing, 2001.

J. *The Sensuous Woman*. New York: L. Stuart, 1969.

James, David E. *The Most Typical Avant-Garde: History and Geography of Minor Cinemas in Los Angeles*. Berkeley: University of California Press, 2005.

Jackson, Earl, Jr. *Strategies of Deviance: Studies in Gay Male Representation*. Bloomington: Indiana University Press, 1995.

Johnson, David K. *The Lavender Scare: The Cold War Persecution of Gays and Lesbians in the Federal Government*. Chicago: University of Chicago Press, 2004.

Jones, William E. *Halsted Plays Himself*. Los Angeles: Semiotext(e), 2011.

Kearns, Michael. "The Gage Boys Are Rolling Again with *L.A. Tool and Die*." *Drum*, no. 34 (January 1981): 20–22.

Kepner, James. "A Gay Camp Looks at the Gay Cult." *Pursuit and Symposium* 1, no. 1 (March–April, 1966): 3.

Kinsey, Alfred Charles, Wardell Baxter Pomeroy, Clyde Eugene Martin, and Sam Sloan. *Sexual Behavior in the Human Male*. Philadelphia: W. B. Saunders Company, 1948.

Kipnis, Laura. *Bound and Gagged: Pornography and the Politics of Fantasy in America*. New York: Grove Press, 1996.

Kitses, Jim. *Horizons West: Directing the Western from John Ford to Clint Eastwood*. London: Palgrave Macmillan on behalf of the British Film Institute, 2004.

Kleinberg, Seymour. *Alienated Affection: Being Gay in America*. New York: St. Martin's Press, 1980.

Klinger, Barbara. "The Road to Dystopia: Landscaping the Nation in *Easy Rider*." In *The Road Movie Book*, edited by Steven Cohan and Ina Rae Hark, 179–204. London: Routledge, 1997.

Kramer, Peter. *The New Hollywood: From Bonnie and Clyde to Star Wars*. London: Wallflower Press, 2005.

Kuhn, Annette. *Ratcatcher*. London: Palgrave Macmillan on behalf of the British Film Institute, 2008.

Levine, Martin P. *Gay Macho: The Life and Death of the Homosexual Clone*. New York: New York University Press, 1998.

Lewis, Jon. *Hollywood vs. Hardcore: How the Struggle Over Censorship Saved the Modern Film Industry*. New York: New York University Press, 2000.

Locke, Robert. "My Brother the Porn Star: An Interview with Richard Locke." *Blueboy* 27 (December 1978): 82–84, 89.

Loney, George. "Shooting Up in New York." *After Dark* 12, no. 10 (February 1980): 34–37.

Loovis, David. *Gay Spirit: A Guide to Becoming a Sensuous Homosexual*. New York: Strawberry Hill Publishing, 1974.

M. *The Sensuous Man*. New York: L. Stuart, 1971.

Mann, William J. *Behind the Screen: How Gays and Lesbians Shaped Hollywood*. New York: Penguin Books, 2001.

Marcuse, Herbert. *Eros and Civilization: A Philosophical Inquiry into Freud*. London: Routledge, 1998. First published 1956 by Routledge & Kegan Paul Ltd.

Marvin, John. "The Great Gay Movie Boom." *Quorum* 2, no. 8 (n.d.).
"Mattachine Society Project Collection." Collection 2008-016. Online Archive of California, ONE National Gay and Lesbian Archives. Accessed May 2, 2017. http://www.oac.cdlib.org/findaid/ark:/13030/kt7w1035mz/.
Meeker, Martin. *Contacts Desired: Gay and Lesbian Communications and Community, 1940s–1970s*. Chicago: University of Chicago Press, 2006.
Meyer, Richard. "Gay Power circa 1970: Visual Strategies for Sexual Revolution." *GLQ: A Journal for Lesbian and Gay Studies* 12, no. 3 (2006): 441–64.
———. *Outlaw Representation: Censorship and Homosexuality in Twentieth-Century American Art*. Boston: Beacon Press, 2002.
Miller, Quinn. "The Bob Cummings Show's 'Artists at "Work"': Gender Transitive Programming and Counterpublicity." *Spectator* 28, no. 1 (2008): 10–28.
———. "Television." *TSQ: Transgender Studies Quarterly* 1, no. 1–2 (2014): 216–19.
"The Motion Picture Production Code." March 31, 1930. Association of Motion Pictures Producers, Inc. Hollywood, CA. Reprinted by Richard Maltby as appendix 1 in *Hollywood Cinema*. 2nd ed. Oxford: Blackwell Publishing, 2003.
"Movie Review: *Some of My Best Friends Are . . .* Two Viewpoints but a Must for You/All." *The Nuntius*, November 11, 1971.
Muller, Eddie, and Daniel Faris. *Grindhouse: The Forbidden World of "Adults Only" Cinema*. New York: St. Martin's Press, 1996.
Muñoz, José Esteban. *Cruising Utopia: The Then and There of Queer Futurity*. New York: New York University Press, 2009.
Nash, Jennifer C. *The Black Body in Ecstasy: Reading Race, Reading Pornography*. Durham, NC: Duke University Press, 2014.
New Line Press Kit for *A Very Natural Thing*. Box 46, Folder 438, Foster Gunnison Jr. Papers, undated, 1945–94, University of Connecticut Libraries.
Newton, Esther. *Mother Camp: Female Impersonators in America*. 2nd ed. Ann Arbor: University of Chicago Press, 1979.
Nystrom, Derek. *Hard Hats, Rednecks, and Macho Men: Class in 1970s American Cinema*. New York: Oxford University Press, 2009.
Ollendorf, Robert H. V. *The Juvenile Homosexual Experience and Its Effect on Adult Sexuality*. New York: The Julian Press, 1966.
Osterweil, Ara. "Close Up: America Year Zero." *Artforum*, January 2017, 191–94.
Overseth, Marcus. "Grows Rapidly: What Kind of People?" *San Francisco Free Press*, December 7, 1969.
Owen, Frank. *Teenage Stories of Action*. New York: Grosset and Dunlap, 1948.
"Pat Rocco Photographs and Papers: Biography." Collection 2007-006. Online Archive of California, ONE National Gay and Lesbian Archives. Accessed August 2, 2017. http://www.oac.cdlib.org/findaid/ark:/13030/kt3k4025zg/admin/.
People of the State of California vs. Robert H. Mizer. Municipal Court of Los Angeles, case no. 23722, 1954.

Physique Pictorial 10, no. 4 (April 1961).

Physique Pictorial 11, no. 4 (June 1965).

"Police Raid at Slave Auction." *Drummer* 1, no. 6 (May–June 1976): 12–14.

Porter, Ronald K. "A Rainbow in Black: The Gay Politics of the Black Panther Party." *Counterpoints* 367, "Sexualities in Education: A Reader" (2012).

Powell, Ryan. "Bijou (Wakefield Poole, 1972)." *Porn Studies* 4, no. 3 (2017): 280–88.

———. "Gothic Spatiality and the Limits of Gay Visibility in *The Boys in the Band*." In *The Boys in the Band: Flashpoints of Cinema, History, and Queer Politics*, edited by Matt Bell, 88–112. Detroit: Wayne State University Press, 2016.

———. "Queer Interstates: Cultural Geography and Social Contact in *Kansas City Trucking Co.* and *El Paso Wrecking Corp.*" In *Queering the Countryside: New Frontiers in Rural Queer Studies*, edited by Mary L. Gray, Colin R. Johnson, and Brian J. Gilley, 181–202. New York: New York University Press, 2016.

Pursell, Caroll W. *The Military-Industrial Complex: A Reader.* New York: Harper and Row Publishers, 1972.

"Raids Jar Hollywood Gays." *The Advocate*, no. 130, January 30, 1974.

Ramakers, Micha. *Dirty Pictures: Tom of Finland, Masculinity, and Homosexuality.* New York: St. Martin's Press, 2000.

Ross, Andrew. "Uses of Camp." In *Camp: Queer Aesthetics and the Performing Subject; A Reader*, edited by Fabio Cleto, 308–29. Ann Arbor: University of Michigan Press, 1999.

Russo, Vito. *The Celluloid Closet: Homosexuality in the Movies*. Cambridge: Harper and Row Publishers, 1981.

Samuels, Stuart. *Midnight Movies*. New York: Macmillan Publishing Co., 1983.

Savran, David. *Taking It Like A Man: White Masculinity, Masochism, and Contemporary American Culture*. New Jersey: Princeton University Press, 1998.

Schaefer, Eric. "Gauging a Revolution: 16 mm Film and the Rise of the Pornographic Feature." In *Porn Studies*, edited by Linda Williams, 370–400. Durham, NC: Duke University Press, 2004.

Schatz, Thomas. "The New Hollywood." In *Film Theory Goes to the Movies*, edited by Jim Collins, Ava Preacher Collins, and Hilary Radner, 8–37. New York: Routledge, 1993.

Schick, Irvin C. *The Erotic Margin: Sexuality and Spatiality in Alterist Discourse*. New York: Verso, 1999.

Schtier, Rachel. *Striptease: The Untold History of the Girl Show.* New York: Oxford University Press, 2004.

Segal, Lynne. *Slow Motion: Changing Masculinities, Changing Men*. London: Virago, 1990.

Shuttleton, David. "The Queer Politics of Gay Pastoral." In *De-Centering Sexualities: Politics and Representations beyond the Metropolis*, edited by Richard Phillips, Diane Watt, and David Shuttleton, 125–46. London: Routledge, 2000.

Siebenand, Paul Alcuin. "The Beginning of Gay Cinema in Los Angeles: The Industry and the Audience." PhD diss., University of Southern California, 1975.

Silverstein, Charles, and Edmund White. *The Joy of Gay Sex: An Inmate Guide for Gay Men to the Pleasures of a Gay Lifestyle.* New York: Crown Publishing Group, 1977.

Silverstein, Mike. "Good Save the Queen." *Gay Sunshine,* no. 3, November 1970.

Sitney, P. Adams. *Visionary Film: The American Avant-Garde, 1943–2000.* 3rd ed. New York: Oxford University Press, 2002.

Staiger, Janet. "Finding Community in the Early 1960s: Underground Cinema and Sexual Politics." In *Swinging Single: Representing Sexuality in the 1960s,* edited by Hillary Radner and Moya Luckett. Minneapolis: University of Minnesota Press, 1999.

Stanton, Mary. *Freedom Walk: Mississippi or Bust.* Jackson: University of Mississippi Press, 2003.

Strub, Whitney. *Perversion for Profit: The Politics of Pornography and the Rise of the New Right.* New York: Columbia University Press, 2011.

Stryker, Susan. *Queer Pulp: Perverted Passions from the Golden Age of the Paperback.* San Francisco: Chronicle Books, 2001.

Suárez, Juan A. *Bike Boys, Drag Queens and Superstars: Avant-Garde, Mass Culture, and Gay Identities in the 1960s Underground Cinema.* Bloomington: Indiana University Press, 1996.

———. "Kenneth Anger: Clothing, Queerness, Magic." In *Birds of Paradise: Costume as Cinematic Spectacle,* edited by Marketa Uhlirova, 277–92. London: Koenig Books, 2013.

Sugrue, Thomas J. *The Origins of the Urban Crisis: Race and Inequality in Postwar Detroit.* Princeton, NJ: Princeton University Press, 1996.

Teal, Don. *The Gay Militants: How Gay Liberation Began in America, 1969–1971.* New York: Stein and Day, 1971.

Terdiman, Richard. *Discourse/Counter-Discourse: The Theory and Practice of Symbolic Resistance in Nineteenth Century France.* Ithaca, NY: Cornell University Press, 1985.

Third World Gay Revolution and Gay Liberation Front. "Gay Revolution and Sex Roles." In *Out of the Closets: Voices of Gay Liberation,* edited by Karla Jay and Allen Young, 252–62. 2nd ed. New York: Pyramid Books, 1974. First published 1971 in *Chicago Gay Pride* as "Statement."

Timmons, Stuart. *The Trouble with Harry Hay: Founder of the Modern Gay Movement.* Boston: Alyson Publications, 1990.

Tinkcom, Matthew. *Working Like a Homosexual: Camp, Capital, Cinema.* Durham, NC: Duke University Press, 2002.

Tompkins, Jane. *West of Everything: The Inner Life of Westerns.* New York: Oxford University Press, 1993.

"Truckers/Work." *The Advocate,* no. 172, September 10, 1975.

Tyler, Parker. *Screening the Sexes: Homosexuality in the Movies*. New York: Anchor Books, 1972.

———. *Sex Psyche Etcetera in the Film*. 2nd ed. Middlesex: Penguin Books, 1971.

Vider, Stephen. "'Oh Hell, May, Why Don't You People Have a Cookbook?': Camp Humor and Gay Domesticity." *American Quarterly* 65, no. 4 (December 2013).

Villarejo, Amy. *Lesbian Rule: Cultural Criticism and the Value of Desire*. Durham, NC: Duke University Press, 2003.

Warner, Michael. *Publics and Counterpublics*. New York: Zone Books, 2002.

Waugh, Thomas. *The Fruit Machine: Twenty Years of Writings on Queer Cinema*. Durham, NC: Duke University Press, 2000.

———. *Hard to Imagine: Gay Male Eroticism in Photography and Film from Their Beginnings to Stonewall*. New York: Columbia University Press, 1996.

———. *Out/Lines: Underground Gay Graphics from Before Stonewall*. Vancouver: Arsenal Pulp Press, 2002.

Welch, Paul. "Homosexuality in America." *Life*, June 26, 1969.

Weston, Kath. "Get Thee to a Big City: Sexual Imaginary and the Great Gay Migration." *GLQ: Gay and Lesbian Quarterly Review* 2, no. 3 (1995): 253–77.

White, Edmund, and Tom Lake. *States of Desire: Travels in Gay America*. New York: Dutton, 1980.

White, Patricia. *Uninvited: Classical Hollywood Cinema and Lesbian Representability*. Bloomington: Indiana University Press, 1999.

Whitman, Carl. "A Gay Manifesto." In *We Are Everywhere: A Historical Sourcebook of Gay and Lesbian Politics*, edited by Mark Blasius and Shane Phelan, 386–87. New York: Routledge, 1997. First published 1970 in *The Red Butterfly* pamphlet.

Williams, Linda. *Hard Core: Power, Pleasure, and the Frenzy of the Visible*. Berkeley: University of California Press, 1989.

———. *Screening Sex*. Durham, NC: Duke University Press, 2008.

Witt, Lynn, Sherry Thomas, and Eric Marcus, eds. *Out in All Directions: The Almanac of Gay and Lesbian America*. New York: Warner Books, 1995.

Wuest, Brian. "Defining Homosexual Love Stories: Pat Rocco, Categorization, and the Legitimation of Gay Narrative Film." *Film History* 29, no. 4 (2017): 59–88.

Youmans, Greg. "Performing Essentialism: Reassessing Barbara Hammer's Films of the 1970s." *Camera Obscura* 81 (2012): 101–32.

Young, Allen. "Out of the Closets, Into the Streets." In *Out of the Closets: Voices of Gay Liberation*, edited by Karla Jay and Allen Young, 6–30. 2nd ed. New York: Pyramid Books, 1974.

Zimmerman, Patricia E. *Reel Families: A Social History of Amateur Film*. Bloomington: Indiana University Press, 1995.

Filmography

Adam and Yves. Dir. Peter de Rome. Hand in Hand Films. 1974.
Aladdin. Dir. Bob Mizer. Athletic Model Guild Prod. 1956.
Always on a Sunday. Dir. Connie B. DeMille. Gay Girls Riding Club Prod. Date unknown.
American Cream. Dir. Rob Simple. Hand in Hand Films. 1972.
Arabian Nights. Dir. John Rawlins. Universal Pictures. 1942.
Ballet Down the Highway. Dir. Jack Deveau. Hand in Hand Films. 1975.
The Big Combo. Dir. Joseph Lewis. Security Pictures, Theodora Prod. 1955.
Bijou. Dir. Wakefield Poole. Poolemar Prod. 1972.
Blackboard Jungle. Dir. Richard Brooks. MGM. 1955.
Booking a Hood. Dir. Bob Mizer. Athletic Model Guild Prod. 1957.
Boy on the Run. Dir. Pat Rocco. Bizarre Prod. 1968.
Boys in Prison. Dir. Bob Mizer. Athletic Model Guild Prod. 1957.
The Boys in the Band. Dir. William Friedkin. Cinema Center Films. 1970.
Boys in the Sand. Dir. Wakefield Poole. Poolemar Prod. 1971.
Boys Out to Ball. Dir. Pat Rocco. Bizarre Prod. 1968.
Butch Easter. Dir. Peter de Rome. 1966.
Casey. Dir. Donald Crane. Palm Features. 1971.
Christmas U.S.A. Dir. Gregory Markopoulos. 1949.
The Collection. Dir. Tim DeSimone. Hand in Hand Films. 1970.
Confidential File. "Homosexuals and the Problem They Present." Dir. Roger Barlow. Written by Paul Coates. KTTV Los Angeles, April 1954.
Cruising. Dir. William Friedkin. Lorimar Film Entertainment. 1980.
Daydreams on a Crosstown Bus. Dir. Peter de Rome. Hand in Hand Prod. 1972.

The Destroying Angel. Dir. Peter de Rome. Hand in Hand Prod. 1976.
Discovery. Dir. Pat Rocco. Bizarre Prod. 1968.
Double Exposure. Dir. Peter de Rome. 1969.
Dust unto Dust. Dir. Tom De Simone. Hand in Hand Films. 1970.
East of Eden. Dir. Elia Kazan. Warner Bros. 1955.
El Paso Wrecking Corp. Dir. Joe Gage. Joe Gage Films. 1977.
Encounter. Dir. Peter de Rome. 1971.
The Erotic Films of Peter de Rome. Dir. Peter de Rome. Hand in Hand Prod. 1973.
The Fire Island Kids. Dir. Peter de Rome. 1971.
Fireworks. Dir. Kenneth Anger. 1947.
Flaming Creatures. Dir. Jack Smith. 1963.
Fragments of Seeking. Dir. Curtis Harrington. 1946.
Gay Sex in the 70s. Directed by Joseph Lovett. Lovett Prod., Frameline, Heartlove Prod. 2005.
Green Thoughts. Dir. Peter de Rome. 1970.
Groovy Guy. Dir. Pat Rocco. Bizarre Prod. 1968.
Hair Revisited. Dir. Pat Rocco. Bizarre Prod. 1970.
Homosexuals on the March. Dir. Pat Rocco. Bizarre Prod. 1970.
Hot Pants. Dir. Peter de Rome. 1971.
Johnny Minotaur. Dir. Charles Henri Ford. Impact Films. 1971.
Jungle Queen. Dir. Lewis D. Collins, Ray Taylor. Universal Pictures. 1945.
Kansas City Trucking Co. Dir. Joe Gage. Joe Gage Films. 1976.
Kiss. Dir. Pat Rocco. Bizarre Prod. 1970.
Kiss Today Goodbye. Dir. Francis Ellie. Manhattan Pictures. 1976.
L.A. Plays Itself/Sex Garage. Dir. Fred Halsted. Eight of Clubs. 1972.
L.A. Tool and Die. Dir. Joe Gage. Joe Gage Films. 1979.
Lonesome Cowboys. Dir. Andy Warhol. Andy Warhol Films. 1968.
Love Is Blue. Dir. Pat Rocco. Bizarre Prod. 1968.
The Luckiest Cat in Town. Dir. Pat Rocco. Bizarre Prod. 1970.
Luminous Procuress. Dir. Steve Arnold. Paramour. 1971.
Making the Boys. Dir. Crayton Robey. 4th Row Films, Crayton Robey Prod. 2011.
The Maltese Falcon. Dir. John Huston. Warner Brothers. 1941.
Marco of Rio. Dir. Pat Rocco. Bizarre Prod. 1969.
Meat Market Arrest. Dir. Pat Rocco. Bizarre Prod. 1970.
The Meatrack. Dir. Richard Stockton. Sherpix. 1969.
Memories. Directed by Pat Rocco. Bizarre Prod. 1968.
Mondo Rocco. Dir. Pat Rocco. Bizarre Prod. 1970.
Mumbo Jumbo. Dir. Peter de Rome. Hand in Hand Prod. 1972.
My Hustler. Dir. Andy Warhol. Andy Warhol Films. 1965.
Narcissus. Dir. Willard Maas. 1956.
Navy Blue. Dir. Francis Ellie. 1979.
A Night at Joani's. Dir. Pat Rocco. Bizarre Prod. 1970.
A Night at the Adonis. Dir. Jack Deveau. Hand in Hand Films. 1978.
The Night Before. Dir. Arch Brown. Hand in Hand Films. 1973.

Normal Love. Dir. Jack Smith. 1963.
Nudist Beach Surfers. Dir. Pat Rocco. Bizarre Prod. 1968.
One Adventure. Dir. Pat Rocco. Bizarre Prod. 1972.
Outrageous! Dir. Richard Benner. Film Consortium of Canada, Canadian Film Development Corporation. 1977.
Pink Narcissus. Dir. James Bidgood. Sherpix. 1971.
The Prisoner. Dir. Michael Redd. Bizarre Prod. 1970.
Prometheus. Dir. Peter de Rome. Hand in Hand Prod. 1972.
The Queen. Dir. Frank Simon. M.D.H., Si Litvinoff Film Prod., Vineyard. 1968.
Rebel without a Cause. Dir. Nicholas Ray. Warner Bros. 1955.
Reflections of an Indian Boy. Dir. Dick Clark. Jaguar Prod. 1972.
The Rejected. Dir. Richard Christian. National Education Television. 1961.
The Room. Dir. Pat Rocco. Bizarre Prod. 1970.
The Sailor and the B-Girl. Dir. Bob Mizer. Athletic Model Guild Prod. 1959.
Saturday Night at the Baths. Dir. by David Buckley. B.T.O. Films. 1975.
Scopo. Dir. Peter de Rome. 1966.
Scorpio Rising. Dir. Kenneth Anger. Puck Film Prod. 1963.
Screaming Queens: The Riot at Compton's Cafeteria. Dir. Victor Silverman and Susan Stryker. Produced in association with ITVS and KQED. 2005.
Screen Test. Dir. Pat Rocco. Bizarre Prod. 1970.
The Second Coming. Dir. Peter de Rome. 1972.
Slave Market. Dir. Bob Mizer. Athletic Model Guild Prod. 1958.
Some of My Best Friends Are . . . Dir. Mervyn Nelson. American International Pictures. 1971.
Someone. Dir. Pat Rocco. Bizarre Prod. 1968.
Song of the Loon. Dir. Andrew Herbert. Sawyer Prod. 1970.
Spy on the Fly. Dir. Ray Harrison. Gay Girls Riding Club Prod. 1966.
Sticks and Stones. Dir. Stan Lopresto. Toktee-O'Kay. 1970.
Terry and the Pirates. Dir. James Horne. Columbia Pictures. 1940.
The Thief of Bagdad. Dir. Michael Powell et al. Alexander Korda Films, London Film Prod. 1940.
Thunderball. Dir. Terrence Young. MGM. 1966.
Underground. Dir. Peter de Rome. Hand in Hand Prod. 1972.
Vapors. Dir. Andy Milligan. 1965.
The Vice and the Badge. Dir. Anon. Zenith Pictures. 1953.
A Very Natural Thing. Dir. Christopher Larkin. Montage Creations. 1974.
A Very Special Friend. Dir. Pat Rocco. Bizarre Prod. 1968.
What Really Happened to Baby Jane? Dir. Connie B. DeMille. Gay Girls Riding Club Prod. 1963.
The Wild One. Dir. László Benedek. Stanley Kramer Prod. 1953.

Index

Pages numbers in italics refer to figures.